Economists
and the Economy

Economists
and the Economy

The Evolution of Economic Ideas
1600 to the Present Day

Roger Backhouse

Basil Blackwell

British Library Cataloguing in Publication Data
Backhouse, Roger.
Economists and the economy, the evolution of economic ideas,
1600 to the present day
1. Economic history
I. Title
330.9

ISBN 0–631–15558–9

Library of Congress Cataloging-in-Publication Data

Backhouse, Roger.
Economists and the economy, the evolution of economic ideas,
1600 to the present day

Bibliography: p.
Includes index.
1. Economics. 2. Economic history. 1. Title.
HB171.B135 1988   330   88–6045
ISBN 0–631–15558–9

Typeset in 10 on 11 pt Bembo
by Photo-Graphics, Honiton, Devon
Printed in Great Britain by T. J. Press Ltd., Padstow, Cornwall

Contents

List of Figures

List of Tables

Preface

This book contains what is, as far as I know, a unique blend of economic history and the history of economic thought. Its main aim is to provide students of economics with some of the historical background they need in order to be able to understand the subject they are studying. In addition, I hope that people whose knowledge of economics is fairly limited may find reading the book a useful way of learning what economics is about. In the following chapters two themes recur. The first is that there are very serious limits to what economics can achieve. One reason for this is that economic ideas are, to a great extent, dependent on historical circumstances. The other is that there are certain problems that economists have never managed to tackle successfully and which are unlikely to be tackled much better in the foreseeable future. The second theme is that advances in economic theory have been fundamental to such progress as has taken place in economists' understanding of the world. Even though it may sometimes appear to be only tenuously related to real-world problems economic theorizing is vital to the health of the discipline.

My main concern in this book is with economic ideas. The economic history I cover is selected to fit in with this. Thus although the book discusses episodes in economic history that I think economists ought to know about, the selection of topics is almost certainly not that which an economic historian, studying the subject for its own sake, would make. Monetary questions, for example, receive a disproportionate emphasis compared with issues of economic development and structural change. The reason for this is simply that economists have paid a great deal of attention to monetary issues, and I need to provide the background to these.

To treat this subject at all comprehensively is beyond the scope of a single volume, let alone a small one. I have therefore had to be selective, providing examples to illustrate my arguments rather than trying to cover everything I would like to include. There are thus numerous topics that are covered all too briefly and others that are not discussed at all. Public finance, for example, has been an important stimulus to economic thought but I have not the space to deal with it without leaving out something equally important. In addition there are numerous economists (for example Alfred Marshall) whose contributions to the subject are more important than is suggested by the attention they receive here. If I were to do them justice, however, the result would be something much closer to conventional histories of economic thought. Readers wanting a more conventional (balanced?) coverage of the history of economic thought as a whole should consult some of the books listed in the Note on the Literature.

The main sources I have used are listed in the Note on the Literature. Where this mentions very few items the reason is sometimes that I have relied entirely on the original sources discussed in the text but it is often the case that the ideas are ones that I have been aware of so long that I have forgotten where I originally got them from. My sources for some of these ideas are given in the book I wrote three years ago. I apologize for any omissions.

I am indebted to those who have read drafts of various chapters and provided helpful suggestions. Without implicating them in any way I would like to thank Peter Burridge, Peter Cain, Mark Casson, Rosemary Clarke, John Creedy, Terence Hutchison, Denis O'Brien and Leonard Schwarz. Preparation of the typescript was made much easier than it would otherwise have been by Professor E. Bergman's marvellously versatile text formatting program, ROFF4. Most of the figures were originally produced using Micro TSP. (The limited resolution of CGA graphics accounts for some of the irregularities in the graphs.) I also owe an enormous debt to my family, Merida, Robert and Alison, who have put up with my spending many long evenings alone with books and a computer.

1

Introduction

1.1 ECONOMICS TODAY

Economics is a peculiar, and frequently misunderstood, subject, its claim to scientific status often being disputed, even by economists. Consider some of the many jokes made about economists.

1 When I consult an economist I want one with only one hand. I'm fed up with 'on the one hand this, on the other hand that . . .'.
2 If you take all the economists in the world and lay them end to end, you still won't reach a conclusion.
3 A physicist, an engineer and an economist are stranded on a desert island, trying to open a can of beans. The physicist tries opening it with a knife, but fails. The engineer tries hitting the can with a stone. 'You'll get nowhere like that', observes the economist helpfully. 'What would *you* do then?', they retort. 'Well,' says the economist, 'assume we have a can-opener, . . .'.

Economists are held to be unable to agree amongst themselves, or even to make up their own minds; they are prone to irrelevant, abstract reasoning, and their forecasts, needless to say, are held, like those of weather forecasters, always to be wrong.

In addition to attacks from outsiders there have been some very strong attacks made by economists. The classic such attack is probably that of Wasily Leontief, a major figure in twentieth-century economics. In his Presidential Address to the American Economic Association, in 1970, Leontief claimed that, despite the outward signs of success,

Much of current academic teaching and research has been criticized for its lack of relevance, that is, of immediate practical impact. . . . The problem is caused not by an inadequate selection of targets, but rather by our inability to hit squarely any one of them. The inadequacy of which I spoke before is caused not by the *irrelevance* of the practical problems to which present-day economists address their efforts, but by the palpable *inadequacy* of the scientific means with which they try to solve them.

He went on to argue that this was due to an imbalance in the discipline.

I submit that the consistently indifferent performance in practical applications is in fact a symptom of a fundamental imbalance in the present state of our discipline. The weak and all too slowly growing empirical foundation cannot support the proliferating superstructure of pure, or should I say, speculative economic theory.

After describing the increasing use of intricate mathematics in economics Leontief continued,

To sum up with the words of a recent president of the Econometric Society, '. . . the achievements of economic theory in the last two decades are both impressive and in many ways beautiful. But it cannot be denied that there is something scandalous in the spectacle of so many people refining the analysis of economic states which they give no reason to suppose will ever, or have ever, come about . . . . It is an unsatisfactory and slightly dishonest state of affairs'. (Leontief, 1971, pp. 24–26.)

Lest it be thought that this is simply the reaction of an applied economist to economic theory, it is worth noting that the president of the Econometric Society quoted by Leontief is Frank Hahn, an economist whose main contributions have been to relatively abstract economic theory.

Disquiet concerning the state of economics, and particularly of economic theory, was at its height in the 1970s, with many commentators speaking of a 'crisis' in the subject. In the 1980s, however, such criticisms have become markedly less frequent. There are a number of reasons for this. One is that people have run out of new, critical things to say about economics. The critical movement has, to a certain extent, run out of steam. More important, there has been a newfound confidence amongst economists. The severe and unprecedented economic shocks to which the world economy was subjected in the 1970s (see p. 160) were one reason for the crisis and these have not been repeated. Even the stock market crash of October 1987 has not challenged economic theory, or disturbed the world economy in the way that the oil shocks of the 1970s did. In microeconomics, theorists have moved away from constructing more and more general models towards working with simpler ones. As a result they are now tackling problems that are much more closely related to real-world problems: examining the implications of uncertainty and limited information (see p. 180), for example, opens up vast new areas to economic analysis. In macroeconomics, the assumption of rational expectations (see p. 162) has provided economists with new techniques for analysing problems. In both macro and microeconomcs opportunities for interesting theorizing have thus been opened up on a large scale.

Despite this confidence, however, a certain unease persists in various quarters. As many awkward questions about the nature of economics have been pushed aside as have been answered. There is thus still an urgent need to think carefully about the nature of the subject and where it is going.

1.2 ECONOMICS AND ITS PAST

The need for a historical perspective

One way to understand contemporary economics would be to look in detail at what is going on in the subject today: to examine economic theories and how they are related to real-world problems; to examine the nature of the data available to economists and the way they use it. If we are to understand the subject properly, however, we need to know more than this, for we need to know something about both economic history (the history of the economies that economists are concerned to analyse) and the history of economic thought (how economists have tried to analyse these economies).

The main reason for this is that the subject matter of economics, unlike that of most sciences, is constantly changing. Not only do we have entirely new problems arising, but where we do have perennial problems the context in which they occur is changing. We cannot assume, for example, that contemporary economies will respond to external shocks (say a collapse in demand for exports) in the same way as, say, the economy of seventeenth-century England would have done. There are many reasons for this. Institutions have changed and developed (for example, we now have a highly developed financial system in which central banks and international institutions play a key role; something that did not exist even a century ago). Communications have improved, specialization has increased and technology has improved. In addition, people have learnt more about the economy, raising the possibility that they may respond to signals in a different way from earlier generations. Such changes are going on all the time, which means that economists have to change their ideas accordingly. If we are to understand the extent and nature of this problem we must study history.

In addition to changing in response to develoments in the economy, economics has changed for other reasons. Political and social changes have led economists to change their perspective on the world, good examples of this being the change in attitudes towards public policy which took place in seventeenth-century England (see p. 48) and the transition from 'colonial' to 'development' economics after the Second World War (see p. 33). Economics has also changed as a result of changing intellectual standards. The now-widespread use of mathematics in economics, for example, has done much more than simply make economic theory more precise: concepts and ideas amenable to mathematical treatment have been examined thoroughly, whilst other ideas (perhaps equally valuable) that cannot be fitted into mathematical models have been neglected. Institutions have changed and developed (for example, we now have a highly developed financial system in which central banks and international institutions play a key role; something that did not exist even a century ago). Communications have improved, specialization has increased and technology has improved. In addition, people have learnt more about the economy, raising the possibility that they may respond to signals in a different way from earlier generations. Such changes are going on all the time, which means that economists have to change their ideas accordingly. If we are to understand the extent and nature of this problem we must study history.

The final point to make is that the criteria we use to appraise any scientific theory, whether in economics or any other subject must take account of how a theory or set of ideas evolves over time. The distinguishing feature of science is not that its theories are known to be true, but that it possesses a mechanism by which theories are tested and inadequate theories discarded. At one time, for example, the theory of phlogiston was a respectable 'scientific theory, but it has now been abandoned in favour of theories that are better able to explain empirical evidence. Similarly, pre-Copernican astronomy was, in its day, a legitimate scientific theory but, as more and more accurate astronomical measurements were obtained, it was shown to be an inadequate explanation of the observed motion of the planets. A while later Copernicus's theory itself met a similar fate. The criteria in terms of which we appraise a scientific theory must, therefore, be dynamic: they must take account of how theories evolve over time (this issue is discussed further on pp. 189–91). It is, therefore, necessary to examine not only science as it is today, but the history of science. Economics is no exception to this.

Approaches to the history of economic thought

There are two main approaches to the history of economic thought: 'absolutism' and 'relativism'. The absolutist approach involves appraising economic thought from a particular point of view, typically that provided by contemporary economics. We can, for example, ask whether Adam Smith's great work, *An Inquiry into the Nature and Causes of the Wealth of Nations*, was logically consistent, and whether the ideas expressed in it make sense in terms of modern economic theory. Such an approach is perhaps most explicit in Mark Blaug's *Economic Theory in Retrospect* (1985). 'Criticism', he writes, 'involves standards of judgement, and my standards are those of modern economic theory' (Blaug, 1985, p. 1). Such an absolutist approach also underlies J. A. Schumpeter's *History of Economic Analysis* (1954), one of the classic books on the subject. Schumpeter describes many of the intellectual and other influences to which economists were subject, but he takes Walras's general equilibrium system (see p. 177) as the standard by which economic theories should be judged.

The alternative approach is relativism: to see economic ideas as dependent for their validity on the historical circumstances in which they were developed. Theories are seen as ephemeral and historically contingent, the result being a vision of the history of economic thought in which progress does not take place, merely changes in the problems. To quote from a recent, very eloquent, relativist account of the history of economic thought,

Economists deal with a universe where data are freakish and not valid universally, and where phenomena emerge which were not only not known before but had not existed before. It is of the nature of economic science that it involves events and phenomena which not only change complexion from time to time but do not also occur at all places. Problems that emerge as crucial at one time may turn out to be totally irrelevant at another time in the same economy, and those that are relevant in the context of one economy may well be irrelevant elsewhere. In economics old theories do not die. And they do not die not because one is built on the other, but because one is independent of the other. (Dasgupta, 1985, p. 2)

Though these two approaches are sometimes presented as alternatives, they are complementary. Though circumstances may explain why economists become interested in certain theories, historical circumstances cannot be used to justify bad theorizing. It is always valid to examine the logical coherence of economic theories, to examine the filiation of economic ideas, and to ask to what extent there has been progress in economic theory. For all the changes in economic phenomena, there are, as we will see in the following chapters, many ideas that can be traced right through the history of economic thought. To this extent the absolutist approach to the history of economic thought is valid. At the same time, however, it is important to recognize that the theories which can be analysed in this way, independently of historical circumstances, comprise only a part of economics. In the words of Alfred Marshall, the dominant figure in economics in the late nineteenth and early twentieth centuries (see pp. 194–5 for a more extensive quotation), 'In my view "Theory" is essential. No one gets any real grip of economic problems unless he will work at it. But I conceive no more calamitous notion than that abstract, or general, or "theoretical" economics is economics "proper". (Marshall, 1925, p. 437.) If economic theories are to be given any meaning they have to be clothed in assumptions and evidence about the real world. When this happens their validity becomes contingent on historical circumstances and the relativist case comes into its own. When the world changes, economic ideas have to be changed or abandoned.

In this book, therefore, absolutist and relativist ideas are intertwined, for we are concerned both with economists' thinking on what was happening around them, and also with the theoretical ideas that provided economists with the framework within which they could tackle these problems. In chapters 2 to 5 we examine how economists have responded to certain economic problems considering in turn problems of economic growth, the regulation of trade and industry, money and inflation, and the problem of employment and economic fluctuations. Underlying attempts to tackle such practical problems, however, has been a developing apparatus of pure theory, and in chapter 6 we turn to see how this has evolved over the centuries. In the final chapter we discuss the role of economic theory in economics, and attempt to weigh up the strengths and limitations of economics as it exists today.

There are a number of reasons for approaching the subject in this way, concentrating on the relationship between economic ideas and the economic background against which they were written. One is that I have adopted a different approach, concentrating on what Schumpeter called 'the filiation of economic ideas', in my *A History of Modern Economic Analysis* (1985). A more important reason is that many of the misunderstandings which people have concerning the scope of economics arise from a failure to appreciate the historical dimension of the subject, rather than from a failure to understand the structure of contemporary economic theory itself. A historical approach, pointing out both the economic history background, and how economists have responded to this, is thus very useful. Finally, adopting such an approach, focusing on how economists have responded to practical problems, makes it easier to tell the story in a less technical manner, which will, I hope, make it accessible to a wider audience than if I were to concentrate on pure theory.

2

Growth and Development

2.1 THE EIGHTEENTH CENTURY

French and English economic growth

The first systematic theories of economic growth were developed in eighteenth-century France and England, well before what has come to be known as the industrial revolution. Though growth rates were lower than in the nineteenth century, the eighteenth century saw substantial growth in both France and England, the two countries achieving similar growth rates for much of the century. In both countries industry appears to have been growing faster than agriculture, though agriculture remained dominant. In France the share of agriculture in 'physical product' (i.e. excluding services) fell from 74 per cent in 1701–10 to 61 per cent in 1781–90. In England the equivalent figure has been estimated at about 65 per cent from 1688 to around 1760 (agriculture as a percentage of total product was of course much lower, probably at around 40 per cent). (Crafts, 1985, p. 16; Deane and Cole, 1965.)

As tables 2.1 and 2.2 show, the French economy was probably growing faster than the English economy for the bulk of the eighteenth century. These figures, however, conceal enormous differences between the two economies. France started the eighteenth century poorer and more backward than England, the main reason for this being a prolonged period of stagnation, from the 1630s to around 1720. During this time prices fluctuated violently, with frequent economic crises during which death rates rose. In addition profits and rents remained low. The result was that by 1720 the population was lower than in 1640, whilst industrial production had not risen, and may have fallen. In contrast, though England suffered from crises and periods of stagnation, these were less severe and less prolonged. Population, together with industrial and agricultural output, rose.

The figures in table 2.2 reflect the substantial progress that was made in English agriculture throughout the eighteenth century, though it is important to realize that by the start of the century productivity was much higher than in France. Crop rotations and the growing of fodder crops were means by which yields were increased. In Norfolk and Suffolk, for example, wheat yields were between 14 and 17 bushels per acre by 1700, compared with only 11–13 bushels per acre a century earlier. By 1750 this

Growth and Development

Table 2.1 French economic growth in the eighteenth
century

	Agriculture	Industry
1701–10	100	100
	0.33%	
1751–60	118	1.9%
	1.31%	
1771–80	153	
	0.13%	
1781–90	155	454

Entries are index numbers and growth rates per annum.
Source: Marczewski (1960), pp. 369–86.

Table 2.2 English economic growth in the eighteenth century

	Industry	Agriculture	Commerce
1700	100	100	100
	0.71%	0.60%	0.69%
1760	153	143	151
	1.51%	0.13%	0.70%
1780	197	147	174

Entries are index numbers and growth rates per annum.
Source: Crafts (1985), pp. 32, 42.

figure had probably increased to 15–20 bushels (Overton, 1987). An
important feature of eighteenth-century English agriculture was the
enclosure of common land, a process which gathered momentum from
the middle of the eighteenth century. The impetus here came from large
farmers, who wanted enclosure in order to be able to improve the land
and adopt new techniques in order to raise productivity. Though it is
possible, as table 2.2 suggests, that the initial effect of enclosures may
have been to lower the growth rate of agricultural output, enclosure made
possible increases in agricultural productivity which would otherwise have
been difficult to achieve. In addition, because population was growing,
and communications improving, there was a growing market for
agricultural produce. Along with this rise in agricultural production went
a rising standard of living, especially in Lancashire and other industrial
regions, where by the middle of the century wages were comparable with
those paid in London.

This was in marked contrast to the situation of French agriculture, which remained much more backward. Subsistence farming, which is supposed to have virtually died out in England by the seventeenth century, was still widespread. Landowners in France were much less involved than were their English counterparts in the cultivation of land, their incomes deriving instead from money payments, labour services, and payments in kind. Where English landlords turned to improvements to raise their revenues, French landlords attempted to extract the maximum from feudal dues owed to them, and they tried to increase the amounts paid by sharecroppers. Pressure for land to cultivate thus came from the peasants, not from the nobility, and thus France did not acquire the large fields which made possible the widespread application of machinery. Except for isolated regions, yields remained low. Associated with all this, the French market was not unified. Taxation and poor communications hampered the movement of produce from one region to another, which meant that not only did prices fluctuate sharply, but famine in one region could co-exist with gluts in others.

England was also much more advanced in industry. Though change was still slow compared with the changes which occurred towards the end of the century, significant advances were made. In industry the use of coal was much more widespread than in France: in 1709 Abraham Darby had successfully used coke for smelting iron ore, whilst in 1712 Thomas Newcomen had installed the first commercially used steam engine. By 1781 over 360 steam engines were in use. As regards the level of production, French industry, as tables 2.1 and 2.2 show, kept pace with English. French industry, however, had changed less, and output per head was lower. In the words of one authority, 'On the eve of the Revolution, the French economy was not basically different from what it had been under Louis XIV: it was merely producing more.' (Crouzet, 1986, p. 155.)

François Quesnay

Prior to Adam Smith's *Wealth of Nations* the only systematic theory of economic growth was that of Quesnay, the leading economist amongst the Physiocrats, the school which dominated French economics in the second half of the eighteenth century. His interest in the problem was prompted by the state of the French economy as he saw it, for he believed that population was declining, and production falling. It is worth noting that although Quesnay believed this to the case, economic growth was, by the middle of the eighteenth century, probably as rapid in France as in England. The long period of French stagnation was, by then, over.

Central to Quesnay's theory of growth was his *Tableau Economique*. This was a table showing how money and goods circulated through the economy, and it was based very firmly on the nature of the French economy in the mid-eighteenth century as Quesnay saw it. Quesnay analysed the economy in terms of two sectors, agriculture and industry. The crucial characteristic was that agriculture produced a surplus over costs, whereas industry did not. Manufacturing was described, somewhat misleadingly, as being 'sterile', but the argument was merely that industry is competitive, and as a result will not be able to produce a profit. Agriculture, Quesnay assumed, might or might not produce a surplus, depending on what production techniques were employed.

Quesnay argued that three types of agriculture could be found in the Europe of his day. There was subsistence farming, where peasants cultivated the land using only their own labour. Such methods did not yield any surplus. Above this came what Quesnay termed *la petite culture*, in which human labour was assisted by oxen, the animals normally being provided by the landlord, and shared amongst a number of sharecroppers. This was more productive, but involved a capital investment. Still more productive was *la grande culture*, in which large landowners used horse-drawn ploughs. Using detailed data on soil yields, prices, the cost of keeping animals, and so on, Quesnay estimated that *la petite culture* yielded a surplus over annual advances (circulating capital, comprising the annual investment in raw material and wages needed to produce the harvest) of 36 per cent. *La grande culture*, on the other hand, will yield a surplus of 100 per cent on annual advances. To obtain an equivalent rate of profit on total capital employed we have to allow for fixed capital. Assuming that the ratio of fixed to circulating capital was 4:1 in *la grande culture*, and 2:1 in *la petite culture*, Quesnay estimated the corresponding profit rates to be 20 per cent and 12 per cent respectively.

An extremely simplified version of the theory underlying the numerical examples analysed in the different versions of Quesnay's *tableau* is shown in figure 2.1. Part (a) of figure 2.1 shows the circulation of money between landlords, industry and agriculture. The process starts with the landlords spending their rents on a mixture of manufactured goods and agricultural produce. This generates incomes in these sectors which leads to further spending, this in turn generating more income. As a result, the total level of spending is greater than that of the landlords' spending which sustains it. At the end of the year, because agriculture yields a surplus, farmers pay rents to the landlords, these rents providing income for the landlords to spend in the following year.

Corresponding to these expenditure flows are flows of goods, these being shown in part (b) of figure 2.1. Most of the flows shown here are the counterparts of the money flows shown in figure 2.1a. Also shown, however, are agricultural advances, the working capital used up during the year as part of the production process. In the same way that the level of rents determines the scale of spending in the economy, it is agricultural advances that determine the level of production. It is thus very important how much produce farmers have left over at the end of the year, for this constitutes the following year's advances, and hence determines the following year's production.

These two flows, of goods and money, are, of course, related. Of particular importance is the dependence of rents on the level of agricultural advances, for it is the latter which, given the rate of profit, determine the

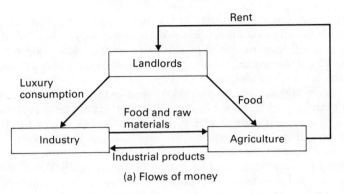

(a) Flows of money

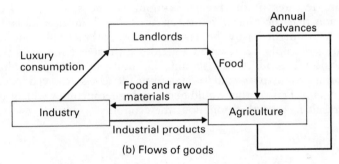

(b) Flows of goods

FIGURE 2.1   *Quesnay's theory of economic growth*

level of agricultural profits, and hence rents. Suppose, for example, that the landlords decided to spend a higher fraction of their income on manufactured goods (presumably luxury goods). The result would be that profits in the agricultural sector would fall, which means that unless this were completely compensated for by a fall in rents, farmers would be able to save less for the following year's advances. The other way of looking at this is to note that higher incomes in the industrial sector will lead to higher consumption of food, leaving less available in the agricultural sector. In the following year agricultural output will be lower. Manufacturing will expand, but because manufacturing does not yield a surplus, this will not compensate for the contraction in agriculture.

Increased spending by the landlords on manufactured goods is thus one possible cause of economic decline. Two others are taxes on agricultural produce and low productivity. If a tax is imposed on agricultural produce, farmers' revenues will be reduced. Quesnay then argued that because they were determined by long-term contracts, rents would change only as contracts came up for renewal. This meant that rents would change very slowly and as a result of this agricultural advances in the following year would be lower. Taxation of rents, in contrast, would not have this effect, for, unless the state spent a different fraction of its revenues on agricultural produce from the landlords, flows of income would not be affected. Similarly, a fall in agricultural productivity would, again assuming rents did not adjust immediately, lower the level of agricultural advances and hence the level of production.

Quesnay's *tableau* thus explained why the French economy was so stagnant, and it provided the basis for a coherent set of policy prescriptions. To raise the French growth rate it was necessary to reduce the taxation of agricultural produce, replacing it with taxes on rents, to reduce expenditure on manufactured goods, or to raise agricultural productivity. Although his numerical examples may look rather artificial, and although it can be argued that he was defending the interests of certain sections of French society rather than undertaking disinterested analysis, the assumptions made by Quesnay constituted a serious attempt to isolate the important features of the French economy as he saw them. Even his assumption that the rate of return on agricultural advances was 100 per cent, which might easily be taken for an arithmetically simple, but unrealistic, example, represented a serious estimate of the potential level of agricultural productivity should the best methods be utilized. If agricultural productivity could be raised to the levels achieved in England and in parts of France, this would generate higher incomes which, in turn, would result in growth throughout the economy.

Adam Smith

Like Quesnay, with whose work he was familiar, and for whom he had a high regard, Adam Smith viewed growth in terms of capital accumulation. Similarly, he saw the task of raising the growth rate in terms of increasing the fraction of resources going into productive activity. The relevant chapter of the *Wealth of Nations* is entitled 'Of the accumulation of capital, or of productive and unproductive labour'. Smith, however, did not take the view that only agriculture was productive. Productive labour was any labour which added to the value of the subject on which it was bestowed. Comparing the labour of a manufacturer with that of a menial servant, for example, he claimed that whilst the labour of both was valuable, and worthy of reward,

the labour of the manufacturer fixes and realizes itself in some particular subject or vendible commodity, which lasts for some time at least after that labour is past.... That subject, or what is the same thing, the price of that subject, can afterwards, if necessary, put into motion a quantity of labour equal to that which had originally produced it. (Smith, 1776, I, pp. 351–2.)

The main aspects of Smith's theory of capital accumulation are shown in figure 2.2. The annual produce of a nation, he argued, divides naturally into two parts: the largest part is used to replace capital used up during the year; the other part constitutes revenue, this including both profit on capital and rent on land. This revenue may be used to support either unproductive labourers, or idle hands, or it may be saved. Savings, along with that part of the annual produce which replaces capital, are used to employ productive labour, the amount of productive labour employed determining the next year's produce. Growth thus depends on the fraction of the labour force employed productively, this in turn depending on the level of saving.

Saving, therefore, was for Smith the key to growth: 'Capitals are increased by parsimony, and diminished by prodigality and misconduct' (1776, I, p. 358), prodigality referring to high consumption, misconduct to investment in unsuccessful ventures (in this context it is interesting to note that Smith regarded bankruptcy as 'perhaps the greatest and most humiliating calamity which can befal an innocent man', comparing it with the gallows (Smith, 1776, I, p. 363). The role of consumption in maintaining demand was something to which Smith attached no importance, for he argued that 'What is apparently saved is as regularly consumed as what is annually spent, and nearly in the same time too; but it is consumed by a different set of people' (Smith, 1776, I, p. 359.) His reasoning was

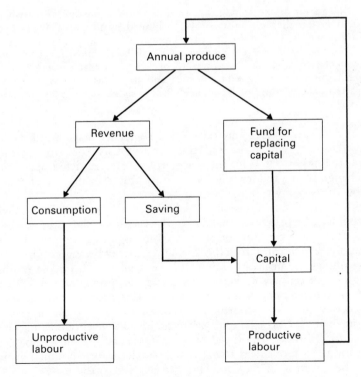

FIGURE 2.2 *Smith's theory of growth*

that, in countries where a tolerable level of security prevails, 'A man must be perfectly crazy who . . . does not employ all the stock which he commands . . . in some one or other of those three ways [consumption, investment in fixed or in circulating capital]' (Smith, 1776, I, p. 301.)

Capital accumulation was, however, only one aspect of the problem of growth, for in Smith's system the growth rate depends not only on the proportion of the labour force employed productively, but also on the productivity of productive labour. It is to explain this that Smith introduces the concept with which he is so closely associated, the division of labour. Division of labour raises productivity, he argued, for three reasons. (1) Workmen's dexterity improves as they perform an operation more frequently. (2) Time is saved, for men do not have to pass so frequently from one operation to another. (3) Machinery can be employed.

Though Smith's most noted example of the division of labour, pin-making, is an example of the division of labour within a factory, he attached far greater importance to the division of labour between firms: to specialization within a country. Men can specialize only if they can exchange their produce for the other goods that they need, and the ability to do this is limited by the extent of the market:

As it is the power of exchanging that gives occasion to the division of labour, so the extent of this division must always be limited by the extent of that power, or, in other words, by the extent of the market. When the market is very small, no person can have any encouragement to dedicate himself entirely to one employment, for want of the power to exchange all that surplus part of the produce of his own labour, which is over and above his own consumption, for such parts of the produce of other men's labour as he has occasion for. (Smith, 1776, p. 21.)

The main means whereby markets can be widened was, Smith believed, water transport, which reduced costs enormously compared with land transport. Regions far from the sea or rivers had restricted opportunities to exchange their produce, and were thus limited in the extent to which division of labour was possible.

Smith viewed the division of labour as the main cause of rising productivity, the first three chapters of the *Wealth of Nations* being devoted to this. It is, however, not correct to see him as anticipating the 'industrial revolution', which dates from the closing decades of the eighteenth century. The examples of mechanization Smith cites all date from the middle of the eighteenth century or before, and, even in the second edition of the *Wealth of Nations*, published as late as 1784, he fails to mention any of the inventions which were shortly to revolutionize the cotton industry. In addition, many of his examples relate to small-scale production. The pin factory, for example, employed only ten workers. He shows no signs of anticipating the movement towards large-scale factory production which was to be a feature of the following century's growth.

2.2 THE INDUSTRIAL REVOLUTION IN ENGLAND

Background

During the eighteenth century economists became aware of the problem of economic growth as something involving the whole economy, not simply foreign trade. Though the changes involved were small in comparison with those which occurred later, there was substantial and noticeable growth, especially in England. Towards the end of the eighteenth century, however, the pace and character of the process of economic growth changed, first in England, and later in the rest of Western Europe.

The most dramatic aspect of this process was the transformation of the cotton textile industry. A series of innovations occurred from the 1770s onwards which reduced costs and led to the rapid rise in production shown in table 2.3. This was a new type of development, for in order to take advantage of the new inventions, large-scale organization involving substantial investment was necessary. In addition, the cotton industry

Table 2.3   The growth of the British cotton industry

	Raw cotton consumption (m.lb)	Gross value of cotton output (£m.)	Value of Exports (£m.)
1760	3.4	0.6	0.3
1773	4.2	0.9	0.3
1782	8.7	4.0	n.a.
1785	16.1	5.4	0.9
1788	24.7	7.0	1.6
1796	26.5	10.0	3.7
1799	41.8	11.1	5.1
1802	54.3	15.0	9.3
1806	63.1	18.9	12.5
1812	65.0	28.3	17.4
1816	99.7	30.0	17.4
1820	141	29.4	15.5
1825	169	33.1	16.9
1830	249	32.1	18.1
1835	331	44.6	22.5
1840	452	46.7	23.3
1845	560	46.7	25.9
1850	621	45.7	27.8
1855	802	56.9	34.9
1860	1050	77.0	49.1

Source: Deane and Cole (1969), pp. 185, 187.

Growth and Development

Table 2.4   The growth of British iron production

	Pig iron production ('000 tons)	Production per furnace ('000 tons)
1740	17	
1788	68	
1796	125	
1806	258	
1810	400	1.8
1825	580	2.2
1828	700	2.5
1840	1400	3.5
1843	1220	3.6
1847	2000	4.6
1852	2700	5.4

Source: 1740–1806 from Landes (1969), p. 96; 1810–52 from Riden (1980), p. 76.

came very quickly to be dominated by foreign trade: by about the turn of the century over half the industry's output was being exported. Associated with this mechanization of the cotton industry was the application of steam power, and the development of the iron industry, as shown in tables 2.4 and 2.5. The movement towards larger-scale in iron production is illustrated by the figures for output per furnace. The growth rates achieved in these two sectors are shown in table 2.6.

Associated with the rise of these industries was a significant structural change, cotton's share of industrial output rising from under 3 per cent in 1770 to 17 per cent in 1801, and to 25 per cent in 1831. At the same time there was a further movement away from agriculture and into industry: in 1760 agriculture employed 53 per cent of the labour force, industry only 24 per cent. By 1800 this had changed to 41 and 30 per cent, and by 1840 to 29 and 47 per cent. This shift away from agriculture was much more rapid than in countries which industrialized subsequently

Table 2.5   Steam engines in Britain

	Non-Watt engines	Watt engines	Total
1712	1	—	1
1781	360	—	360
1795		150	
1800	830	500	1200–1330

Source: Mathias (1983), p. 123. See Harris (1967).

Table 2.6 Growth rates in the cotton and iron industries

	Cotton	Iron
1700–60	1.37	0.60
1760–70	4.59	1.65
1770–80	6.20	4.47
1780–90	12.76	3.79
1790–1801	6.73	3.79
1801–11	4.49	7.45
1811–21	5.59	−0.28
1821–31	6.82	6.47

Figures are percentages per annum. Cotton is growth rate of retained raw cotton imports; iron is growth rate of pig iron output.
Source: Crafts (1985), p. 23.

Table 2.7 Growth rates of output and national product

1700–60	0.7	0.7
1760–80	1.5	0.7
1780–1801	2.1	1.3
1801–31	3.0	2.0
1831–60	3.3	2.5

Figures are percentages per annum.
Source: Crafts (1985), pp. 32, 45, 81, 84.

(Crafts, 1985, p. 62). Despite the size of the structural changes which took place, there was no dramatic rise in the growth rate either of industrial production, or of national income (see table 2.7). Firstly, the rise in cotton and iron production was accompanied by enormous falls in prices relative to prices in other sectors. The result was that their shares of output rose by much less than the growth rates of output would suggest. Secondly, 'unmodernized' sectors still accounted for the bulk of economic activity.

Corresponding to this gradual rise in the overall growth rate was a gradual rise in the share of output being devoted to investment, as shown in table 2.8.

The English classical perspective

At the same time as developments in the cotton and iron industries were, albeit very gradually, laying the foundations for a transformation of the British economy, there emerged the English classical vision of the process of economic growth. The origins of the classical theory lay in Smith's

Table 2.8 Investment as a percentage of output

1700	4
1760	6
1780	7
1801	7.9
1811	8.5
1821	11.2
1831	11.7

Source: Crafts (1985), p. 73.

Wealth of Nations, but new ideas were introduced into his theory with the result that something very different emerged. These ideas were the Malthusian theory of population growth, and the Ricardian theory of rent (called Ricardian, though it was developed independently by a number of economists).

Malthus's theory, first expounded in his *Essay on Population* in 1798 and developed in subsequent editions, was that, if unchecked, population would outgrow the supply of food. Population was capable of growing in a geometric ratio (1, 2, 4, 8, 16, . . .) whereas the supply of food could grow only in an arithmetic ratio (1, 2, 3, 4, 5, . . .). Population growth thus had to be restrained below its potential rate by checks operating on either the birth rate (preventive checks) or the death rate (positive checks). Such checks included moral restraint (primarily postponing the age of marriage), vice (including birth control) and misery (starvation).

It is tempting to relate Malthus's theory to the population explosion that England was experiencing (see table 2.9), but to do so would be a mistake. When he wrote the first edition of his *Essay*, Malthus believed that the British population had been stationary since the time of Gregory King (who estimated it at 5.5 million in 1688). The first census, in 1801, revealed that there had been enormous growth since then, but Malthus took little notice of this. As regards the causes of this rise in population growth, recent research suggests that Malthus may have been right in stressing variation in marriage rates. When the cost of living was high, fewer marriages took place than when it was low, this resulting in a lower birth rate. Malthus's theory, however, was intended as a universal theory, not an explanation of what was happening around him. It was put forward to refute the notion that social reform could be used as a means of improving society: its message was that unless a means were found to curb the birth rate, population would expand until people were reduced to subsistence.

If Malthus's population theory owed little to contemporary economic events, the opposite was true of the theory of rent, published simultaneously by West Torrens, Malthus and Ricardo in 1815. Napoleon's attempt to exclude Britain from European trade meant that grain prices rose sharply

Table 2.9   The growth rate of population

	Population (million)	Annual percentage growth rate
1691	4.9	0.0
1701	5.1	0.3
1711	5.2	0.3
1721	5.4	0.2
1731	5.3	−0.2
1741	5.6	0.6
1751	5.8	0.3
1761	6.1	0.6
1771	6.4	0.5
1781	7.0	0.9
1791	7.7	0.9
1801	8.7	1.1
1811	9.9	1.3
1821	11.5	1.5

Source: Wrigley and Schofield (1981), pp. 528–9.

in years of scarcity. The area of land under cultivation rose, until by 1815 virtually all wasteland was uncultivable. In addition there were numerous enclosures, much land being turned over from rough grazing to more intensive cultivation. Along with the rise in grain prices went large increases in rents.

The Ricardian theory of rent was a generalization from this experience. As agricultural output expands, less and less fertile land has to be brought into cultivation. Rent is the premium which can be charged for the use of land more fertile than the least fertile land being cultivated. Suppose, for example, that there are five plots of land, A, B, C, D and E, capable of yielding harvests of 100, 70, 50, 40 and 30 bushels of wheat respectively. Suppose that the capital and labour required to work each plot of land costs £50, and that the price of wheat is £1 per bushel. Plots A, B and C will be cultivated, but plots D and E will be too infertile to be worth cultivating. Plot C is only just fertile enough to be worth cultivating, so its owner will be unable to obtain any rent. In contrast, the owners of plots A and B will be able to obtain rents of £50 and £20 respectively. Now suppose the price of wheat rises to £1.25 per bushel. It will now be just worth cultivating plot D, but D's owner will obtain no rent. The rise in the price of wheat will raise rents on plots A, B and C to £75, £37.50 and £12.50 respectively.

The Malthusian theory of population and the Ricardian theory of rent were the main components of Ricardo's theory of growth (developed in his *Principles of Political Economy and Taxation*, 1817). As in Smith's theory, capital accumulation led to increased production, but the effects of this were very different. Firstly, Malthus's population theory implied that any rise in wages above subsistence would simply lead to population growth, forcing wages back down to subsistence. Any rise in production would thus be accompanied by population growth and an increased demand for food. Because of the scarcity of fertile land, less and less fertile land would have to be brought into cultivation, and the price of food, together with rents, would rise. This would result in a rise in wages, for otherwise workers would not be able to survive, the result being a fall in profits. Eventually this process would result in a level of profits so low that there would be no incentive to invest, and growth would come to an end. The economy would reach a stationary state.

During the period after 1815 economists accumulated a lot of evidence that was inconsistent with Ricardo's theory. Census returns showed that the birth rate was falling up to the 1840s, despite the fact that food prices were not rising. Thus by the early 1830s most economists had abandoned the Malthusian population doctrine. One of the first to break with it was Nassau Senior who wrote, in 1929, that 'in the absence of a disturbing cause, food has a tendency to increase faster [than population], because, in fact, *it has generally done so*' (quoted in Blaug, 1986, p. 96). In addition, the evidence that food production had increased substantially (population rose by 9 million from 1801 to 1831, with wheat imports never exceeding 500,000 quarters a year) whilst employment in agriculture had risen much more slowly than population as a whole (7 per cent compared with 34 per cent) cast serious doubts on the existence of diminishing returns in agriculture.

Evidence on whether the rate of profit was declining is, even today, hard to obtain and inconclusive, though it has been claimed that profits were falling in industries, such as cotton textiles, where raw materials accounted for a high proportion of costs. When prices were rising, raw materials prices usually rose faster than prices of manufactured goods and when prices fell they fell more slowly (Church, 1980, Introduction, p. 27). In both the cotton and iron industries entrepreneurs were forced to innovate in order to survive in the face of increased competition and falling profit margins. The fall in the price of cotton goods is shown by the figures in table 2.3 which show that cotton output (measured by consumption of raw cotton) rose much faster than the value of goods produced. This perspective is consistent with the views of contemporaries: in 1833 witnesses before a Parliamentary select committee were unanimous in considering the level of profits to be no more than adequate. Even though contemporaries may have had reason to believe that the rate of profit was falling, however, there was evidence to suggest that this was not due to diminishing agricultural productivity. The failure of the wheat price to rise, even before the Corn Laws were repealed in 1846, is one piece of evidence. So too is the evidence cited above that agricultural productivity was rising. In addition we have McCulloch's conclusion that although rents had, he estimated, risen by about £30m. between 1815 and 1845, the level of rents in England was still 'moderate'. It thus seems reasonable to conclude that there was enough evidence available to cast serious doubt on the Ricardian theory. Economists such as McCulloch and J. S. Mill who continued to support it did so in the face of evidence to the contrary.

Ricardo's theory of growth had very direct implications for economic policy, for it implied that the sole obstacle to growth was the rising cost of subsistence. If the problem of diminishing returns in agriculture could be overcome by trade, with manufactured goods being exported in order to buy food, growth could continue indefinitely. There would, he argued, always be a market for increased production, for increased production would create its own demand. Free trade in corn, therefore, was the policy required to make growth possible. The Corn Laws, which protected British agriculture by imposing a tariff on imported corn, had to be removed. It is thus justifiable to argue that Ricardo had an optimistic view of the prospects for economic growth, for the barriers to growth were only political.

Ricardo's view that growth would never be constrained by a shortage of demand, did not go unquestioned. One of its major critics was Malthus, who tried, somewhat ineffectively, to show that growth might falter if demand were insufficient. The core of his argument was that consumption out of wages could not, by itself, create enough demand to sustain production, for the value of production must exceed wages. The additional consumption necessary to sustain demand could, Malthus argued, come from consumption out of rents. If consumption out of rents were too low, demand would be insufficient to cover production and a general glut would result. The correct response to such an argument is that demand can also be created by investment: provided that savings are all spent on purchasing capital equipment, no shortage of demand need emerge. Malthus's reason for stressing the need for consumption was that investment will lead to higher production, which means increased investment may make a glut worse rather than better.

Malthus's arguments failed to make much headway against the Ricardian view for a number of reasons. The major one was that he never managed to formulate his ideas in a logically consistent way. His opponents (Ricardo and Say) were thus able to point out his errors, without being forced to re-examine their own theories. A different type of reason was that Malthus's ideas could be seen as involving a return to a Physiocratic view of the world, in which agriculture is dominant (remember that for Quesnay it was landlords' expenditure which sustained economic activity). Malthus was initially very hostile to industrialization and, though he softened his views considerably in later editions of his *Essay*, he was never as enthusiastic about the benefits of manufacturing-based growth as were Ricardo and the other leading economists of the period. Malthus's position as the champion of the agricultural interests and the landowning classes may have been one reason why his views on gluts did not receive much support. Such a position was becoming unpopular as the role of industry in the economy increased.

It may seem strange, in view of the transformation which was taking place in the cotton industry, that in this account of classical writing on growth, no mention has been made of inventions, and the use of new machinery to raise productivity. An economist who did recognize the significance of new inventions and mechanization, including the inventions that were transforming the cotton industry, was J. R. McCulloch, writing mostly in the 1820s and 1830s. His analysis of growth, stressing capital accumulation and division of labour, owed more to Smith than to Ricardo. McCulloch claimed, however, that Smith had stressed invention too little compared with the division of labour. Invention, he argued, provided limitless opportunities for growth: technical progress would reduce the price of manufactured goods, offsetting any rise in the price of agricultural goods, thus removing the need for wages to rise as an economy grew. Furthermore, because he accepted the view that the subsistence wage was psychologically determined, rising over time, McCulloch realized that technological progress might permanently raise wage rates, for rises in wage rates would not necessarily result in population growth.

A major problem in the years after 1815 was the so-called 'machinery question': there was a widespread popular fear that the introduction of labour-saving machinery would throw people out of work. Outbreaks of machine-breaking, both in industry and in agriculture, occurred regularly in times of commercial crisis. Of particular concern was the plight of the hand loom weavers, for their numbers had increased enormously as a result of cotton spinning being mechanized before weaving. The enormous increase in cotton production led to an increase in the number of hand-loom weavers. When power looms began to be introduced the result was enormous distress amongst the ranks of the hand-loom weavers. Wage rates amongst hand-loom weavers, for example, fell from £1.15 per week in 1805 to 41p per week by 1818, and to 30p by 1831. The problem confronting economists was to decide whether such distress was a permanent consequence of the introduction of new machinery, or merely a temporary effect.

The classical economists analysed this problem in two ways. The most common was to argue in terms of the 'wages fund'. The argument was that if capitalists were suddenly to increase their fixed capital (machinery) this would reduce the amount of circulating capital (the wages fund) available to employ labour. The result would thus be that a sudden increase in machinery would lead to a fall in employment. This was the position Ricardo adopted in the third edition of his *Principles* (1821). In previous editions he had assumed that the introduction of cost-reducing machinery must be to the benefit of everyone. The other approach was that of McCulloch, who in 1821 argued that the crucial issue was what happened to output. If labour-saving machinery were introduced, costs and hence prices would fall. If the labour displaced by the machines were to be re-employed it was necessary that these price reductions stimulate demand and increase output. This was exactly what was happening in the early nineteenth-century cotton industry, which was characterized by a cycle of improved machinery, falling costs and rising output. Far more than Ricardo, therefore, McCulloch was aware of, and understood, the transformation which was taking place in British industry.

Marx

The first volume of Karl Marx's *Capital* was published in 1867, with subsequent volumes appearing much later after his death. His ideas on how a capitalist economy grows were, however, formed in the 1840s. This decade, sometimes referred to as 'the hungry forties', was one of great hardship for many members of the working class, especially in the very severe depression of 1842. Industrialization had gone a long way but it had probably not at that stage brought about any rise in living standards. It was only from the 1850s that real wages began to rise significantly and, in addition, the government began to take action on issues such as public health, sanitary conditions and education. For the working classes the 1840s may well have been the worst decade of the nineteenth century.

Although Marx was German and steeped in German philosophy, his economics was purely English in origin, being based on Ricardo. Like many socialists before him, he took up Ricardo's labour theory of value and used it as an argument that profits were the result of capitalists' exploiting workers. The capitalist buys labour power at its value, which is its cost of production, namely the cost of the workers' subsistence. Because this is less than the value of the commodities workers produce, the capitalist is left with a surplus. If the worker is, for example, forced to work for 12 hours, and it takes only four hours to produce his or her subsistence, eight hours of 'unpaid' labour will have been provided. This 'unpaid' labour is the surplus extracted by the capitalist, and constitutes the capitalist's profits.

Marx's theory of growth is based on his 'reproduction schemes'. These were inspired by Quesnay's *Tableau Economique* (see pp. 9–12) and showed how capital reproduced itself from year to year. He divided the economy into two 'departments', or sectors: department I produces capital goods and department II consumer goods. Making certain assumptions about the 'rate of exploitation' (essentially the ratio of profits to wages), the 'organic composition of capital' (the ratio of fixed capital to capital used to employ labour or, in other words, capital per head) and how capitalists allocate their profits between consumption and investment, Marx was able to show, using a series of numerical examples, how capital would grow over time. Though not fully appreciated by orthodox economists until the 1960s, these reproduction schemes were remarkable exercises in the theory of economic growth.

Marx's main interest, however, was not in abstract economic theory but in the future of capitalism. His vision of this was based on his prediction that the organic composition of capital would rise steadily, with increased mechanization and the substitution of capital for labour. Given a constant rate of exploitation (profits divided by wages) this implies that the rate of profit (profits divided by the capital stock) must fall. Faced with this situation capitalists respond by trying to increase the rate of exploitation: they innovate, they try to increase the length of the working day and they try to push wages below the subsistence level. In addition, this process of increased mechanization will throw people out of work, increasing the 'reserve army' of the unemployed. The working class will become pauperized, mechanization reducing work to mere mechanical activity, causing a deterioration in working conditions.

Though we may dispute the route by which Marx reached these conclusions, this picture of capitalists' being forced to innovate in the face of severe competition, with dire consequences for the working class, fits well with the situation facing British industry in the 1830s and 1840s (see p. 20). From the 1850s onwards, however, when real wages began to increase steadily and conditions for the working classes improved, Marx's vision of a process in which the position of the working class became more and more intolerable, eventually resulting in a revolution, seemed less and less appropriate.

2.3 GROWTH IN TWENTIETH-CENTURY INDUSTRIAL COUNTRIES

Introduction

In 1952 Moses Abramovitz, surveying the economics of growth claimed that, in contrast to most other areas of economics, 'the problem of growth lacks any organised and generally known body of doctrine' (Abramovitz, 1952, p. 132). Smith, Ricardo and Mill had, he argued, examined the links between growth and the distribution of income; others (such as Marx, the German historians and the American Institutionalists) had investigated the rise and decline of capitalist institutions; whilst others (such as Tawney, Weber and Veblen) had considered the role of mental attitudes in fostering the growth of science and its application to industry. In addition there had been work on the theory of saving and population growth which was relevant to problems of growth, as was statistical and historical research into the subject. None of this, however, had been organized into a useful hypothesis capable of explaining differences in growth rates.

Since then the position has changed in that, for a number of reasons, economic growth became the subject of a large amount of research. In the 1950s, once the immediate postwar problems were out of the way, the Western world entered a period of sustained growth. In addition, Keynesian economics provided an enormous theoretical stimulus: Keynes's concepts of saving, investment and national income were clearly relevant to the question of long-term growth, facing economists with the task of extending Keynes's theory to deal with the problem. This task was made easier by economists' increased knowledge of mathematics. Finally, due above all to the work of Raymond Goldsmith, Simon Kuznets and their associates at the National Bureau of Economic Research in the US, and Colin Clark in Britain, economists had available an unprecedented amount of statistical material on growth.

The Harrod–Domar Model

The theory which initiated what has been described as 'the snowball of modern growth theory' is what has come to be known as the Harrod–Domar model. Although Harrod's version of this model (1939) came first, Domar's model (1946) is easier to follow. Its starting point is that investment performs two functions. It generates aggregate demand, via the multiplier, and it leads to an increase in productive capacity. From this Domar derived the condition that if demand was to grow at the same rate as productive capacity, the growth rate must equal s/v, where s is the average propensity to save and v is the 'incremental capital output ratio' (ICOR). The ICOR is the level of investment required to raise productive capacity by \$1, so $1/v$ is the increase in productive capacity that results from investing \$1. If the multiplier is $1/s$ and demand is to rise by \$$(1/v)$, investment must rise by \$$(s/v)$. The equilibrium growth rate, the growth rate that must occur if demand and supply (productive capacity) are to grow at the same rate, is therefore s/v. If investment does not grow at this rate then either (if investment is growing too fast) output will be rising at an unsustainable rate, or (if investment is growing too slowly) output will be growing too slowly, and productive capacity will be becoming less and less fully utilized (secular stagnation).

In this theory, s and v are both assumed to be constant. The main reason for this was that it made the problem simpler, though Domar did suggest that over long periods of time s and v might in practice be constant. Kuznets's work suggested that s had been constant at about 12 per cent from 1879 to 1941, whilst v was thought to be just over 3. The implication of these numbers was that if there was to be a continued balance between output and productive capacity, investment would have to grow at 3–4 per cent each year. Between 1879 and 1941 US national income had grown at 3.3 per cent per annum.

Though his model was very similar, Harrod posed the problem in a different way. He christened the growth rate s/v the 'warranted' growth rate, for this was the growth rate warranted by the level of saving in the economy. Against this was set the 'natural' rate of growth, the rate determined by the rate of growth of the labour force and the rate of technical progress (the rate at which potential output per head is growing). The problem, he argued, was that there was no reason why the natural and warranted growth rates should be the same: s, v and n all depended on different factors. This problem was made worse because, for reasons we will not go into here, if the actual growth rate were not equal to the warranted rate, it would move further and further away from it. In other words, the warranted rate of growth was not stable.

Contemporary growth theory

The Harrod–Domar model was the starting point for an enormous literature on the theory of economic growth. In this literature, theoretical issues were without question dominant. Beyond the concern to explain what came to be called certain 'stylized facts' about long-run growth (that output per head and capital per head both increase, and that the capital–output ratio neither rises nor falls, and that the distribution of national income between capital and labour is approximately constant) there was only a limited concern with facts about the real world. Economists were concerned to extend the Harrod–Domar model, and to solve the resulting theoretical puzzles.

The dominant approach came to be known as 'neoclassical' growth theory. The main characteristic of neoclassical growth models is that markets are assumed to be perfectly competitive, with firms organizing production so as to maximize their profits, and with prices determined by supply and demand. To see how such models work, suppose that an economy is growing at rate s/v, and that this growth rate is greater than the rate of population growth. This means that demand for labour will be rising faster than supply, and that the wage rate will rise. Firms will respond to this by adopting more capital-intensive methods in order to reduce their labour costs, and so v will rise. This will lower s/v, bringing the growth rate down towards the rate of population growth. Similarly, if growth is too sluggish, with the result that unemployment is emerging, wages will be pushed downwards. The result will be that firms will have an incentive to use more labour and less capital, and so v will fall; s/v will rise. Competitive forces, therefore, will act so as to bring s/v into line with the growth rate of the labour force. It is possible to show, therefore, that the economy will converge towards a growth path on which it is growing at a rate determined by the growth rate of the labour force. In neoclassical growth theory, therefore, Harrod's problems are both solved. Variations in v will bring the warranted rate into line with the natural rate, and the responses of factor prices to supply and demand will ensure that the economy moves towards the natural rate of growth.

The basic neoclassical model was, especially during the 1950s and 1960s, extended in an enormous number of directions: to distinguish between two sectors, one producing consumption goods, the other investment goods; to allow for a variety of different capital goods, with all the problems that involves; to bring in the government, and government debt; to allow for changes in the fraction of income saved.

Central to most aggregative neoclassical growth models is the concept of the aggregate production function: the relationship between the level of output, and inputs of capital and labour. This was the subject of one of the most heated controversies in post-war economics, over whether or not it was meaningful to use an aggregate measure of capital in a production function. The argument is that in neoclassical theory the quantity of capital performs two functions simultaneously. The first is that it is a measure of the stock of capital goods in the economy: the amount of capital in this sense determines the amount that can be produced. The second function of capital in neoclassical models is that it measures the value of the capital stock for the purpose of calculating profits: profits are calculated as a percentage of capital invested. The Cambridge criticism of neoclassical theory, of which Joan Robinson was the main architect, was to argue that it was impossible to find a measure of capital that could perform these two functions simultaneously. Joan Robinson and her followers claimed that this invalidated any theory in which wages and profits were based on marginal productivity.

The resulting controversy was known as the Cambridge controversy on the grounds that the main participants were based either in Cambridge, England (Joan Robinson) or in Cambridge, Massachusetts (Robert Solow). It lasted for over a decade and attracted a great deal of attention but was inconclusive. Cambridge (England) 'won' in that their arguments about the aggregate production function were shown to be correct. On the other hand, neoclassical economists continued to defend marginal productivity theory; they used aggregate production functions as simple illustrations. Though some things were learned about the concept of capital, it can be argued that this was an example of theoretical energy that might better have been directed at other, more down-to-earth, problems.

Statistical research into growth

At the same time as growth theory was being developed on the basis of Keynesian economics it was becoming possible, for the first time, to approach the problem statistically. One of the simplest and most attractive approaches was to look for relationships between the distribution of production between sectors and the level of wealth. Colin Clark, for example, in one of the earliest and most influential works on the subject, analysed economies in terms of the distribution of the workforce between primary industries (agriculture, forestry and fishing), secondary industries (manufacturing, mining and building) and tertiary industries (other activities, including communications, transport and services). Low real incomes, he argued, were associated with a high proportion of the workforce employed in the primary sector, and a low proportion in the tertiary sector. China, for example, with an income of 120 units (see p. 34) per capita, had 75–80 per cent of its workforce in the primary sector. Europe and Argentina, with incomes in the range 500–1000 units, had between 33 per cent and 40 per cent employed in the tertiary sector, whilst the US, with an income level of 1380 units, had 50 per cent of its workforce in the tertiary sector.

The significance of such cross-country comparisons was reinforced by evidence on how the shares of different sectors had changed over time within countries. Clark found that the share of primary activities normally declined over time, with that of the tertiary sector rising. The share of

Table 2.10   Denison's estimates of the sources of growth, 1950–62

Sources of growth	US		Germany		UK	
Labour	1.12		1.37		0.60	
Employment		0.90		1.49		0.50
Hours of work		−0.17		−0.27		−0.15
Age–sex composition		−0.10		0.04		−0.04
Education		0.49		0.11		0.29
Capital	0.83		1.41		0.51	
Dwellings		0.25		0.14		0.04
International assets		0.05		−0.08		−0.05
Nonresidential structures		0.43		1.02		0.43
Inventories		0.10		0.33		0.09
Land	0.00		0.00		0.00	
Total factor input	1.95		2.78		1.11	
Advances of knowledge	0.76		0.76		0.76	
Changes in the lag in the application of knowledge (measured relative to the US) etc.						
Reduction in the age of capital	. .		0.04		0.00	
Other	. .		0.80		0.03	
Improved allocation of resources						
Contraction of agric. inputs	0.25		0.77		0.06	
Contraction of self-employment	0.04		0.14		0.04	
Reduction in trade barriers	0.00		0.10		0.02	
Balancing of the capital stock	. .		0.26		. .	
Economies of scale						
Growth of national market	0.30		0.63		0.22	
Growth of local markets	0.06		0.07		0.05	
Income elasticities	. .		0.91		0.09	
Irregularities in pressure of demand	−0.04		. .		−0.09	
Output per unit of input	1.37		4.48		1.18	
National income	3.32		7.26		2.29	

Figures are contributions to average annual growth rates in percentage points. A pair of dots indicates that the figure concerned was not calculated.
Source: Denison (1967), pp. 298, 308, 314.

secondary industries rose at first, and later, as tertiary activities became more important, declined. The share of secondary industries, for example, reached its maximum in Britain around 1901 and in the US around 1920. This pattern was something that could be explained in terms of shifts in the pattern of demand. For example, as people become more wealthy they spend a smaller fraction of their income on food, hence the declining share of agriculture.

These inquiries bore no relation to the theories of growth which were developed during the 1950s and 1960s. More closely related to growth theory were attempts to estimate the contributions of different factors to growth. This work was based on the theory that under perfect competition factors will be paid their marginal products. The wage rate will thus measure the output that would be lost if employment were reduced by one person. Similarly, the rate of profit measures the output that would be lost if the capital stock were $1 smaller. It follows from this that if, for example, wages comprise 75 per cent of output, and profits 25 per cent, a 1 per cent increase in employment will result in a 0.75 per cent increase in output, and a 1 per cent increase in the capital stock will raise output by 0.25 per cent. This can be used to calculate the contributions of labour and capital to growth. Continue this example by assuming that output has risen by 15 per cent over some period, with the capital stock increasing by 12 per cent and employment by 8 per cent. Labour force growth has contributed 0.75x8 per cent = 6 per cent to the growth of output, and capital has contributed 0.25x12 per cent = 4 per cent. Thus, of the 15 per cent growth in output, 6 per cent is due to labour force growth, 4 per cent to capital accumulation, with the remaining 5 per cent being due to other factors, such as technical progress.

Although he was not the first to adopt this approach to growth, the economist who took this approach furthest was Edward Denison. In order to explain why different countries grow at different rates he took the US and eight European countries and calculated the contributions of various factors to growth. However, rather than simply calculate contributions of capital and labour, he adopted a much more detailed classification of factors of production, deriving estimates such as those shown in table 2.10.

To get an idea of how these figures are calculated, consider some examples. The value of education is measured by comparing the earnings of people with different numbers of years of education. If workers with 12 years of education earn 50 per cent more than workers with only seven years, then this part of their earnings is assumed to measure the productivity of an extra five years of education. Given data on how the educational qualifications of the workforce have changed we can thus work out the contribution of education to growth. As another example, consider the contribution of movement out of agriculture. The argument here is that productivity is lower in agriculture than in other sectors of the economy, so that if labour moves out of agriculture, average productivity will be raised, raising the growth rate. The contribution of this factor is calculated from data on agricultural and non-agricultural productivity, together with figures on numbers employed in agriculture. Many of the figures in this table are based on a large degree of guesswork. The contribution of increasing returns to scale, for example, is based on the assumption that when inputs increase by 10 per cent, output rises by 11 per cent in the US and by 11.1 per cent in Germany and the UK. Reasons were given as to why such figures were plausible ones, but they were nothing more than intelligent guesses.

One of the most significant items in table 2.10 is the item entitled 'advances in knowledge'. This is simply a residual: what is left over after the contributions of all other factors have been deducted from the actual growth rate. It was assumed that the US, which had the highest levels of productivity, was using the best available techniques, and that where other countries' residuals were higher than the American, this was caused by their catching up with the US. The US residual, therefore, was taken as measuring advances in knowledge.

Denison's attempt to explain differences in growth rates was an impressive achievement, but serious doubts have been raised concerning the value of his estimates. One problem is that there is an enormous amount of guesswork involved and the assumptions made are very strong, in particular the assumption that factor payments measure marginal productivities. In addition, the theory of marginal productivity, which is the basis for the whole approach, has been questioned (see pp. 26–7). Even if such problems were overcome, however, there would still remain the problem that key issues are left unexplained. The rate of technical progress, for example, is unexplained. In addition, there may be links between the various 'contributions' to growth: it is possible, for example, that had hours per worker been higher, total employment would have been lower. Thus it is very hard to use such estimates to draw conclusions about policies that would raise growth rates.

Economists have reacted to the work of Denison and others doing similar work in a number of ways. One response is to reject the whole approach, arguing that the estimates are based on so many unjustifiable assumptions that they are meaningless. An alternative approach is to use such methods much more modestly. Denison's work was ambitious in two ways: he tried to obtain highly detailed estimates of how different factors contributed to growth; and he used his estimates to make comparisons across very different economies. A much more modest use of his methods is found in more recent attempts to estimate what has come to be called 'total factor productivity growth', or 'multi-factor productivity growth'. This is simply the residual after deducting the growth in output attributable to capital and labour, using simple aggregate measures of both employment and the capital stock. The way such measures are used is shown in the next section.

The productivity slowdown of the 1970s

Growth theory and estimates of contributions to growth are of only limited usefulness in explaining growth rates, with the result that economists have had to use more ad hoc methods to analyse problems to do with growth. To illustrate this we consider the problem of the slowdown in productivity growth which occurred during the 1970s. The extent of the slowdown is shown in table 2.11. After 1973 the growth rate of output per head fell in virtually all Western industrial countries. The task confronting economists was to explain this in order to be able to predict whether or not it would continue, and to advise on the appropriate policies to pursue.

The 1970s were a time of enormous economic upheaval. Many Western economies were expanding very rapidly for the first 2–3 years of the decade, and commodity prices began to rise significantly in 1972. Then, towards the end of 1973, the major oil exporting countries succeeded in forming an effective cartel which raised the price of oil from $2.7 per barrel in 1973 to $9.8 per barrel in 1974 (these prices are for Saudi Arabian oil). Associated with this rise in the price of oil was a temporary shortage as the Arab–Israeli war resulted in the closure of the Suez canal. Then in 1979, following the revolution in Iran, the price of oil was raised again, the price rising from $12.7 in 1978 to $28.7 in 1980 (see figure 5.14).

These fluctuations had severe repercussions on the rest of the world. (1) Such a dramatic rise in the price of oil was very inflationary. (2) Oil importing countries suddenly found themselves with large trade deficits, and because they could not immediately find alternatives to oil, they had to reduce their imports of other goods. Because there was no corresponding rise in imports by oil producers, the result was a large fall in world demand. Output fell and unemployment rose very substantially in many industrial countries. (3) The rise in the price of oil meant that it now became worth conserving energy, and adopting techniques that used much less energy than previously. Capital equipment that was profitable only at low energy prices became obsolete. (4) Because of the need to pay more for oil imports, oil importing countries had to export more. This meant that they had to adjust to producing goods for export instead of goods for the home market. (5) For some countries, such as Norway and the UK, it now became profitable to develop new sources of oil, such as the North Sea. The result of these, and other shocks, was that the 1970s saw lower growth and higher and more variable inflation rates than in the previous two decades.

Output per head could have grown more slowly after 1973 for two reasons. One is a fall in the growth rate of capital per worker: the shocks to which industrial countries were subject could have reduced investment and hence capital accumulation. The other is that the disturbances after 1973 could have reduced the output obtainable from given inputs of capital and labour. Here the concept of total factor productivity proved a useful

Table 2.11 The growth rate of output per head

	US		UK		France		Germany	
	Economy	Manufacturing	Economy	Manufacturing	Economy	Manufacturing	Economy	Manufacturing
1962–9	2.7	3.1	3.1	4.5	5.2	6.3	5.3	5.9
1969–73	2.6	3.2	3.9	4.1	5.7	5.4	5.2	4.8
1973–5	0.3	−0.3	0.7	−1.3	2.6	2.8	4.0	5.2
1975–9	2.1	3.0	2.0	1.2	5.0	6.1	4.5	5.0

Source: Sachs (1979), p. 275.

framework through which to tackle the problem. Early studies (e.g. Denison, 1979) suggested that after 1973 there had been a slowdown in the growth rate of total factor productivity: the slowdown was not due to a slowdown in the rate of capital accumulation. Though such work was a useful starting point, however, it did not settle the issue. Firstly, it was argued that there were problems with the way in which capital inputs were calculated. It was argued (for example Baily, 1981) that due to the economic disturbances in the 1970s, and in particular to the rise in energy prices, depreciation had been much more rapid than the statisticians had allowed for, and that the reason for the slowdown was that capital had been rendered less efficient. Secondly, irrespective of whether or not these arguments were accepted, there remained the problem of explaining why these changes had occurred. Was it the sharp rise in energy prices? Was it the rise in unemployment and the period of relative stagnation which followed both oil price rises? Was it the need to adjust to exporting a greater volume of output to pay for oil imports? Growth accounting provided concepts that made it a lot easier to discuss these issues, but neither growth theory nor statistical evidence could be used to provide definitive answers.

2.4 GROWTH IN DEVELOPING COUNTRIES

The emergence of development economics as a problem

It was in the 1950s that development economics emerged as a separate branch of economics, concerned with the situation of countries, mostly in Africa, Asia and Latin America, variously described as 'poor', 'emergent', 'less-developed', 'underdeveloped' or 'developing'. At this time the subject of 'colonial economics' came to be displaced by development economics, the change of terminology reflecting both a new political situation and very substantial changes in the way such economies were viewed. On the political front there was the breaking up of the European empires: within five years of the war, India, Pakistan, Ceylon, Burma, the Philippines, Indonesia, Jordan, Syria, Lebanon and Israel became independent. In addition, the UN provided a forum in which these countries, along with the long-independent states in Latin America, could express their concerns.

Alongside these political changes there was a changed perspective on the problems confronting poor countries. 'Colonial economics' had adopted a static perspective, not envisaging any significant change in the colonies' economic situation. The emphasis was on their position as exporters of primary produce, the main objective being, implicitly at least, stabilization. The desire was to avoid the trade fluctuations which caused such problems during the inter-war period. The term 'development' was normally used to denote the development of natural resources, something separate from the problem of increasing the welfare of a colony's inhabitants. This view was reflected in the British doctrine of the 'dual mandate' (with parallel doctrines in other colonial powers) whereby the colonial government was thought to have two responsibilities: development and the welfare of colonial peoples. After the war such a perspective became less and less tenable. Newly independent countries wanted development, not stability. Furthermore, the Soviet Union's success during the war showed that it was possible deliberately to develop a backward economy.

A further stimulus to research on the problem of economic development was provided by statistical work on national income which showed, for the first time, the extent of the gap between rich and poor countries. One of the most influential early contributions was that of Colin Clark, who produced estimates of national income across different countries in 1940, long before the countries concerned produced their own national income statistics. His conclusion was that

the world is found to be a wretchedly poor place. An average real income per worker of 500 IU ['International Unit', defined as the amount of goods and services that $1 would purchase in the USA from 1925 to 1934] or less (in round figures a standard of living below £2 or $10 per breadwinner) is the lot of 81% of the world's population. A standard of living of 1000 IU per worker per year or more is found only in USA, Canada, Australia, New Zealand, Argentine, Great Britain and Switzerland, containing between them 10% of the world's population. Another 9% of the world's population is found in the principal industrial countries of Europe with an average real income per head between 500 and 1000 IU. About 53% of the world's population, including the whole populations of India and China, enjoys a real income per head of less than 200 IU. Average real income per breadwinner in China and India is about 120 and 200 IU respectively. . . . Two-thirds of the world's whole output of economically valuable goods and services was . . . produced in the so-called industrial countries containing less than one-third of the world's population, and nearly half of the world's output in four countries. (Clark, 1940, pp. 2–3)

Clark's estimates were subject to considerable criticism, and better ones were developed over subsequent decades, but the stark contrast between the wealth of a number of rich, mostly industrial, countries and the rest of the world remained. The problem was compounded by the fact that the rich countries appeared to be growing fairly rapidly, whereas the most poor countries were stagnating. Hans Singer, one of the leading figures in post-war development economics, in 1949 felt confident enough to claim that average world income was then lower than in 1913, the reason being that rapid population growth in poor countries meant that an increasing fraction of the world's population was living in poor countries where the standard of living was not increasing at all. As statistical evidence accumulated, this picture seemed to be confirmed. For example, Simon Kuznets, though he raised serious doubts about Clark's methods, produced similar results, shown in table 2.12. Western Europe was approximately ten times wealthier than Asia and Africa, with the United States even wealthier. In comparing these figures it is crucial to remember that the

Table 2.12   Kuznets's estimates of the distribution of world income

Region	1938			1949		
	Pop	*Inc*	*I/P*	*Pop*	*Inc*	*I/P*
United States	6.1	25.9	429	6.5	40.9	626
Canada, Australia and New Zealand	1.0	3.7	370	1.0	3.5	350
Western Europe	10.1	27.7	275	10.0	21.5	214
USSR	7.9	8.1	102	8.4	11.2	133
Other Europe	8.4	10.8	129	6.4	6.0	94
Latin America	6.0	4.2	71	6.6	4.4	66
Asia	53.2	17.3	33	52.4	10.5	20
Africa	7.3	2.3	32	8.6	2.0	24

Pop: Percentage of world population
Inc: Percentage of world income
I/P: Income per capita (an index with world percapita income = 100)

Source: Kuznets (1956), p. 17.

changes from 1938 to 1949 reflect above all else the effects of the war. This explains the decline in European income relative to that of the US.

Early development economics

One of the earliest and most influential theories of why poor countries were poor was that of Ragnar Nurkse. He started from Adam Smith's observation that division of labour was limited by the extent of the market, but reinterpreted this to imply that where the market was limited there were few opportunities for investment. At the same time, low incomes meant that savings were low. The result was a vicious circle in which income, investment and savings remained low. Other economists added features to this story, but the basic explanation of why poor countries remained poor remained the same. Leibenstein introduced Malthusian arguments to show why it was difficult to raise per capita incomes. Scitovsky and others stressed the importance of externalities and the need to build up an infrastructure of basic services. Transport facilities and education, for example, are things that are essential for development but which are unlikely to be provided in sufficient quantities by the private sector.

One criticism of this type of argument is that it overlooks the opportunities provided by foreign trade. Foreign trade provides access to markets larger than are available at home, providing greater opportunities for investment. In the 1950s, however, it was argued few countries were in a position to use international trade as a means of escaping from the vicious circle of low income and low investment. The reason was that most poor countries produced goods for which the income elasticity of demand was very low: as incomes in rich countries rose, demand for the goods produced by most poor countries grew very slowly. In addition, synthetic substitutes were available for an increasing number of primary products (e.g. rubber, jute, cotton). Because demand for their products was growing relatively slowly, poor countries had very limited scope for increasing their export earnings.

Some economists (notably Hans Singer and Raul Prebisch) went significantly further than this, arguing that there had been a secular deterioration in the terms of trade facing non-industrial countries: the prices of their products were rising more slowly than prices of industrial products. The implication of this was that poor countries' exports would buy an ever-decreasing quantity of industrial goods. Prebisch and economists working for the ECLA (the UN Economic Commission for Latin America) fitted this into a larger theory, arguing that the reason for the deterioration in the terms of trade was the bargaining position of workers in industrial countries. Productivity in both rich and poor countries was rising, but whereas in rich countries this led to rising real wages, in poor countries the result was falling prices. The result of this was that poor countries' goods became cheaper relative to the goods produced by rich countries (the terms of trade moved in favour of rich countries), causing the gains from trade to be distributed unequally. Rich countries, Prebisch claimed, gained more from trade than poor countries.

In analysing the situation of developing countries at this time, enormous stress was laid on the need for investment, and the need to raise saving. Low incomes were considered severely to restrict the ability of poor countries to save, and hence their ability to grow. The Harrod–Domar model, discussed above, provided a simple way of highlighting this problem. According to this model, the growth rate was determined by the savings ratio divided by the ICOR (incremental capital ouput ratio – the amount of capital required to increase output by 1 unit). If the ICOR is 4 (most countries were thought to have ICORs of about 3 or 4) this means that 4 per cent of output must be invested if output is to rise by 1 per cent. Suppose that a poor country's population is growing by 3 per cent p.a. (again a typical figure). Given an ICOR of 4 the country will have to save 12 per cent of its output simply in order to maintain living standards, a 12 per cent savings ratio being required in order to sustain 3 per cent growth in output. As poor countries were thought to be capable of saving only about 5 per cent of their income, the implications of this were very pessimistic.

The importance of raising investment was emphasized in the Arthur Lewis's growth model (Lewis, 1954, 1955) the most influential model of development produced during the 1950s. This model assumed that a developing country comprised two sectors: a backward, agricultural sector, and an advanced industrial sector. There was assumed to be surplus labour in agriculture, the marginal product of labour being either zero or very low. Growth occurred when investment took place in the industrial sector, for this would raise demand for labour, and hence industrial wage rates, attracting labour out of agriculture. As profits earned in the industrial sector were reinvested, so demand for labour would rise still further, and a higher and higher fraction of the workforce would be employed in the industrial sector, this process coming to a halt only when labour was no longer scarce. In this theory, as in the Harrod–Domar model, investment is crucial. If sufficient savings cannot be mobilized to increase the size of the industrial sector, the process of growth and development will not get started.

How then could growth be got going? One answer was for foreign aid to make up for the shortage of domestic savings. If investment could be financed by foreign aid the growth rate could be increased, and incomes raised to the point where domestic savings would be sufficient to finance further growth. The other answer was planning. Economists such as Nurkse and Scitovsky argued that a 'big push' was required for industrialization (seen as almost synonymous with development) to get started. In the words of Paul Rosenstein-Rodan, a leading advocate of the theory of the big push, 'Proceeding "bit by bit" will not add up in its effects to the sum total of the single bits. A minimum quantity of investment is a necessary, though not sufficient, condition of success. This, in a nutshell, is the contention of the theory of the big push' (Rosenstein-Rodan, quoted in Meier, 1970, p. 396). If industries are expanded on a large scale each industry will reinforce the others: they will buy each others' products; consumers' incomes will be raised enabling them to buy the goods produced; all firms will benefit from things such as the creation of an industrial workforce. Such development was something which clearly required extensive planning.

This view of the world is often labelled 'structuralist'. Economic change was thought to be constrained by obstacles, bottlenecks and constraints, with people finding it hard to adapt. Neither supplies nor demands would respond to prices: supplies because of the shortage of entrepreneurs, and the influence of custom and tradition; demands because of poverty. In addition, developing countries were believed to be handicapped by their having a structure of production very different from that of developed countries. The task of planning, therefore, was to change the economic structures of developing countries, so that they resembled more closely those of developed countries. In particular, it was thought necessary to develop manufacturing industry, and to encourage a shift away from agriculture. Planners tried to work out which industries needed to be expanded in order to achieve the desired pattern of production, and to identify likely bottlenecks, thus ensuring that they would not arise. Of particular importance was ensuring that growth would not come to a halt because of shortages of foreign exchange. One strategy, popular in certain Latin American countries, was 'import substitution': developing industries which could produce substitutes for manufactured goods that would otherwise have to be imported from developed countries.

Rostow's theory of the take-off

In the 1960s discussions of economic development came to be dominated by ideas put forward in Rostow's *The Stages of Economic Growth: a Non-Communist Manifesto* (1960). His starting point was not twentieth-century underdeveloped countries, but the experience of those countries, in particular Europe and the USA, that had industrialized successfully. On the basis of their experience Rostow distinguished five stages of economic growth: traditional society; the pre-conditions for take-off; the take-off into self-sustained growth; the drive towards maturity; and the age of high mass consumption. Of particular interest was the take-off into self-sustained growth, for it was this which distinguished rich countries from poor ones. The take-off was deemed to have occurred in 1783–1802 in Britain; in 1843–60 in the USA; in 1850–73 in Germany; in 1878–1900 in Japan; and in 1890–1914 in Russia. Countries such as Turkey, Argentina, China and India were diagnosed as having started their periods of take-off, though because it remained incomplete it was then too soon to judge whether or not it had been successful.

Rostow argued that certain developments were required before any economy could take off into self-sustained growth. Social and economic structures have to be changed so that the society concerned is in a position to be able to exploit the fruits of modern science. The idea has to spread that economic progress is desirable, and people have to emerge who are willing to take risks in the pursuit of profit or modernization. Banks and institutions for mobilizing capital have to appear. Roads and communications have to be built. This, however, occurs within the context of a slowly-growing, traditional society. The transition to the take-off occurs only when three things happen: (1) investment rises from about 5 per cent of output to 10 per cent; (2) there emerges at least one leading manufacturing sector, with a high rate of growth; (3) there exists, or there emerges rapidly, a political, social and institutional framework which exploits the impulses to expansion in the modern sector, giving growth an on-going character.

Though there were other important aspects of his thesis, Rostow, like many students of development economics in the 1950s, emphasized the role of capital accumulation. His main argument as to why the investment ratio had to rise from 5 to 10 per cent was based on the Harrod–Domar model discussed above. However, because his ideas were based on an interpretation of the historical experience of industrial countries, they could be tested. This happened very quickly, and considerable doubts were raised about his thesis. In particular, Kuznets produced statistics which cast grave doubts on Rostow's claim that investment ratios had in fact risen sharply to about 10 per cent during the period of take-off. In addition, Gerschenkron argued persuasively that it was impossible to fit even the experience of all the European countries that had industrialized into a single framework. There was, he claimed, great variety to be found. If

Rostow's framework was inadequate to deal with the European experience, it was hard to believe that twentieth-century developing countries must follow the same pattern.

The experience of poor countries after 1950

The 1950s and early 1960s were years when confidence in development economics, and in what could be achieved by planning, was high. India started its series of five-year plans in 1952, many countries following with plans of their own, or with plans worked out in association with international organizations such as the World Bank. The outcome of this effort, however, was rather different from what had been anticipated, and as a result many economists were forced to change their perspective on development.

After 1950 most less developed countries achieved high growth rates of per capita income. As table 2.13 shows, the average was 3.4 per cent p.a. The assumption that such countries were too poor to be able to save, and hence to grow, proved unfounded. This high average growth rate, however, conceals an enormous diversity in the experiences of individual countries. The experience of the fastest-growing region in table 2.13, the Middle East, can be explained in terms of oil resources, but putting this case aside, there is a marked difference between the 4.2 per cent acheived by China, and East Asia's 3.9 per cent, and the much lower growth rates achieved in South Asia, Africa and Latin America. At the country level the diversity is even greater. Libya, Iraq, Taiwan, South Korea, Iran, Hong Kong, Jamaica and Israel grew at over 4.5 per cent p.a., whilst per capita incomes actually fell in Rwanda, Burundi, Upper Volta and Madagascar, with a further five African and Latin American countries

Table 2.13   GNP per capita, 1950–75

| Region | 1974 US $ | | Annual growth rate |
	1950	1975	
South Asia	85	132	1.7
Africa	170	308	2.4
Latin America	495	944	2.6
East Asia	130	341	3.9
China (People's Republic)	113	320	4.2
Middle East	460	1660	5.2
Developing countries	160	375	3.4
Developing countries excluding China	187	400	3.0
Developed countries	2378	5238	3.2

Source: Morawetz (1977), p. 13.

showing hardly any growth. The picture is complicated by the fact that it was not the countries that were initially poorest that grew most slowly. Latin America was initially relatively rich, but grew slowly; whereas China and East Asia were initially poor, but grew fairly rapidly.

This diversity in growth performance was matched by the enormous variety of ways in which countries grew. For some countries, in particular the oil exporting countries, development of natural resources and the export of primary commodities was the driving factor. Other countries, such as South Korea, Taiwan and Hong Kong, pursued market-orientated strategies, relying on entrepreneurial skills to develop efficient manufacturing industries, able to compete in world markets. China followed its own distinctive strategy. It thus became clear that there was no single route to development. In addition, not all the countries expected to succeed did so. India, for example, has remained very poor, despite all the attempts to plan for a higher rate of growth.

Whilst for some countries (such as India, Pakistan or Bangladesh) any rise in the living standards of the bulk of the population is clearly contingent on a substantial rise in per capita incomes, the experience of developing countries since 1950 has shown that the relationship between growth and living standards is more complicated than had been assumed. It has become clear that rapid growth of national income does not necessarily mean that the poverty is being eliminated more rapidly, or that standards of life are rising faster than if growth were slower. A simple, but very important, measure of well-being is life expectancy. As is shown by a comparison of tables 2.13 and 2.14 there is no simple connection between growth rates and rises in life expectancy. East Asia, for example, grew more rapidly, yet had a lower increase in life expectancy than South Asia. A similar picture emerges when we consider other measures of how well so-called basic needs' are being satisfied. Measuring basic needs by looking at things such as the supply of calories or proteins, housing quality, literacy and school enrolments, and the provision of doctors, nurses and hospital beds, there appears to be little if any connection

Table 2.14   Life expectancy at birth

Region	1950–5	1965–70	Change
South Asia	41	49	8
East Asia	45	52	7
Africa	36	43	7
Latin America	52	60	8
China (People's Republic)	48	60	12
Developed countries	65	70	5

Source: Morawetz (1977), p. 48.

between rapid growth and the degree to which basic needs have been satisfied (Morawetz, 1977, pp. 54ff; World Bank, 1978, pp. 71ff).

Contemporary development economics

Since the 1960s there has occurred what has been described as a resurgence of neoclassical development economics, this being defined in the following way:

a neoclassical vision of the world is one of flexibility. In their own or their families' interests, people adapt readily to changing opportunities and prices, even if they do not like doing so and even though they may take their time. Businesses pursue objectives roughly consistent with the assumption that they maximize risk- and time-discounted profits. . . . There is usually a variety of ways of making things such that production methods can be expected to change when input prices change. . . . Although demand and supply always depend to a greater or lesser extent on expectations of an uncertain future, nevertheless most markets usually tend to achieve an equilibrium without wild price fluctuations. In short, the price mechanism can be expected to work rather well [though by no means perfectly]. (Little, 1982, p. 25)

Development economists have thus, since the 1960s, placed much greater emphasis on prices, and on how people in poor countries respond to price incentives.

One reason for this change is that economists have learnt that many of the assumptions made during the 1950s were not justified. (1) Poor countries have managed to achieve relatively high savings, achieving growth rates of per capita income that would have been thought impossible 30 years ago. In the words of Paul Rosenstein-Rodan, one of the pioneers of development economics in the 1940s,

The postwar period of development is a history of triumph – not of failure. The increase in life expectancy, the fall in infant mortality, the rates of growth, the achievements in any number of developing countries – nobody at the end of the Second World War would have expected so much. A billion people are still hungry, but it would now be 2 billion without the achievements that have been made. (Rosenstein-Rodan, 1984, pp. 220–1)

(2) The experience of countries such as Taiwan and South Korea has shown that the general export-pessimism of the 1950s is unjustifiable. Certainly some countries have problems in finding products that they can export, but many countries can. (3) The assumption that there was excess labour in agriculture was recognized to be false. At certain times of the year it may be impossible to employ everyone, but at other times (particularly for planting and harvesting) virtually the whole agricultural labour force is fully employed. Thus labour cannot normally be removed from agriculture without some reduction in output. In addition, it is now recognized that there is substantial scope for raising productivity in

agriculture. Land drainage, irrigation, and the use of fertilizers or high-yielding varieties of wheat or rice may contribute more to raising output per head than many forms of industrial investment.

Neoclassical development economics has also received a strong impetus from what has happened to general microeconomic theory. If, for example, we are to analyse the behaviour of peasant farmers deciding whether or not to invest in fertilizers or high-yielding varieties of rice, we need to allow for the risks involved. This requires a theory of how people choose when there is uncertainty about the future, and sufficient mathematics to enable us to work out the answer. It is only in the past 20 years or so that economists have had widespread access to such techniques.

Associated with this resurgence of neoclassical development economics has been a changed perspective on planning. Planning in the 1950s was generally structuralist: it focused on the economy as a whole, and was aimed at altering the relative importance of different sectors in the economy – often increasing manufacturing at the expense of agriculture. The targets in such plans were frequently not achieved, and by the 1960s many economists had come to the conclusion that planning had failed. The neoclassical response to this is to argue this was, at least in part, because structuralist planning was concerned with the wrong things.

Planning can be concerned with three levels: individual projects (for example, a new fertilizer plant, steel works, or irrigation project); particular industries; or the economy as a whole. Structuralist planning started at the last of these levels, working out what the structure of the economy should look like, inferring from this what had to happen in individual industries. Only at the end would the planner work out what projects should be undertaken. The result was that resources might be allocated to a particular sector, even though there were in fact no worthwhile projects to be undertaken there. Resources were thus allocated inefficiently and it could be argued that under such circumstances failure to meet planning targets was often a good sign. Planning should, it is argued, start at the other end, with the evaluation of individual projects to see which ones are worth undertaking. Though it may sometimes be necessary to plan at an industry level, this will frequently be unnecessary, for prices will contain enough information on the value of the project. At an economy-wide level planning will rarely be needed, for the price mechanism will take care of overall resource allocation. Consider, for example, the decision as to whether to build steel plants in a developing country. The structuralist approach was to argue that such plants would reduce dependence on imports, and to decide how many plants to build it was necessary to work out how much steel would be demanded by other sectors of the economy. The neoclassical approach is to observe that steel can be bought and sold on the world market. This means that if a country can make steel cheaply enough for building steel mills to be profitable, they should be built, any surplus steel being sold on the world market. If such plants are unprofitable it is more efficient to continue relying on imports.

Neoclassical planning therefore concentrates on project evaluation, and on prices. Particularly important are so-called 'shadow prices'. These are prices, to be used in project evaluation, designed to ensure that all the social benefits and costs associated with a project are correctly taken into account. To facilitate this process, the OECD (Organization for Economic Cooperation and Development) and UNIDO (United Nations Industrial Development Organization) published manuals on how such shadow prices should be calculated. It is as yet too early to know how successful these techniques will turn out to be.

2.5   CONCLUSIONS

The problem of economic growth has been a major concern of economists over a long period. The factors on which their attention has been focused have changed over time in response to the changing nature of the economy, though the process has sometimes been a slow one. It took a long time, for example, for industrialization and its implications to be fully recognized. Of particular importance has been a certain tension between formal models of the process of economic growth and much wider, and more informal, discussions of the factors causing economic growth. The problem is that formal models can show only the 'mechanics' of growth: the relationship between inputs and outputs; between saving, investment and the growth of output. The determinants of productivity (and hence the 'causes' of growth) are left unanalysed by such formal models. For example, education is clearly important in raising the productivity of labour but it is neglected in growth theory simply because of the difficulties involved in quantifying educational output in a satisfactory way. In contrast, informal discussion can encompass all possible causes of growth. Such explanations frequently appeal to common sense (the importance of education, for example) but given a very loose framework it is generally impossible to test one explanation against another. Cross-country comparisons can provide suggestions as to important factors, but little more is possible. The historical experience of growth is so varied that there is little hope that simple schemes such as that of Rostow will ever be able to explain the pattern. One of the lessons from history appears to be that there is no single pattern: the nineteenth-century leaders in economic growth (Britain, Germany, USA) were all very different; so too are the twentieth-century success stories (Japan, USSR, Korea, Taiwan, China).

There has, nonetheless, been considerable progress in dealing with problems of growth. Models of growth are technically much better, and they are much more clearly specified. At the same time, growth theory has, with some justification, been picked out as one of the areas where much theorizing has lost contact with any real-world problems, the Cambridge controversies being an oft-cited example. It can be argued, however, that even if the results are not enough to justify the enormous research effort that went into tackling these problems, we have, nonetheless, learned something, and in addition we now understand much better than previously the limitations of certain types of model. Although such models do not provide general explanations of growth, they do provide some useful concepts that can be used to clarify issues. The concepts of total factor productivity and shadow prices are perhaps two of the most useful.

3

The Regulation of Trade and Industry

3.1 INTRODUCTION

This chapter deals with a wide range of problems related to what is often described as the issue of *laissez-faire* versus state intervention. Even more than is the case elsewhere in this book, the amount of relevant material means that it is possible to consider only a series of examples illustrating some of the main changes that have taken place. The starting point is what is usually called the age of 'mercantilism', in the seventeenth and eighteenth centuries when most European governments became involved in regulating, sometimes in very great detail, both industry and trade. The chapter then moves on to consider Britain during the industrial revolution, important not only because industrialization eventually changed the structure of the world economy creating new economic problems, but also because this was the setting against which Adam Smith and his successors challenged 'mercantilist' policies, arguing the case for free trade. The extent to which they advocated *laissez-faire* is something we shall have to consider.

After this the focus of attention moves away from Britain towards the US and Germany. This is for three main reasons. The first is that, especially in the second half of the nineteenth century, with the enormous expansion that took place in the German and US economies, Britain became progressively less important in the world economy. The second reason is that it is important to consider the movement away from free trade which took place during the second half of the nineteenth century, Germany and the US being the most important countries involved (Britain clung to free trade right into the twentieth century). The third reason is that towards the end of the nineteenth century industry became much more concentrated, especially in Germany and the US, raising new problems for economists to tackle. Attention is therefore focused on the US, where the issue of industrial concentration and monopoly received a great deal of attention.

When it comes to the twentieth century the selection of topics is much more arbitrary. The New Deal is discussed because not only did it involve a significant increase in state intervention in what was by then the world's largest economy, but also because it was based on some interesting, now somewhat unorthodox, ideas. As an example of contemporary discussions of trade policy the chapter considers the formation of the European Economic Community. As examples of contemporary industrial policy it considers the recent movement towards de-regulation in the US and some of the arguments about nationalization and de-nationalization in the UK. Though this is but a small fraction of the issues that could be discussed, it is enough to illustrate some of the ways in which discussions of government policy have changed over the centuries.

3.2 ENGLAND IN THE SEVENTEENTH CENTURY

Before the Civil War

Throughout the seventeenth century English trade and industry were subject to extensive regulation and interference, but the nature of this regulation changed very substantially during the seventeenth century, especially after the Civil War. Before the Civil War the major objectives of government policy were to maintain public order and to keep royal revenues high. The interests of the crown, not those of the country as a whole, were paramount, the resulting policies being a major grievance of the business and landed classes.

One of the main forms of government regulation was the creation of monopolies. The system of patents, whereby individuals were granted monopolies over specific activities, was originally designed to encourage innovation and to provide some protection for industries which were seen as vital for national defence. The monopolies set up by Elizabeth in copper, saltpetre and gunpowder were aimed at making England independent of foreign suppliers. However, because the over-riding objective of policy was the establishment of royal power the system came to be used in a very different manner. Under James I, monopolies were created specifically to be sold or to be given to individuals in payment for services to the crown. The enforcement of patents was farmed out to individuals who had the right to keep the fines they collected. These individuals enforced patents only in cases where it was worth their while, ignoring many infringements. In such cases businessmen were effectively buying exemptions from the patents. The public thus lost far more from the system of monopolies than the crown gained. Pym, one of the Stuarts' main critics, claimed that the wine monopoly cost the public £360,000 a year, of which the king got only £30,000.

The basis for Tudor and early Stuart policy towards industry lay in mediaeval theories according to which the right to trade was a privilege bought from either the local landowner or the crown. The government had the right to grant individuals patents, and to create monopolies. It became clear, however, that the creation and sale of monopolies was nothing more than a very inefficient way of raising revenue. Furthermore, from the end of the sixteenth century onwards, some monopolies were successfully challenged in the courts as being an infringement of the economic freedom of the subject and as being contrary to common law (see Heckscher, 1955, p. 283). These court cases were reinforced by legislation, the most important of which was the Monopolies Act of 1624. This rejected any patents of monopoly which were not confined to new industries and it allowed a monopoly for an invention only for a limited number of years, thus laying the foundations for modern patent law.

Underlying all this period's legislation was the notion of an ordered, controlled society. Even the Statute of Monopolies specified that its prohibition of monopoly was not to apply to the city of London, to any 'town corporate', or to any companies or societies of merchants 'erected for the maintenance, enlargement or ordering of any trade or merchandize' (Heckscher, 1955, p. 285). Trade needed to be ordered and governed if it was to prosper, this being the function of gilds and trading companies. It was no offence to grant a patent or a monopoly to a group of sellers in order that trade could be regulated.

To achieve this goal of an ordered, stable society there were many measures designed to uphold the status quo, many of which served to restrict industry and the development of a capitalist economy. In the sixteenth century, for example, legislation was passed restricting the number of sheep one man could own, and the number of looms that clothiers and weavers could own.

One of the most wide-ranging such measures was the Statute of Artificers (1563) which attempted to regulate the market for labour. Though it was based on legislation dating back to the fourteenth century, it survived, albeit with major amendments, till the early nineteenth century. This contained a number of major provisions. (1) There was a requirement that all men, except those involved in certain specified occupations, be available to work in agriculture. In addition, handicraft workers and artisans were obliged to help with the harvest when this was necessary. (2) Rules about apprenticeship, including who was eligible to enter different forms of apprenticeship, were tightened up. (3) Justices of the Peace were empowered with the task of fixing wage rates, taking account of the cost of living. (4) No-one was to be allowed to move from one locality to another unless he could prove that he had been released from his employment. The idea underlying this statute was that of an ordered, regulated society in which the seeking of individual gain was severely curtailed. The regulation of wages reflected the mediaeval idea of the just price, as opposed to the idea of prices determined by supply and demand.

Another major area of government regulation was foreign trade where the government's objectives were again to provide order and to increase royal revenues. 'Regulated companies', such as the Merchant Adventurers, were gilds for foreign trade. Each company had a monopoly of trade with a certain region and it made rules about who was allowed to trade and how. It was individual members, not the company itself, that shipped goods and bore any risks. Restricting trade in this way achieved both of the government's objectives: the companies regulated trade, and the small number of wealthy, favoured traders were beholden to the government, providing a willing source of loans.

The notion that markets needed regulating if they were to be orderly extended also to the money markets. Restrictions on the export of coin and bullion were imposed. This was in part a response to the crown's shortage of money and the resulting desire to keep as much money in the kingdom as possible. There was also, however, the desire to regulate the money market. Foreign exchange dealings might provide a means for speculation, or for avoiding the usury laws which restricted the rate of interest that could legally be charged on loans. If foreign exchange dealings were forced to take place only at the proper exchange rates, these undesirable transactions could be eliminated and order could be imposed on the market.

After the Civil War

In the 1650s, under Oliver Cromwell, the whole basis of economic policy changed. Policy was no longer dictated by the interests of the crown, but was for the benefit of a more widely defined national interest. In the sphere of foreign trade there were two aspects to the new policy. The first was the Navigation Act of 1651 which, amended in 1660, laid the basis for England's foreign trade policy throughout the eighteenth century. This Act laid down that the colonies, chartered or proprietory, should be subordinated to Parliament, thus making a coherent imperial policy possible and ensuring that trade was monopolized by English shipping. The second aspect of the new policy was the use of England's now powerful navy to promote English trading interests. A series of wars against the Dutch ended their dominance of trade to the East and West Indies. Jamaica, the base for the eighteenth-century slave trade, was captured and the basis for British rule in India was laid. Other naval actions made the seas safe for English shipping. The result was that England became the entrepot for most of Europe's colonial trade, and the shipping industry expanded enormously.

The Navigation Acts and the power of the English fleet made the old regulated trading companies superfluous. They made possible the transition from a system based on trading companies to one based on a national monopoly. Both colonial traders and domestic producers were protected from foreign competition but, within this framework, they were free to compete with each other. With the Navigation Act of 1651, according to one historian, 'we have arrived at a fully fashioned conception of economic policy in an essentially national form. . . . Henceforth the merchant was here to work out his destiny, free of formal organization, within a general protective framework of national legislation' (C. Wilson, quoted in Hill, 1967, p. 124.) More succinctly, the Middle Ages in trade and colonial policy had ended.

This policy continued after the Restoration and the revolution of 1688. The trading companies gradually lost their privileges, though the East

India Company survived. The Dutch were defeated by 1674. An alliance with Portugal opened up the Portuguese empire alongside the Dutch to English traders, whilst the War of the Spanish Succession gave them access to the Spanish empire.

The revolution also marked the end of the Middle Ages in industry and commerce. The government lost its power to grant monopolies, and gild regulations became ever more difficult to enforce. The revolution of 1688 further extended the rights of businessmen. Parliament refused to enforce the Elizabethan machinery of industrial regulation. Freeholders were granted the freedom to work mineral deposits found in their own lands (hitherto mines believed to contain gold or silver could be worked by the royal monopolists without compensation) and the Mines Royal and the Mineral and Battery Works, the two established mining companies, lost their monopolies. At the same time restrictions on labour were reduced. The clause in the Statute of Artificers preventing the relatively poor from working in the clothing industry was repealed; it was ruled that the Statute of Artificers applied only to agricultural workers; and apprenticeship regulations broke down.

At the same time, whilst industry and internal trade were becoming much more free, a system of industrial protection emerged. In the 1690s customs duties were increased in order to raise finance for wartime expenditure, but these duties remained and developed into a system of protection for British industry, of which the Board of Trade, established in 1696, was the symbol.

Arguments for economic freedom

Associated with this upheaval in economic policy during the seventeenth century was an equally profound change in the way men viewed the nature of economic activity. During the years after 1640 the scope for private initiative, as we have seen, widened considerably. At the same time diversification and the exploitation of new markets came to be seen as preferable to the protection of a stable agrarian order, which was the basis of much Tudor and early Stuart economic policy. These changes occurred for two reasons. There were the political changes, which shifted power from the crown to Parliament, and hence to the business community. In addition, there were changes in the market. Regulation of the cloth industry, for example, collapsed as the industry responded to new market opportunities. Similarly, as the threat of famine receded after the 1640s, increasing employment came to be seen as a better way of helping the needy than controlling the grain trade.

During the 1640s men started to discuss trade in a new way, with a number of writers arguing the case for free trade, where free trade meant freedom from the regulations and restrictions imposed by the established trading companies. They wanted the rules governing entry into different activities to be relaxed. An anonymous author, for example, argued that if the Merchant Adventurers' restrictions on the cloth export trade were removed, prices would fall, but this would be compensated for by a rise in sales. Lower prices, he argued, would lead not to a glutted market, but to higher sales and higher profits. This approach was followed by other writers, who argued that increasing the number of merchants could increase industry, and that when the Merchant Adventurers were allowed to restrict trade the result was that cloth remained unsold, and men unemployed. In these pamphlets the view was emerging that increasing wealth involved increasing the riches of a large number of people, not simply a small privileged group.

Prior to the Civil War the major contribution was the balance of trade doctrine (discussed further in chapter 4). The term was coined by Edward Misselden in 1622, and taken up by Thomas Mun in his widely read *England's Treasure by Forraign Trade* as an argument against controlling exchange rates and bullion flows. Trade in goods, he argued, was primary. It is because more goods are being imported than are being exported that money flows out of the country, and it is futile to try to remedy this by preventing the movement of bullion. The freedom to export bullion was a particular interest of the East India Company, of which Mun was a director, the reason being that the company was unable to export English goods to pay for its imports from Asia. Asian countries required gold and silver.

The significance of Mun's use of the balance of trade doctrine was twofold. On the one hand it could be used to argue that there were economic laws which were above the sovereign: bullion flows and the foreign exchanges were determined by the conditions of trade, not by royal decree. On the other hand, the balance of trade theory provided a theory of growth, in which the merchant was the key figure. If a country exported more than it imported this led to higher production. Furthermore, the resulting favourable balance of trade would cause money to flow into the country enabling this higher production to be financed. In Mun's hands, therefore, the balance of trade was an argument for economic freedom. It was, however, based on a very one-sided view of the process of growth, emphasizing production and the role of the merchant. Demand, and the role consumption, were neglected.

In the last three decades of the seventeenth century the use of the balance of trade theory changed. French and Dutch competition placed English clothiers in a defensive position, struggling for markets. In addition, Indian cotton goods began to appear on a large scale on the English market, displacing traditional woollen goods. As a result a number of clothiers took up the balance of trade theory to argue for restrictions on trade. In their writings the cloth industry, not the merchant, was seen as the key to prosperity. They proposed measures including: restricting imports of cloth; setting the poor to work; improvements in agriculture in order to reduce the cost of living, and hence the clothing industry's costs; allowing the import of raw materials free of any customs duty; and either taxing or banning the import of consumers' goods. These measures, it was argued, would lead to a favourable balance of trade, and to a prosperous domestic industry.

Whilst the balance of trade theory was being used to argue for protection of English industry, new arguments for economic freedom were being put forward by writers such as Barbon (1690), North (1691) and Martyn (1701). In these writings consumption, even of imported textiles, was seen as worthwhile: it provided an incentive to work, as well as being desirable in itself. Trade was seen as something from which all nations could benefit, not, as in the balance of trade theory, as a struggle in which one nation's gain was another's loss. All trade was considered profitable. In the words of Roger North,

the loss of a trade with one nation, is not that only, separately considered, but so much of the trade of the world rescinded and lost, for all is combined together. . . . there can be no trade unprofitable to the publick; for if any prove so, men leave it off; and wherever the traders thrive, the publick, of which they are a part, thrives also. (Roger North's preface to North, 1691, p. viii)

Government interference, he argued, would not benefit the country as a whole:

to force men to deal in any prescrib'd manner, may profit such as happen to serve them; but the publick gains not, because it is taking from one subject, to give to another.

The most developed theory was probably that of Henry Martyn. Importing Indian cottons, he argued, would leave labourers with more to spend on English goods. If men did become unemployed, this would depress wages, lowering costs for English manufacturers. Importing cotton goods, therefore, was beneficial to the economy, and rejecting the benefits of cheap textiles was akin to rejecting the benefits of new inventions.

Theories such as those of North and Martyn were able to explain England's rapidly increasing wealth in the period after 1660, something of which contemporaries were well aware. This was something that the balance of trade theory failed to explain. More important, perhaps, they provided a much better insight into the workings of a market economy: of the way prices were determined, and the way markets co-ordinated economic activities. Due to the attention paid to consumption as well as production, which contrasted with the balance of trade theory's one-sided stress on production, internal trade was no longer seen as sterile.

Mercantilism

England continued its policy of protecting industry and regulating foreign trade for the benefit of English merchants and seamen throughout the eighteenth century. This was the system described by Adam Smith in *The Wealth of Nations* as 'the mercantile system'. Since Smith's time the term 'mercantilism' has come to be used to describe both the period's economic policies, and the economic theories used to support those policies. The mercantile system, Smith argued, was based on the notion that money constituted wealth, for the nation as well as the individual; and that foreign trade was the means by which this wealth was to be increased (as evidenced by the title of Mun's *England's Treasure by Forraign Trade*, the main work cited by Smith in this context). The mercantilists, Smith claimed, went on to argue that trade and industry should be regulated so as to achieve a favourable balance of trade, thereby increasing the nation's stock of money.

It should, however, be clear by now that simply to dismiss either the period's economic policies, or its economic ideas, as 'mercantilist', is to do the seventeenth century an injustice. Over the century, and especially after the Civil War, very profound changes took place in the way economic policy was conceived, and in the arguments used to argue for different policies. After the revolution the whole basis of government regulation of trade and industry changed, away from a mediaeval conception of the economy as centred on the crown, to one centred on the nation as a whole. Not only was policy designed for the benefit of the nation as a whole (or at least those represented in Parliament), but the system was based on individual initiative and enterprise, albeit within a national monopoly sustained by the state. Simply to focus on the existence of customs and restraints on trade throughout the period is to ignore the very important shift away from a mediaeval conception of economic policy, towards one much more modern. This was in marked contrast to the situation in France, to which we now turn.

3.3 FRANCE UNDER THE *ANCIEN RÉGIME*

The system of Colbert

In the late seventeenth-century economic policy in France was dominated by Jean Baptiste Colbert, Louis XIV's most important minister from the death of Cardinal Mazarin in 1661, until his own death in 1683. Colbert was responsible for instigating a system of industrial regulation which went beyond anything attempted in England or anywhere else in Europe. Industries were subsidized, attempts were made to set up new industries, and royal manufacturing concerns were established, all in an attempt to increase France's productive capacity. In addition, in order to improve the quality of French goods, something that was necessary if exports were to be increased, detailed regulations were imposed, these laying down in great detail both specifications for goods, and the methods by which they were to be produced. To increase the supply of labour, emigration of skilled labour was prohibited, and measures were taken to increase the birth rate. In addition, Colbert built roads, bridges and canals in order to improve communications within France. To complete the process of economic unification he attempted, albeit unsuccessfully, to eliminate internal customs barriers.

Externally, Colbert was an advocate of the view that one nation's gain was another's loss. If France were to increase her trade, he argued, she had to take trade from other countries, and the quickest way to do this was to take it by force. He expressed these ideas very concisely in 1669, when he wrote,

Commerce is carried on by 20,000 vessels and that number cannot be increased. Each nation strives to have its fair share and to get ahead of the others. The Dutch now fight this war [of commerce] with 15,000 to 16,000 vessels . . . the English with 3,000 to 4,000 . . . and the French with 500 to 600. The last two countries can improve their commerce only by increasing the number of their vessels and can increase the number only . . . by paring away from 15,000 to 16,000 Dutch ships. (Quoted in Clough and Rapp, 1975, pp. 214)

One aspect of this view of trade was the struggle for bullion: the only way a country could increase the amount of money circulating within it was to take bullion from other countries. To do this it had to export more than it imported in order to achieve a favourable balance of trade.

Colbert's economic ideas were far from original, but his policies are important. According to Heckscher, the greatest historian of the period,

Colbert's achievements hold a special interest chiefly because he . . . formulated his economic programme as a complete whole and realized the connection between measures taken in different spheres. His work consequently indicates with particular clarity how the abolition of internal tolls was just one part of the general attempt at economic unity within the state and fitted in with the whole mercantilist system of trade – with its policy of hindering imports, encouraging exports and free trade within the country, attracting the precious metals and having a rapid circulation of money within the country. (Heckscher, 1955, I, p. 81)

Boisguilbert

For most of the seventeenth century no significant economic writings were published in France, presumably because of the censorship. One of the first major writers on economic questions was Pierre de Boisguilbert, whose writings started in the 1690s. Boisguilbert was severely critical of the French government's policies, seeing the situation facing the country as one of widespread economic decline and poverty. Particularly important was the depression in agriculture, which had suffered from Colbert's policy of stimulating industrial development.

A major reason for these problems, according to Boisguilbert, was the burden of taxation and its arbitrary nature: the amount of tax a man would have to pay, and when it was going to be demanded, were very uncertain. This uncertainty made it hard for businessmen to invest. In addition, taxation reduced consumption, partly by inducing people to hoard money as a precaution against tax demands, and partly because it redistributed income from the poor to the rich. Government interference in industry and agriculture also reduced people's ability to consume. This reduction was important, because consumption created income: 'Consumption and income are one and the same thing and the ruin of consumption is the ruin of income' (quoted in Hutchison, 1988, p. 109).

Boisguilbert argued that competitive markets brought about a harmony of interests.

Nature, or Providence, alone can preserve justice, provided, once again, that no one interferes; and this is how they achieve it. They establish first an equal need to sell and buy with regard to every sort of good, with the moving spirit, in all markets, both with sellers and buyers, being solely for profit. It is with the aid of this equilibrium, or balance, that the seller and the buyer alike are equally forced to listen to reason and to submit to it. (Quoted in Hutchison, 1988, p. 112)

His conclusion was that the state should leave nature free ('*laisse faire la nature*'), and should intervene simply in order to protect individuals and prevent violence. Like his English contemporaries such as North and Martyn, Boisguilbert saw how the market might co-ordinate economic activities, and he saw the importance of consumption. Such views contrasted sharply with those of Colbert and his successors.

The Physiocrats

The ideas of men such as Boisguilbert were taken up and developed in the second half of the eighteenth century by the Physiocrats, pre-eminent amongst whom was Quesnay, whose *tableau economique* is discussed in chapter 2. It was the Physiocrats who coined the phrase '*laissez-faire, laissez-passer*', their main justification for this policy being that there was a harmony of interests inherent in the natural order. If the rule of nature were followed, they argued, people would work for others in the belief that they were working for themselves. The word 'physiocracy' means 'rule of nature'.

The main distinguishing feature of physiocratic economics was the view that agriculture played a unique role in the economy, as the only sector capable of producing a surplus. Growth, as Quesnay's *tableau* showed, depended on the production of an agricultural surplus, and this depended on agriculture being profitable. The Physiocrats were thus very critical of French economic policies, which favoured industry and placed great burdens on agriculture. French agriculture was largely conducted by peasants, each cultivating a small amount of land at a low level of productivity. If landholdings could be increased and investment raised, so that modern methods could be employed as in England and Holland, productivity could be increased enormously. One problem was the difficulty faced by farmers in getting credit, due to the length of the harvest cycle, and the uncertainty involved. Another problem was the restrictions placed on trade in grain, designed to prevent famine, but resulting in lower profits and lower production. The Physiocrats thus argued for free trade in grain, including the freedom to export, in order to raise farmers' profits and hence stimulate growth.

This desire for high agricultural prices took precedence over the Physiocrats' belief in *laissez-faire*, for though they favoured agricultural exports they were hostile to exports of manufactured goods. Demand for French manufactured goods, seen primarily as luxury goods, would be volatile, leading to periodic spells of unemployment. In addition, exporting manufactured goods conflicted with their policy of encouraging agricultural exports: manufactured exports were possible only if wages were sufficiently low, and this required a low price of grain, whereas exporting grain would keep the price of grain high. In the words of Quesnay, 'Happy the land which has no exports of manufactures because agricultural exports maintain farm prices at too high a level to permit the sterile class to sell its products abroad' (quoted in Spiegel, 1983, p. 193). Thus although the Physiocrats did argue for *laissez-faire*, and although they made very important contributions to economic theory (see also pp. 9–12), their views on regulating trade and industry were somewhat anachronistic.

3.4 BRITAIN DURING THE INDUSTRIAL REVOLUTION

Background

Long before the industrial revolution, regulations governing industry had largely ceased or fallen into neglect, the main work of demolishing such regulations having taken place, as explained above, as early as the seventeenth century. The main exception was the Law of Settlement, which restricted labour mobility in order to prevent the poor from becoming a burden on the parishes to which they might move, and which lasted into the nineteenth century. The main form of regulation to remain in force was the system of colonial trade established by the Navigation Acts, together with a system of protective tariffs. The woollen industry, in the eighteenth century still the largest single occupation outside agriculture, for example, was protected by a host of restrictions. The export of raw wool, sheep and rams was prohibited; between 1719 and 1825 skilled workers were forbidden to emigrate; and until 1843 textile machinery could not be exported. In addition, to widen the home market for wool, the import of silks and printed cotton goods was prohibited. Within these barriers *laissez-faire* prevailed: with the exception of foreign trade, the age of *laissez-faire* had begun in the late seventeenth century.

It was only in the nineteenth century that free trade, in the sense of a demand for the lowering or elimination of tariff barriers, became a major issue. A theoretical challenge (considered below) to the system of protection was launched by Adam Smith and his followers. In addition, business interests began, once the wars against France were in the past, to see commercial advantages in freer trade. In 1820 a group of merchants, prompted by economists, as it is reasonable to call the members of the Political Economy Club, petitioned Parliament for free-trade policies, and over the following 20 years pressure increased enormously. One of the main reasons for this was the growth of the cotton industry, determined to get its raw materials as cheaply as possible and concerned to find export markets for the rapidly increasing quantity of cotton goods being produced. The problem was that exporters were having to extend their markets outside the British Empire into areas which had relatively little connection with the world market, such as Brazil, south-east Asia, Australia and the west coast of Africa. The only way these countries could pay for British cottons was by providing primary produce (coffee, cocoa, sugar, timber, hides, grain or wool) in exchange. Because such goods were subject to high British tariffs it was often prohibitively expensive to import them, which meant that the market for British exports was thereby restricted. A related problem concerned shipping costs. If produce from countries outside the empire could not be imported into Britain, ships going to such countries would have to return empty, thus making exporting much more expensive.

A different issue arose with trade to countries with stronger governments, such as the US and countries in northern Europe. The danger here was that such countries would retaliate against British tariff discrimination by imposing tariffs of their own. Still further issues were raised by one particular aspect of the system, the tariff on imported corn, but this is so important that it is discussed separately below.

During the 1820s there was some movement in the direction of freer trade. Huskisson, as President of the Board of Trade in the 1820s, greatly simplified the system of tariffs, and a series of commercial treaties was negotiated with other European countries whereby tariff barriers were reduced on a reciprocal basis. At about the same time the few remaining trading monopolies were removed: the East India Compay lost its monopoly of trade with India in 1813, and of its trade with China in 1834; the Levant company its monopoly of trade with the near east in 1825. The movement towards free trade was, however, slow.

It was in the 1840s that the main movement towards free trade took place, one of the reasons for this being that even once the arguments in its favour were accepted, there remained the enormous problem of finding an alternative source of revenue. It was not until Peel managed, in 1841, to re-introduce income tax, introduced during the Napoleonic Wars and later abandoned, that free trade was a possibility. The budget of 1842 reduced all customs duties, though maintaining discrimination in favour of imperial produce. The 1845 budget completed the process, abolishing altogether duties on many goods including raw cotton, wool, cattle and butter. Duties on non-empire timber, coffee and sugar were reduced substantially, timber from £2.75 to 50p per load, coffee from 6p to 1p per lb, and sugar from £3.15 to £1.70 per cwt (though the old rate remained on sugar produced using slaves). With these tariff reductions, together with the repeal of the Corn Laws in 1846 (discussed below) the movement towards free trade was virtually complete. The Navigation Acts were abolished in 1849.

Adam Smith

As was explained in chapter 2, Adam Smith's work antedates the industrial revolution. It is, however, vital to consider his views on *laissez-faire*, for not only did they provide the starting point for subsequent writing on the subject, but they remained influential throughout the nineteenth century (and beyond). Postponing for a while arguments related specifically to foreign trade, there are two main strands to Smith's argument about *laissez-faire*. The first of these is his claim that industry is limited by the stock of capital, which means that its total cannot be increased by government regulation.

> The general industry of the society can never exceed what the capital of the society can employ. . . . the number of those that can continually be employed by all the members of a great society, must bear a certain proportion to the whole capital of that society, and can never exceed that proportion. No regulation of commerce can increase the quantity of industry in any society beyond what its capital can maintain. (Smith, 1776, I, p. 475)

If government regulation could not alter the level of activity, all it could achieve was to divert resources from one activity into another.

This leads in to the second strand to Smith's argument, which is that individuals will use their resources in such a way as to produce maximum benefit to society, and that, by implication, government regulation can only be harmful (governments have, he argued, much poorer information than the people who are actually involved). His simplest explanation of why this will be the case is that national revenue comprises simply the value of the goods that everyone in society produces, and therefore that if each person maximizes the value of his or her own produce, national revenue will be maximized. The problem with this argument is that it ignores the fact that when one person increases his or her income, the value of someone else's produce may be reduced. The problem is thus much more complicated than Smith suggests. His argument here is worth quoting at some length, however, because it is the place where his famous 'invisible hand' makes its appearance.

> But the annual revenue of every society is always precisely equal to the exchangeable value of the whole annual produce of its industry. . . . As every individual, therefore, endeavours as much as he can both to employ his capital in support of domestic industry, and so to direct that industry that its produce may be of the greatest value; every individual necessarily labours to render the annual revenue of the society as great as he can. By preferring the support of domestic to that of foreign industry, he intends only his own security; and by directing that industry in such a manner as its produce may be of the greatest value, he intends only his own gain, and he is in this, as in many other cases, led by an invisible hand to promote an end which was no part of his intention. . . . By pursuing his own interest he frequently promotes that of the society far more effectually than when he really intends to promote it. (Smith, 1776, I, pp. 477–8)

Although Smith's argument in this paragraph is very weak, he makes it clear elsewhere in the *Wealth of Nations* that it is competition that produces this result.

All systems either of preference or of restraint, therefore, being taken away, the obvious and simple system of natural liberty establishes itself of its own accord. Every man, as long as he does not violate the laws of justice, is left perfectly free to bring both his industry and capital into competition with those of any other man, or order of men. (Smith, 1776, II, p. 208)

In earlier chapters Smith had shown that competition would ensure an optimal allocation of resources through ensuring that the same returns were earned in different activities:

The whole of the advantages and disadvantages of the different employments of labour and stock [capital] must, in the same neighbourhood, be either perfectly equal or continually tending to equality. If in the same neighbourhood, there was any employment evidently either more or less advantageous than the rest, so many people would crowd into it in the one case, and so many would desert it in the other, that its advantages would soon return to the level of other employments. (Smith, 1776, I, p. 111)

Smith, therefore, argued the case for *laissez-faire* much more cogently than had any of his predecessors, but he nonetheless saw numerous exceptions to this rule. He supported the Navigation Acts, on the grounds that they encouraged the British shipping industry, vital for defence. Defence of the realm, he considered, was in this instance more important than wealth. He defended the imposition of tariffs either to protect infant industries, or in retaliation against other countries. Finally, and this is a major exception to the rule of *laissez-faire*, the government had the duty of

erecting and maintaining certain public works and certain public institutions, which it can never be for the interest of any individual, or small number of individuals, to erect and maintain, because the profit could never repay the expence to any individual or small number of individuals, though it may frequently do much more than repay it to a great society. (Smith, 1776, II, p. 209)

An example he gave was roads. Even if a road-owner could impose a toll, he would not have an adequate incentive to maintain a main road adequately, for most traffic would use the road irrespective of its condition, and the owner would get much the same revenue however much he spent on maintenance.

Smith, therefore, was not hostile to government intervention in the economy. His arguments about competition and 'the invisible hand' were not directed against government activity in general but against a specific set of regulations which he saw as restricting individual initiative and harming growth.

Foreign trade

The economists writing in England at this time were able to discuss issues of commercial policy much more effectively than previous generations had been able to do, mainly because they had much better theories of international trade to work with. There were two main approaches. The first was that of Adam Smith and, following him, J. R. McCulloch, who explained trade in terms of 'absolute advantage': a country exports those goods it can produce more efficiently, and therefore more cheaply, than its neighbours; and it imports those goods that can be produced more efficiently abroad, and which can thus be obtained more cheaply abroad than at home. Foreign trade thus benefits a country through enabling it to buy from the cheapest possible source. Free trade maximizes such gains. More important, however, was the fact that free trade would encourage specialization and the division of labour (see chapter 2). Labour and capital, Smith argued, would migrate to those regions where resource endowments allowed them to be used most effectively. Foreign trade thus supports economic growth, raising profits, in just the same way as internal trade.

The alternative approach was that put forward by David Ricardo and Robert Torrens, who argued that trade was determined not by which country could produce goods most efficiently, but by 'comparative advantage'. This is best explained by looking at Ricardo's example, taken from his *Principles of Political Economy and Taxation* (1817), in which Portugal produces both cloth and wine more efficiently than England. Changing Ricardo's numbers slightly to simplify them, assume that in England a barrel of wine is worth 1.5 rolls of cloth, whereas in Portugal, because wine can be produced much more easily, a barrel of wine is worth only 0.5 rolls of cloth. Ricardo showed that in this example, even though Portugal can produce both cloth and wine more efficiently than England, it will be profitable, to both countries, for English cloth to be traded for Portuguese wine, provided that the price of a barrel of wine is somewhere between 0.5 and 1.5 rolls of cloth. Rather than produce its own cloth, Portugal would do better to specialize in producing wine, obtaining cloth through trade: the cost of each roll of cloth would then be, say, 1 barrel of wine instead of 2.

A crucial aspect of this theory, which distinguishes it sharply from Smith's, is that capital and labour cannot move freely from one country to another. To see why, assume that the only cost is labour, and suppose that wages were the same in both countries. Portugal would then be able to produce both wine and cloth more cheaply than England, and would thus export both goods to England. The result, however, would be a that gold and silver would be sent from England to Portugal to pay for the goods being imported. This would lower English prices and wages, and raise Portuguese prices and wages (the quantity theory of money). This process of money flows, falling English prices and rising Portuguese prices would continue until cloth, the good in which England's productivity shortfall is least, becomes cheaper in England than in Portugal. England will then start exporting cloth, which will pay for its imports of wine. If labour were completely mobile, wages would have to be the same in England as in Portugal, which would mean that this process of adjustment could never occur: Portuguese industry would simply expand, and English industry would disappear, for it would never be able to compete successfully.

This theory of comparative advantage, developed by Ricardo and Torrens, was, however, incomplete, leaving a number of important things unexplained. Particularly important is the question of what prices will be established. In the example above, all we could say was that after trade the price of a roll of cloth must be between 0.5 and 1.5 barrels of wine. This gap in the theory was filled by John Stuart Mill, who, in his *Principles of Political Economy* (1848) provided a more general explanation of trade in terms of supply and demand.

the Equation of International Demand . . . may be concisely stated as follows. The produce of a country exchanges for the produce of other countries, at such values as are required in order that the whole of her exports may exactly pay for the whole of her imports. This law of International Values is but an extension of the more general law of Value, which we called the Equation of Supply and Demand. We have seen that the value of a commodity always adjusts itself as to bring the demand to the exact level of the supply. (Mill, quoted in O'Brien, 1975, p. 183)

Though it shows only a part of what is going on, the essence of Mill's theory can be explained using figure 3.1. As its price rises, each country will produce (supply) more cloth, and consume (demand) less. If production exceeds supply, then the country is an exporter of cloth; if it is less, an importer. Equilibrium occurs where total supply equals total demand, at a price level such as *P*, where the amount of cloth country A wishes to export equals the amount B wishes to import. For reasons that we will not go into here, this is known as Mill's theory of 'reciprocal demand'. Though Mill has generalized Ricardo's assumptions, his theory forms a

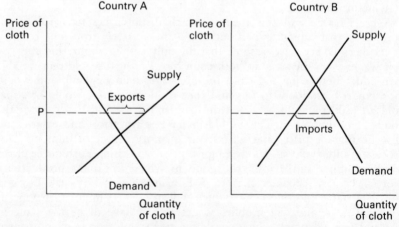

FIGURE 3.1 *Mill's theory of international trade*

natural extension of Ricardo's theory of comparative advantage, built on similar assumptions, notably that capital and labour are immobile between countries.

The significance of these theories, and the reason why so much time has been spent going through them, is that the classical economists (Smith and his successors) had a much better theory of international trade on which to base their policy prescriptions, than any of their predecessors. Compared with these theories of trade, the analytical tools available to Hume and Cantillon, let alone writers such as North, Martyn or Boisguilbert, were very limited. This meant that Ricardo, Mill and their contemporaries could tackle issues that their predecessors were quite unable to deal with. For example, in discussions of free trade, one issue was whether the imposition of a tariff could improve a country's terms of trade: the price of its exports divided by the price of its imports. If the terms of trade could be improved in this way, then a country could benefit from imposing a tariff. If the other country retaliated by imposing a tariff of its own, of course, both countries would be worse off than if there was free trade. It was because he believed a tariff could improve a country's terms of trade that Torrens, for example, argued that free trade should come about only on a reciprocal basis. A country should not adopt free trade unilaterally, but should negotiate commercial treaties whereby other countries also reduced their tariffs. Using a theory such as Mill's theory of reciprocal demand it was possible to work out the exact circumstances under which a tariff would, or would not, improve a country's terms of trade. Apparently abstract theory, therefore, had a direct bearing on important policy questions.

The main arguments used by the classical economists in defence of free trade, however, were based on much less formal theory. Great use was made of Smith's theory, much more informal than Ricardo's, which stressed the role of trade in stimulating growth. Trade, it was argued, extended the market, providing opportunities for profit, and stimulating growth, whereas protection, imposed by a state operating on the basis of very imperfect knowledge, distorted trade, reducing the stimulus to growth, and encouraging smuggling and corruption. Though this owed much to Smith's theory of growth, and even more to his vision of the process of economic growth, it was not something for which any formal theory was required.

The Corn Laws

Of the many protective tariffs that existed in early nineteenth-century England, the one to arouse by far the most controversy was the Corn Laws. There was opposition to the Corn Laws throughout the period after 1815, and in 1839 the Anti Corn Law League was founded. By 1846, according to one historian, the Anti Corn Law League was the most powerful national pressure group England had known, and upon their techniques of mass meetings, travelling orators, hymns and catechisms, a good deal of later Victorian revivalist and temperance – and even trade union – oratory was based. (Mathias, 1983, p. 275)

When repeal did come, it split the Conservative Party, ending Sir Robert Peel's ministerial career.

The history of agricultural protection in England goes back a long way. Adam Smith criticized the Corn Laws, which imposed tariffs on imported corn, and which provided bounties to corn exporters, but the Corn Laws which were the object of so much attention in the early nineteenth century had their origin in the Napoleonic wars. During the war Napoleon's attempted blockade of England, together with a series of bad harvests at a time when England's industry and population were expanding rapidly, caused the price of corn to rise dramatically, leading farmers to extend the area under cultivation. When peace came, farmers feared the consequences of lower prices and, amidst much controversy, Parliament passed the Corn Laws of 1814 and 1815. The bounty on exporting was repealed as an irrelevance: Britain had long since ceased to export corn. More important, the import of corn was prohibited whenever the price was below £4 per quarter, free import being allowed as soon as it exceeded this level. This price reflected the high wartime prices and hence gave British farmers, except in years of extreme scarcity, a monopoly of the home market. This policy led to some sharp fluctuations in the price of corn and in 1828 it was replaced by a sliding scale of duties, according to which the rate of duty fell gradually as the price of corn rose. The Corn Law remained in force until, after modification in 1842, it was repealed by Peel in 1846.

The reason why the Corn Laws raised such controversy was that they were thought to benefit agricultural interests (whether it was farmers or landlords who gained was a matter of dispute) at the expense of the rest of the economy. Farmers received a higher price for corn, whilst manufacturers were forced to pay higher wages than if corn had been cheaper. In addition, 'dear bread' was an emotive issue, for the high price of corn was thought both to lower workers' living standards, and to raise the cost of labour to industrialists. Underlying all this, the Corn Laws focused attention on two different visions of Britain's future: one where agriculture retained its primacy; the other in which Britain exploited its comparative advantage in manufacturing to become the workshop of the world, coming to rely increasingly on imports of cheap food. Given the social consequences of industrialization in the early nineteenth century this was an emotive issue (think, for example, of William Blake's 'Jerusalem'). When repeal did come it was as a response to the depression of the early 1840s, a time of widespread hunger and social unrest. It was hoped that repeal of the Corn Laws, along with the wider movement towards free trade, would encourage more rapid industrial growth, thus getting the country out of a dangerous economic and social situation.

The classical economists were almost unanimous in arguing for the repeal of the Corn Laws. The most well-known of their arguments for repeal was Ricardo's: indeed, it can be argued that Ricardo's whole theory of distribution and growth (see chapter 2) originated in the Corn Law debate of 1814–16 (see Blaug, 1958). His theory was carefully constructed to show that the only barrier to economic growth was diminishing returns in agriculture, which caused rents to rise at the expense of profits, thus reducing savings and hence growth. It was an argument that, if the Corn Laws were not repealed, growth must come to an end because of the rising cost of food. The theory also implied a clear conflict between the interests of landlords and the industrialists and workers. It was the landlords, whose rents were kept high, who benefited from the Corn Laws, with industrialists and workers standing to gain from their repeal.

Although Ricardo's theory of diminishing returns and rising rents is the most well-known one, it was neither the only, nor the most widely used, argument for the repeal of the Corn Laws put forward by the classical economists. One of the most influential writers on the subject was J. R. McCulloch, whose views on the subject were very different from Ricardo's (see O'Brien, 1970, pp. 378–95). McCulloch put forward four main arguments for repealing the Corn Laws. The one on which he laid most stress was that the Corn Laws increased price fluctuations. If there was a poor harvest, prices would rise sharply because imports were effectively prohibited until prices had risen a long way. If there was a good harvest, prices would fall dramatically, perhaps by as much as 50 per cent, before it would be possible for any surplus wheat to be exported. Related to this argument was the argument that farmers did not in fact gain from the Corn Laws, even though they thought they did. One reason why they did not gain was price fluctuations. The other was that the Corn Laws, by raising the cost of living, resulted in more capital flowing abroad than would otherwise have been the case, and this resulted in lower growth, to everyone's disadvantage. Finally, McCulloch argued that the Corn Laws posed a threat to public order, for people believed, albeit incorrectly, that there was a clash of class interests. This reason alone was enough to justify their repeal.

These two reasons, that they increased fluctuations in wheat prices and that they did not in fact benefit farmers, were the main reasons why McCulloch argued for the repeal of the Corn Laws. In addition to these he also used Ricardo's arguments about diminishing returns, though he placed very little stress on it. Finally, he used Smithian arguments about free trade and optimal resource allocation. The Corn Laws, he claimed, cost the British public between £19m. and £36m., of which landlords received only about 20 per cent: the rest constituted a loss due to the misallocation of resources resulting from the Corn Laws.

The classical economists thus put forward a variety of arguments in favour of repealing the Corn Laws. After they were repealed there was no dramatic fall in wheat prices until the 1870s, when the American mid-west began to produce large quantities of cheap wheat, and when the development of steamships reduced the cost of transporting wheat across the Atlantic. Wheat prices were, however, more stable. McCulloch's perspective, stressing the effects of the Corn Laws on price fluctuations, would seem to have been vindicated.

The Factory Acts

In the first half of the nineteenth century there was some movement, albeit extremely slow, away from complete *laissez-faire* in industrial policy, the main aspect of this movement being the Factory Acts, which restricted hours of labour. The first significant act regulating employment in cotton factories was Peel's Act of 1819, which restricted the labour of children under 16 to 12 hours a day and prohibited that of children under nine. This act, however, was very limited, and the provisions for inspection were inadequate to ensure that it was properly enforced. The next major legislation was Althorp's Act in 1833, which specified a 12-hour day for children aged between 14 and 18, and an 8-hour day for children aged between 9 and 13. During the decade or so after this act, discussion was dominated by the Ten Hours movement, the goals of which were achieved in two stages. In 1844 children's hours were reduced to 6½ day, and that of young persons (boys under 18 and girls under 21) to 12 a day. Then, in 1847, the Ten Hours Bill secured a 58-hour week for young persons and for women of all ages. This act was further extended in the 1860s and 1870s.

In other industries regulation came later. It was not until 1842 that the Mines Act prohibited the employment of children under 10 and women in mines. In agriculture, child labour was unregulated until 1867. Child chimney sweeps were prohibited only in 1864. With the extension, in 1878, of the regulations governing the textile industry to all industries, and with the coming, in the 1880s, of compulsory education, we are into a different era.

In the debates over the factory acts the classical economists' arguments were centred on two main issues. The first was their belief in freedom of contract. They were thus generally opposed to regulating the hours of adult men, who were considered free either to accept or reject the terms they were offered (the situation with women was more complicated, reflecting differences of opinion over the extent to which women were, or ought to be, free agents). There was similarly widespread agreement that children were not free agents, and that their labour should be regulated. Views about the appropriate 'age of consent' varied, and the age tended to rise over time, reflecting current legislation.

One of the major problems involved in attempting to regulate child labour was that the hours of labour of adults and children were related: an adult spinner needed children working with him to perform certain tasks. One result was that industrialists tried to get round the factory legislation by working children in shifts, a system which enabled men's hours to be kept high, and which made it much harder to tell whether the regulations governing child labour were being followed. The link between adults' and children's hours was one reason for the popularity of the Ten Hours movement: restricting the hours worked by women and children was a way of reducing adult hours, but without running up against objections concerning freedom of contract. Once this became clear, in the 1840s, many economists opposed the Ten Hours movement.

The classical economists also produced a number of economic arguments about the likely effects of factory legislation. The most well-known argument is probably that of Nassau Senior who claimed, in 1837, that, given the level of fixed capital investment in the cotton industry, a reduction in the working day from 12 hours to ten would completely wipe out profits. The most important aspect of his thesis was that he assumed output would fall in proportion to hours. This was an assumption that few of his fellow economists questioned, despite the evidence that Ashley and other campaigners for factory legislation produced to suggest that productivity rose when hours were reduced. A second argument, used by Torrens, Scrope and others in the 1830s, was that the root cause of the problem of child labour was the Corn Laws, which had raised the price of food and depressed real wages. Factory legislation might be desirable, but only because the Corn Laws had not been repealed.

In the 1840s Torrens introduced an argument based directly on the classical theory of growth. Taking for granted that reducing hours would reduce output in proportion, and that less output would be produced from the existing capital stock, he argued that either wages or profits must fall. The rate of profit, he claimed, was already approaching its minimum, which led him to issue the following warning: 'Enact your Ten Hours Bill and one of two events must inevitably ensue:– the manufactures of England will be transferred to foreign lands, or else the operatives must submit to a reduction of wages to the extent of 25 per cent.' (Quoted in Blaug, 1959, p. 140.) The belief that the government should not intervene in contracts between free agents (employers and adult men) was based on the assumption that people knew what was in their best interests and that as a result competition would result in the working day being set at its optimal length. Though Henry Fawcett said this explicitly, claiming that because employers were maximizing profits the working day would be chosen so as to maximize output per man-hour, this assumption was for the most part only implicit. An economist who consistently rejected this assumption was J. S. Mill. He pointed out that there was an important exception to the principle of non-interference:

The case in which it would be to the advantage of everybody, if everybody were to act in a certain manner, but in which it is not in the interest of an individual to adopt the rule for the guidance of his own conduct, unless he has some assurance that others will do so too. There are a thousand such cases; and when they arise, who is to afford the security that is wanted, except the legislature? (Quoted in Blaug, 1959, p. 137)

At first (in 1832) he applied this to women and children: they end up working longer hours than each alone might have wished. In 1848, in his *Principles of Political Economy*, he applied this to adult, male labour as well. Despite Mill's arguments, however, the notion of free agents continued to dominate the debate.

The classical economists were not in the vanguard of the movement for restricting hours of work, but neither were they completely hostile towards it. Though, with the notable exception of J. S. Mill, they upheld the principle that the state should not intervene in contracts between free agents, they nonetheless admitted very important exceptions to the rule of *laissez-faire*: to portray them as unthinking advocates of *laissez-faire* is as misleading as to suggest that they were leading the struggle for factory reform. As regards the arguments they used to defend their position, these owed relatively little to formal economic theory.

3.5   PUBLIC UTILITIES, PROTECTION AND ANTI-MONOPOLY POLICY IN THE NINETEENTH CENTURY

Background

By 1851, the year of the Great Exhibition, Britain was unquestionably the world's leading industrial power, dominating world trade, and producing a massive proportion of the world's output of manufactured goods: perhaps two-thirds of the world's cotton goods, and half of its iron. Indeed, it has been claimed that the movement towards free trade took place not because the economic case for it came to be accepted, but because British manufacturing had nothing to fear from foreign competition. By the 1870s, however, this position was being challenged, particularly by the US and Germany, both of which were growing very rapidly.

In addition, new industries were developing, very different in character from the cotton textile industry so important in Britain's industrial revolution. Steel-making and the chemical industry required a high input of fixed capital and had to be organized on a large scale if they were to be efficient. These industries came to be dominated by Germany and the US. The background to discussions of trade and industrial policy at the end of the nineteenth century was thus very different from at its beginning. For the first time there was effective, and sometimes bitter, competition between a number of industrial countries, changing the context in which discussions of commercial policy had to take place. At the same time industry was, at least in some areas, becoming more concentrated, thus raising the question of how governments ought to deal with monopolies. This problem was especially acute in the US.

The growth of railways in the nineteenth century is shown in table 3.1. Railways were very important for several reasons. They were large undertakings in themselves, involving a massive investment in fixed capital. Furthermore, railways, along with the telegraph, contributed to

Table 3.1 The growth of railways in the nineteenth century (length of railway line open, in kilometres)

	UK	France	Germany	US
1830	157	31	—	37
1840	2,390	410	469	4,535
1850	9,797	2,915	5,856	14,518
1860	14,603	9,167	11,089	49,288
1870	21,558★	15,544	18,876	85,170
1880	25,060	23,089	33,838	150,091
1890	27,827	33,280	42,869	268,282
1900	30,079	38,109	51,678	311,160
1910	32,184	40,484	61,209	386,714

Source: Mitchell (1978), Table F1; Mitchell (1983), Table G1. The asterisked figure is for 1871.

an enormous improvement in communications, breaking down local markets, and making the emergence of larger organizations much easier. In the US railways not only opened up the west, but they were a vital factor in the concentration of industry which took place towards the end of the century: not only were they a major industry in their own right, but control over railways was used by men such as Rockefeller and Vanderbilt as a means to eliminate competitors and to dominate other industries.

Railways and public utilities

In addition to their playing a major role in the development of the economies of Europe and the US, railways, along with other public works, were in themselves an important stimulus to economic theorizing. This was especially true in France, where a number of engineers in the *Ecole des Ponts et Chaussées* (literally, School of Bridges and Highways) made important contributions to economic theory. The most important of these was Jules Dupuit. Dupuit's starting point was the argument that the utility of something to a consumer depends on how much of it he or she can consume. He illustrated this with the example of a town's water supply:

Water is distributed in a city which, situated at a height, could procure it only with great pains. There was then such a value that the hectoliter per day was 50 francs by annual subscription. It is quite clear that every hectoliter of water consumed in these circumstances has a utility of *at least* 50 francs. (Dupuit, 1853, as quoted in Ekelund and Hebert, 1983, p. 261; see also Dupuit, 1844, p. 86.)

Now suppose pumps are installed, reducing the cost of water to 30 francs per hectolitre.

What happens? First, the inhabitant who consumed a hectoliter will continue to do so and will realize a benefit of 20 francs on his first hectoliter; but it is highly probable that this lower price will encourage him to increase his consumption; instead of using it parsimoniously for his personal use, he will use it for *needs less pressing, less essential*, the satisfaction of which is *worth more than 30 francs*, since this sacrifice is necessary to obtain water, but is worth *less than 50*, since at this price he relinquished his consumption.

Each additional hectolitre of water will be worth a smaller amount than the previous one.

   Dupuit plotted the value of the last unit of water against consumption, as in figure 3.2 (see Dupuit, 1844, pp. 106–110). This curve is at the same time the marginal utility curve (for it gives the value, or utility, to the consumer, of an additional unit of water), and the demand curve: if the price is p', the consumer will purchase q' units; if it is p'', he will purchase q'' units. He went on from here to investigate both the behaviour of a monopolist faced with this demand curve, and the question of the socially optimal tariff rate.

   Suppose now that figure 3.2 depicts the marginal utility-cum-demand curve for railway travel over a particular line, and that the cost of carrying

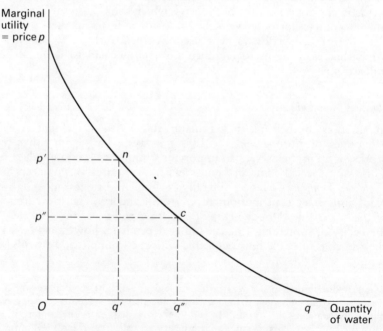

FIGURE 3.2 *Dupuit's theory of demand and utility*

additional passengers is zero. Suppose that the fare is set at p'; q' journeys will be made. Dupuit showed that the value (utility) of these journeys to the consumer would be given by the area of the triangle $pp'n$. The first journey is worth p, but the consumer pays only p', enjoying a surplus of $p-p'$. The next journey is worth slightly less, yielding a slightly smaller surplus, and so on until the qth journey which is worth only p', yielding no surplus at all. From the railway company's point of view the surplus is given by the rectangle $Op'nq'$, for each journey yields a revenue of p', whilst costing nothing. If there are fixed costs, of course, the railway's profits will be less than this. Finally we have the triangle $nq'q$, which is the lost utility. If travel were free, q journeys would be undertaken, yielding a surplus of Opq: when a higher price is charged, part of this potential surplus still goes to the consumer, part goes to the railway company, the rest being lost.

Dupuit was thus able to show a clear conflict of interest. The maximum benefits were obtained by charging a zero price (or a price equal to marginal cost, if the marginal cost of travel were not zero), whereas the railway owner, typically a monopolist, would choose a higher price so as to maximize revenue.

The rise of protectionism in the US and Germany

At the start of the nineteenth century Germany was divided into many states. The Congress of Vienna, in 1815, reduced the number of German states to 39, with four free cities. One of the first steps towards German union was the Zollverein, or customs union, set up, for a variety of political and economic reasons, in 1834. This was gradually enlarged to include all the German states by 1867. The Zollverein abolished all internal tariffs, imposing a common external tariff. This external tariff was, however, only moderately protective, for the Prussian agricultural interests, which favoured free trade, were still strong.

In Europe free trade came more slowly than in Britain, because there was the fear that British competition would crush domestic industries, without allowing other industries to grow up to replace them. In the 1860s, however, tariff barriers fell, due to a series of commercial treaties. The result was that in the 1870s few activities were restricted by heavy taxation. After that, however, this policy was reversed. Germany raised tariff barriers in 1879, followed in the 1880s by most European countries, the major exception being Britain. These tariffs were high but they did not prohibit trade, the reason being that governments wanted revenue. Furthermore, many tariffs were used as bargaining counters: the raising of tariffs was frequently followed by commercial treaties which mitigated their effects. At the same time, subsidies were provided to exporters.

Apart from Britain, which pursued a free trade policy throughout, the major exception to this pattern was the US, which pursued a high tariff policy during the Civil War and maintained it throughout the period up to 1913. The tariff was an important political issue, the Republicans, representing northern industry, favouring protection, and the Democrats, who represented both southern agricultural interests and consumer interests, favouring freer trade. It was frequently argued by Democrats that the tariff fostered trusts, and that industries were being protected which were sufficiently strong not to need protection. Despite this bias towards free trade, however, Democratic politicians favoured protection whenever the interests of their constituents were at stake. Thus although tariff rates fluctuated they never fell very far: for virtually the whole period from 1861 to 1913 tariffs covered over half of US imports, the average tariff rate on dutiable goods being over 40 per cent. It was not until 1913 that any substantial reductions were made.

List's arguments for protection

During the nineteenth century many writers, both European and American, advocated protection. The one who stands out, however, is Friedrich List. List was instrumental in organizing support for the Zollverein and in the 1820s was also involved in US debates over protection. His ideas thus did not simply stem from German experience but also owed much to early US advocates of protection, such as Hamilton. His most important work, *The National System of Political Economy* (1841) remains, despite its many inadequacies, the classic nineteenth-century argument for protection.

   List's theory was based on the idea that countries progress through three stages of development: an agricultural stage; a stage in which new industries had been established; and a stage in which a country had well-established industries. In the first stage a policy of free trade was appropriate, for it would enable people to learn from more advanced countries. Free trade was also appropriate in the third stage, a stage which he considered only Britain to have reached, the reason being that free trade would 'stop farmers, manufacturers and merchants from falling into idle habits and to encourage them to maintain the supremacy they have achieved' (List, 1841, p. 158; quoted in Henderson, 1983, pp. 167–8). It was in the second stage that protection was needed if what List called a country's 'productive' forces were to be built up. There were a number of reasons for this. One reason was increasing returns to scale. In an earlier work, List had written that:

A man may manufacture 1,000 yards of broad cloth a year, and sell a yard for 6 dollars, and he may lose money; but he may manufacture 20,000 yards of the same quality, and not get more than 4 dollars a yard, and he may make money. This circumstance has a mighty influence on the rise and fall of manufacturing power. (Quoted in Henderson, 1983, p. 151)

Industry had to be provided with time to become large enough to survive. This problem was exacerbated by the ability of well-established industries in countries such as Britain to compete unfairly: because of their large size and their lower costs such industries could make their profits in their home markets, selling their goods more cheaply abroad, undermining the ability of small local firms to compete. Once large foreign firms had driven local competitors out of business, they would have a monopoly and be able to raise prices. Another reason for needing a protective tariff was to ensure balanced growth. Not only would balance in a country's economy render it less vulnerable to disruptions in foreign trade, but the different sectors of the economy would stimulate each other, each providing a market for the others' produce, and supplying each other with raw materials. List argued that a policy of protection might well result in the country being less wealthy in the short term. This, however, was a price worth paying, because the development of a country's 'productive forces' was more important than simply material wealth (he rather misleadingly suggested that this was a major difference between his perspective and Adam Smith's).

List did not claim that protection was right for all countries, only the US and Germany (the two countries with which he was most concerned) being thought at the right stage to benefit from protection. He criticized Britain for being too slow in moving towards free trade once its industries had become established. In addition, he argued that colonial trade benefited all the countries involved, both developed and undeveloped.

The evidence List adduced for his thesis was primarily historical. He cited countries that had declined through failing to protect and encourage industries: he blamed Portugal's lack of industry on the Methuen Treaty of 1703 whereby Portuguese industry was exposed to British competition which it was unable to withstand. The towns of the Hanseatic League had failed to stimulate German industry, their trading policies benefiting foreigners instead. In contrast, British industry had prospered because of state intervention. This started with protection of the woollen industry, which enabled Britain to dominate European and overseas markets, and continued with both protective tariff policies, and the use of political and military power to secure markets for British goods. He argued that it was by this policy that England 'acquired power, and by her political power gained productive power, and by her productive power gained wealth' (List, 1841, p. 46; quoted in Henderson, 1983, p. 172).

The tariff reform campaign in Britain

Although free trade was maintained in Britain until the 1920s, protection became an important political issue in the 1880s, and even more so in the period from 1896 to 1903. This controversy is worth considering in some detail because it illustrates very well some of the problems involved in using economic theory to settle problems of economic policy. The 1880s were a time of depression, with British industry suffering at the hands of foreign competition, and protection was suggested as a remedy. It was in 1896, however, that protection rose to the top of the political agenda, when Joseph Chamberlain, as Colonial Secretary, promoted the idea of an 'Imperial Zollverein', with free trade internally and a common protective tariff. Due to opposition from colonies that wanted to be able to protect their own industries from British competition, this scheme was modified to one of imperial preference, whereby Britain would discriminate in favour of colonial food and raw materials, and the colonies would discriminate in favour of British industrial goods. After some moves in this direction the process came to a halt in 1903, when Chamberlain failed to get the government to agree to a tariff on grain imports: without a tariff it was impossible to discriminate in favour of colonial produce. Chamberlain thus started a campaign to convert both the Conservative Party and the electorate to a policy of tariff reform.

In the tariff reform controversy there were not merely two, but an enormous variety of standpoints. There were extremists on both sides: some tariff reformers claimed this to be a remedy for virtually every economic problem; whilst on the other side there were those for whom to question free trade came close to blasphemy. Even within less extreme opinion there was a wide range of attitudes. In part this was because political arguments were, right from the start, inseparable from economic ones. For Chamberlain, for example, tariff reform was merely part of a political programme in which imperial unity and social reform were the over-riding issues. In contrast the Prime Minister, Balfour, defended protection as improving Britain's bargaining position in a world in which other countries had tariffs.

Against both these positions were ranged free traders who included not only politicians but a substantial number of academic economists. The most significant expression of academic opinion came in what was described as the manifesto of the 14 professors, contained in a letter to *The Times* on 12 August 1903, the signatories to which included Alfred Marshall, the leading British economist. This letter was an attempt to use the authority of scientific, academic economics to oppose the protectionist cause, but its outcome was to emphasize the lack of unanimity amongst economists. Though there were exceptions, free trade was generally supported by economists sympathetic towards economic theory while protection was supported by those favouring a more historical approach to the subject.

Perhaps the most important economic aspect of the controversy concerned the effect of a tariff on food prices: would the so-called 'stomach taxes' raise the price of food? This was a problem ideally suited to Marshall's theory of supply and demand and we might think that the use of this theory would have helped to resolve the controversy. This was, however, not the case, the reason being that the tariff reformers used many arguments that could not be fitted into the framework of supply and demand. These included not only political arguments but also important dynamic arguments about the effects of a tariff in stimulating industry and employment in Britain and in encouraging the development of new sources of food supply in the colonies.

Empirical evidence also proved incapable of resolving the controversy. The protectionists claimed that tariffs had been an important cause of

German and American industrial success but the free traders could point to other factors, such as natural resources, to explain this. Statistical evidence could not even establish conclusively that British industry was weak without protection: not only were the statistics subject to enormous margins of error but they could be interpreted in different ways.

These issues were complicated enough but there were still further economic issues. For example, one reason why tariff reform became more popular within the Conservative Party was that men saw that revenue from a tariff could be used to finance military expenditures and social welfare measures without the increases in direct taxes that Winston Churchill and Lloyd George, in the Liberal Party, were demanding. Another issue was the link between the gold standard and trade policy, some free traders arguing that the system of international economic relations, of which the gold standard was a part, was founded on free trade.

A further problem was that politicians took remarks made by economists and simplified, or distorted, them to suit their own interests. For example, early in 1903 Ashley, an economist who supported tariff reform, made the following remark: 'the older writers minimised unduly the difficulty with which labour transfers itself from one industry to another, even a closely allied one.' In Chamberlain's hands this argument was changed into something rather different: 'This doctrine, this favourite doctrine, of the "transfer of labour" is a doctrine of pedants who know nothing of business, nothing of labour. It is not true. . . . You cannot teach men who have attained to skill and efficency in one trade, you cannot teach them on a moment's notice, skill and efficency in another.'

Free trade, together with the desire to avoid the 'dear loaf' was one of the main issues on which the Liberal victory in the 1906 election was based. The Unionist Party was converted to protection, but for reasons different from those underlying Chamberlain's original campaign: protection was seen primarily as a remedy for high unemployment, and as a means of raising revenue.

Anti-trust policy in the United States

In the 1880s the problem of anti-competitive practices became an important political issue in the US. One form of organization which became very popular was the 'pool', or cartel. The loosest form of pool simply involved agreeing on a market area for each firm, but other pools involved a group of firms pooling their output, selling it, and distributing the profits on an agreed basis. Pools, however, were subject to two problems. They were difficult to enforce, and their legality was doubtful: in many states the common law concepts of conspiracy and restraint of trade were applied to them, in addition to state legislation. Pools thus gave way to 'trusts'. These involved several companies in an industry granting control over their stock to a group of trustees. Since these trustees then controlled several companies, they could often control an industry.

Although there was some action that could be taken against restrictive practices in the 1890s such action was largely ineffective, and there was pressure for Federal legislation. The problem of railroads was tackled in 1887 with the Interstate Commerce Act. This prohibited pooling arrangements and discriminatory tariffs, and it declared that railway rates must be 'reasonable'. The Interstate Commerce Commission was set up to supervise the railroads. This was followed, in 1890, with the Sherman Antitrust Act which had two main prohibitions:

(1) Every contract, combination in the form of trust or otherwise, or conspiracy, in restraint of trade or commerce among the several States or with foreign nations, is hereby declared to be illegal. . . . (2) Every person who shall monopolize, or attempt to monopolize, or combine or conspire with any other person or persons to monopolize any part of the trade or commerce among the several States, or with foreign nations, shall be deemed guilty of a misdemeanour. (Quoted in Neale, 1970, p. 3)

Either private parties or the Justice Department might instigate proceedings under the act, and in addition to fines and imprisonment, the act specified that an injured party might obtain 'treble damages': three times the damages sustained as a result of the monopoly or conspiracy.

The Sherman Act appears very radical, but in practice was much less so, for it left too much scope for judges to interpret in a way that favoured business. In the most important case in the 1890s, it was ruled that the American Sugar Refining Company, which controlled 95 per cent of the sugar market, was not in violation of the Act. Size and market control, the court argued, did not in themselves prove that the Act had been violated. Moreover, the American Sugar Refining Company was a manufacturing company, and as manufacturing was only 'indirectly' related to 'commerce and trade', it was not covered by the Act! Though the Sherman Act was applied successfully against a pool in 1899, it was also applied to labour unions: it was ruled that unions could be prosecuted as

Table 3.2   Mergers in US manufacturing, 1895–1913

1895	43	1905	226
1896	26	1906	128
1897	69	1907	87
1898	303	1908	50
1899	1208	1909	49
1900	340	1910	142
1901	423	1911	103
1902	379	1912	82
1903	142	1913	85
1904	79		

Source: Nelson (1959), p. 37; quoted in Niemi (1975), p. 257.

conspiracies in restraint of trade. Given this interpretation of the Sherman Act, it is hardly surprising that mergers and business concentrations continued. As table 3.2 shows, the period from 1898 to 1902 saw a mergers on a massive scale, not matched by any other years in the period from 1895 to 1913.

Two factors brought this spate of merger activity to an end. One was the end of the stock market boom (mergers are always more frequent when the stock market is rising). The other was that under Theodore Roosevelt and Taft the Sherman Act was applied more vigorously. The most notable decisions were those to break up the Standard Oil Company and the American Tobacco Company, both in 1911. These decisions were not the result of new legislation but simply the result of the courts interpreting the Sherman Act in a different way. Antitrust legislation was made much more precise in 1914 with the Clayton Act, which prohibited (1) price discrimination when the effect of this was to lessen competition; (2) exclusive-dealing and tying contracts; (3) the acquisition of competing companies; and (4) interlocking directorates. In addition, the Act made it clear that labour unions were not conspiracies in restraint of trade. This was complemented by the Federal Trade Commission, also set up in 1914, which had the power to issue orders requiring businesses to cease illegal practices.

Economists on anti-trust policy

To illustrate the contribution that economists made to this debate we will consider the ideas of Seligman and J. B. Clark. Edwin R. A. Seligman was critical of relying on competition. Competition, he argued, could work only if labour and capital moved from one industry to another in response to differences in profitability. This did not occur:

In the industrial undertakings of the present day the capital invested is often fixed, not circulating, capital, and cannot easily be transferred to a more lucrative business. It is difficult to gauge the superior profitableness of some competitive enterprise; and even when it has been gauged, it is still more difficult at once to transfer the capital. (Seligman, 1925, p. 220; the articles from which this was taken were originally published in 1887)

Competition was thus limited. Furthermore, there were, he argued, some industries where competition was positively undesirable: these were what Seligman called 'economic', or 'industrial' monopolies, nowadays usually called 'natural monopolies'. These occur where large capital investments are required, the method of operation requires 'unity and harmony of management', and output can be increased without a proportionate increase in capital: in other words, where there are increasing returns to scale. Such industries included waterworks, docks, gasworks and all media of transportation. In these cases, Seligman claimed, the disappearance of competition had often reduced costs and benefited the public.

In addition to these natural monopolies, there were monopolies that resulted from industrial combination, a phenomenon which, according to Seligman, was to be found in 'almost every department of wholesale trade . . . [there being] scarcely a trade throughout the land without its combinations' (Seligman, 1925, pp. 221–2). As a result it was no longer possible to maintain that prices were everywhere regulated by competition. This, however, was not altogether bad, for combinations resulted in more stable prices and levels of production, and were preferable to 'cut-throat' competition. The choice confronting the government, Seligman maintained, was either to leave combinations alone, or to regulate them, and of these the latter was preferable. 'Competition,' he declared, 'has had its day and has proved ineffective' (Seligman, 1925, p. 223).

This view that competition had proved ineffective was not shared by J. B. Clark (not to be confused with his son, J. M. Clark). Like Seligman, Clark accepted that there were many industries where increasing returns to scale prevailed, and where concentration was likely to ccur. Concentration did not, however, imply monopoly, the reason being the existence of potential competition. A business may consolidate into one giant corporation, with the public being forced to buy from it, and yet continue to charge normal prices not much above its production costs, on the grounds that a higher price would invite competitors into the market:

The great company prefers to sell all the goods that are required at a moderate price rather than to invite rivals into its territory. This is a monopoly in form but not in fact, for it is shorn of its injurious power; and the thing that holds it firmly in check is *potential competition*. The fact that a rival *can* appear and *will* appear if the price goes above the reasonable level at which it stands induces the corporation to produce goods enough to keep the price at that level. (Clark, 1907, pp. 380–1; Clark's italics)

The ideal situation, he claimed, was where a single corporation produced all the goods, and sold them at such a price so close to cost as to afford competitors no incentive to enter the industry. In practice price will be limited by potential competitors' costs, which will typically be higher than the 'monopolist's' costs, thus affording the latter a margin of profit.

The state, however, Clark argued, should not adopt a policy of *laissez-faire*, for it needs to ensure that potential competitors are not kept out of the market by unfair means. To do this the state had to take steps to eliminate certain anti-competitive practices, the major ones all involving discrimination between individuals:

[1] the 'trust' . . . can enter the particular corner of the field where a small rival is operating, sell goods for less than they cost, and drive off the rival, whilst maintaining itself by the high prices it exacts everywhere else. . . . [2] it may reduce the price of one variety of goods, which a particular competitor is making, and crush him whilst it makes a profit on all other varieties of goods. . . . [3] it may resort to the 'factors agreement', by refusing to sell at the usual wholesalers' rate any of its products to a merchant who handles products of its rivals.

If corporations were deprived of the power to treat different individuals differently, such practices, which Clark saw as underlying monopolies, would become impossible. Potential competition would then curb the power of monopolies to 'tax' the public, giving the public both the benefits of large-scale organization (low costs) and those of competition (prices close to costs). This outlawing of anti-competitive practices was what Clark saw as the 'natural method' for curbing the power of monopoly. Where it proved insufficient there were other methods: the state might, for example, set itself up as a producer, not so as to obtain a monopoly, but to ensure competition.

3.6 SOME TWENTIETH-CENTURY ISSUES

The New Deal

In 1933, immediately after winning the Presidential election, Franklin Roosevelt introduced what he called the 'New Deal'. The purpose of this programme was to lift the US economy out of the worst depression in its history, which meant that measures to alleviate the crisis in the banking system, and to stimulate inflation, were paramount (this 'macroeconomic' aspect of the New Deal is discussed in chapter 5). The measures undertaken in order to achieve the short-term goal of recovery, however, also had longer-term implications in that they involved an enormous extension of government regulation of the economy. The issues of recovery and reform were inextricably bound together. It is this other aspect of the New Deal, the extension of government regulation, with which we are concerned here. The measures will be considered under three headings: agriculture, industry and unemployment relief.

In agriculture the main need was seen as being to raise farm incomes, which had collapsed in the depression, sending many small farmers into bankruptcy. In 1933 measures were taken to reduce output of cotton, wheat, corn, hogs (pigs) and tobacco, through providing farmers with an incentive to reduce the acreage devoted to these products. The following year this was extended to an even wider list of products. New marketing arrangements were set up, to improve the prices farmers received. Other measures involved providing aid to farmers to encourage soil conservation, providing electricity to rural areas, flood control, and aiding farmers who wished to move to farms in more viable locations. As a result, agriculture became one of the most highly regulated sectors of the economy.

The first measure taken to regulate industry was the National Industrial Recovery Act (NIRA) of 1933. Its aim, according to Roosevelt, was to assure 'a reasonable profit to industry and living wages to labor with the elimination of piratical methods and practices which have not only harassed honest business but also contributed to the ills of labor' (quoted in Scheiber, et al., 1976, p. 374). Rather than introduce direct government regulation of industry, the NIRA made provision for the setting up of 'codes of fair competition'. These codes were to be worked out by all interested parties working together, though in practice they were determined by large firms and unions. These codes set, amongst other things, limits on hours worked, and minimum wage rates. This attempt to regulate industry came to an end, however, in 1935, when the Supreme Court ruled it unconstitutional. This working together with big businesses in order to curb what were seen as the effects of unbridled competition was accompanied by a weakening of the Sherman Antitrust Act. Legislation passed in 1937 made it legal for states to allow agreements between manufacturers and retailers which fixed minimum prices for trade-marked goods. The New Deal policies thus encouraged the development of monopoly.

One of the most important of Roosevelt's policies was the establishment in 1933 of the Tennessee Valley Authority. The TVA was to operate hydro-electric plants established during the First World War and to develop industry and agriculture in the Tennessee Valley. It was given powers to control soil erosion, instigate flood control measures, and to build and operate both further hydro-electric plants and industrial enterprises. The extension of government activity involved in this attempt at economic planning was denounced as socialism, but the venture proved immensely successful.

The New Deal also involved a large programme to relieve unemployment and its effects. Workers were given the right to belong to unions and attempts were made to improve unions' bargaining power: employers were forced to enter into collective bargaining and they were forbidden to interfere in workers' attempts to bargain through a union. Programmes were introduced to employ people directly. The Civilian Conservation Corps was set up to undertake public works projects such as flood control and reforestation. On a larger scale, the Public Works Administration, set up at the end of 1933, employed over 4 million by the beginning of 1934. To increase workers' security, unemployment insurance and old age pensions were introduced in the Social Security Act of 1935 (prior to this such schemes existed only at state level, and then only in some states). To relieve the problem of poverty and poor living conditions, the US Housing Authority was set up in 1937, with power to make loans and provide subsidies for slum clearance and the building of low-rent housing.

The New Deal thus resulted in a massive increase in the role of the state, which became involved to a much greater extent than before in virtually all aspects of economic activity. The government was moving away from strict *laissez-faire* towards a mixed economy in which capitalist industry was controlled by the government. Though the impact of the New Deal must not be overestimated, for there had been moves in this direction during the 1920s and because the measures introduced by the New Deal were not completely successful, there was nonetheless a significant change in the government's attitude towards regulating industry.

John Rogers Commons

The economist who has been described as 'the intellectual origin of the New Deal, of labor legislation, of social security, of the whole movement in this country [the US] towards a welfare state' (Boulding, 1957, p. 7), was John Rogers Commons. His contribution was not to provide any formal theory of how increased regulation might work, but was to provide a new perspective from which to view the problem of how a capitalist economy worked and to provide a justification for piecemeal, pragmatic reforms.

Commons's starting point was the fact of scarcity. Conflicts over scarce resources, he argued, would be settled by physical force unless there were constraints which prevented this. To impose such contraints collective action was required:

If transactions are to go on peaceably without resort to violence between the parties, there must always have been a fifth party to the transaction, namely a judge, priest, chieftain, . . ., who would be able to settle the dispute with the aid of the combined power of the group to which the parties belonged. (Commons, 1924, p. 67)

Society comprised, Commons argued, a number of 'going concerns', such as the state, the family, the church, the corporation, the trade union, each of which had its own set of 'working rules' governing the behaviour of its members. These going concerns, together with the working rules which enabled them to survive, were the institutions which society had evolved to overcome the conflicts created by the problem of scarcity. The existence of external arbitrators, and in particular the legal system, makes it possible for disputes to be settled on the basis of what is reasonable, the final arbitrator being the Supreme Court of the United States. 'Reasonable value', a concept to which Commons attached great importance, was 'the court's decision of what is reasonable between plaintiff and defendant. It is objective, measurable in money, and compulsory' (Commons, 1936, p. 244).

The main requirement of working rules was seen as workability: that they must enable the institution to survive. Working rules must, therefore, change over time to reflect new problems and new circumstances. One way this came about was through the legal system: the courts have to decide, on the basis of what they consider reasonable, whether or not certain practices are desirable, taking into account not only statute law but also the good and bad practices of similar persons under similar circumstances. It is because of this that the courts are able to change working rules in response to new economic circumstances. Another way to change working rules was through the political process, the task of policy makers being not to search for ideal solutions but to try to find workable improvements. Government regulation of industry and trade, therefore, was, for Commons, not something special but simply one of many ways in which individuals' activities were constrained so as to enable society to function in a tolerable manner.

Commons had an enormous influence on legislation, particularly in the 1920s and before, both in his home state of Wisconsin and at the Federal level. Though his work was wide-ranging, one of his main concerns was with labour problems, such as factory legislation and unemployment insurance. Largely due to Commons's work, Wisconsin was, up to 1934, the only state to introduce unemployment insurance. His influence on the New Deal itself was less direct. His ideas were a major part of the intellectual environment in which those economists directly concerned with formulating policy worked. He was also important because of his students, many of whom became involved in formulating and implementing the New Deal programmes. Though the economists associated with the programmes did have ideas of their own (Rexford Tugwell, for example, one of Roosevelt's principal economic advisers, went much further than Commons in advocating economic planning) the New Deal policies were very much piecemeal, and pragmatic responses to specific, urgent economic problems. They were not the result of any attempt to apply new theoretical ideas. As such they can justifiably be seen as being the outcome of Commons's overall approach.

Nationalized industries in the UK

As our first example of post-war policy towards trade and industry we consider nationalized industries in the UK. Nationalized industries became important after 1945, the programme of the Labour government elected in that year including taking a number of major industries into public ownership. Coal, gas, electricity, iron and steel, road and rail transport, and the national airlines were all nationalized with the result that by 1951 about 20 per cent of British industry was in the public sector. The question of public ownership remained a political issue, steel being denationalized (privatized, to use the modern terminology) when the Conservatives returned to power in 1951, only to be re-nationalized by Labour in the 1960s. In industries which remained under public ownership there were the issues of how much should be invested and what objectives the industries should be pursuing. The list of nationalized industries was extended as governments, for a variety of reasons, took over private companies. Docks were nationalized by a Conservative government to solve problems there, whilst British Leyland was bought by the government in order to prevent the firm going into liquidation. Then after 1979 a programme of privatization was initiated, with Jaguar, Cable and Wireless, British Telecom, Sealink Ferries, British Gas, British Airways and the British Airways Authority being sold to private investors.

When considering these industries, economists were faced with two main issues. (1) Should industries be nationalized or, once in the public sector, privatized? (2) How should state-owned industries be run: in particular how should their pricing policy and the level of investment be determined? The main contribution to the first of these issues was by Harold Hotelling (1938). Hotelling's argument, which formed the basis of most subsequent discussions of the issue, was that prices should be proportional to marginal costs (the cost of producing an additional unit of output), not to average costs. In deriving this rule Hotelling followed the argument of Dupuit (see p. 67). Hotelling went beyond Dupuit in paying attention to the fact that if there are high fixed costs, as is typically the case in industries such as gas, electricity and transportation, an industry which adopts a marginal cost pricing rule will run at a loss. He showed that if such losses were met by imposing lump-sum taxes the adoption of a marginal cost pricing rule could make everyone better off than if prices were set to cover costs. Suitable taxes, Hotelling thought, included income taxes, inheritance taxes and taxes on the site value of land. In addition, he claimed, part of the necessary revenue could be raised by charging high prices for goods that were in short supply: there was no harm, he thought, in charging higher prices for travel at peak times when space on trains was scarce, for not only would this raise additional revenue, but it would also serve to ration the available space.

Hotelling's arguments were subject to considerable criticism, and as a result his thesis had to be weakened. For example, it was pointed out that income taxes affected the decision as to how many hours to work, and as a result could not be regarded as lump-sum taxes. It was also shown that welfare would be maximized only if prices equalled marginal costs in *all* industries: it was not enough that prices all bore the same proportion to marginal cost. Later, in the 1950s, it was shown that if there were private sector monopolies, the adoption of marginal cost pricing in the public sector might reduce welfare, not increase it. A different approach was taken by Ian Little who took issue with Hotelling's whole approach on the grounds that it took costs as given, completely neglecting the issue of providing incentives to productive efficiency. It was, he claimed, far more important that managers were given well-defined objectives, and that their performance was monitored in terms of these objectives. Marginal cost pricing rules did not allow for such appraisal.

These arguments, however, had little, if any, impact on the way nationalized industries were run. The objectives of nationalization in the 1940s were never clearly defined, the motives for it being political as much as economic. Nationalized industries were required to break even, but this was not enough to ensure that resources were properly used. As regards their pricing policy, they were prevented from discriminating against particular groups of consumers but this was often taken to justify charging prices that were not closely related to costs. Where prices were related to costs they were usually related to average costs, with all consumers paying the same price, whatever the costs of supplying different consumers. All rail passengers, for example, paid the same fare per mile despite the fact that some services cost much more to provide than did others. In addition to these problems, the methods used to appraise and control investment were inadequate, with no effective methods for evaluating different investment projects. In the 1960s some attempt was made to prescribe more specific objectives, but these emphasized commercial considerations, such as the requirement to break even or the need to earn a certain rate of return, not the public interest. Stricter financial controls were introduced in order to ensure that these objectives were met.

Privatization in the UK

Dissatisfaction with the way nationalized industries were run has provided one of the motives for privatization: it is believed that market forces will force privatized firms to be efficient. Such ideas are reinforced by the now extensive literature which views managers as responding to the particular incentives they face. Provided that they meet any external constraints, managers may have an incentive either to seek to expand the scale of their business, or to seek a quiet life, rather than to pursue policies that will promote the public interest. These problems are even greater when 'the public interest' is ill-defined and there are few if any criteria by which managerial success or failure can be judged. Privatization, it is claimed, will provide managers with the incentive to run their businesses efficiently.

A major problem with such arguments is that they fail to distinguish between the effects of ownership and the effects of competition. In addition to any incentive schemes which link managers' rewards to profits, there are two things that provide managers in the private sector with an incentive to produce goods as efficiently as possible: the possibility of bankruptcy, and the threat of takeover. Privatization means that a firm may go bankrupt but if it is sufficiently large (for example, British Telecom or British Gas) there will be no real threat of takeover. The incentive to produce goods efficiently will thus be limited. In addition, whether or not firms set prices that reflect costs depends not on whether they are in the public or the private sector, but on whether the markets in which they sell their products are competitive or not. There is thus no reason why a large private sector monopoly should be any more efficient than if it were in the public sector. To achieve efficiency, competition may be as important as whether industries are publicly or privately owned, if not more so.

Privatization has, however, been pursued for a variety of objectives, not simply as a means of making nationalized industries more efficient. The government has been concerned to reduce the power of public sector trade unions, to promote wider share ownership and to raise revenue. In addition there are the political implications of reducing the extent of public ownership, plus the fact that privatization is something the government can cite as one of its successes, simply by reciting a list of industries it has managed to privatize. These various objectives may easily conflict. For example, if a nationalized industry's monopoly power is removed before privatization, its market value will be much lower than if it is sold as a monopoly. There is also pressure from managers to keep nationalized industries intact, which runs against increasing competition. As a result, it seems fairly safe to say, the economic issues discussed in the previous paragraph have had relatively little impact on the nature of the privatization programme.

Deregulation in the US

By the 1970s certain US industries were subject to extensive regulation. The Interstate Commerce Commission (ICC) governed the rates that could be charged for rail and road transport. The Civil Aeronautics Board determined which routes different airlines could operate, and the fares they could charge. The Federal Communications Commission regulated AT&T's (American Telephone and Telegraph) monopoly of telecommunications. Dealing in shares was closely regulated by the New York Stock Exchange. During the 1970s, however, opposition to such regulations increased, and by the mid-1980s many of them had been removed. The Airline Deregulation Act was passed in 1978, routes being deregulated by the end of 1981, with fares following a year later. In 1980 road and rail transport were deregulated, regulation being retained only in those sections of the market where effective competition was absent. In telecommunications the pressure came as a result of new technology (particularly the use of satellites and ptical fibres) which dramatically reduced the costs of providing long-distance services. A number of firms argued that they should be allowed to compete with AT&T and, during the 1960s, they succeeded in negotiating the right to build and operate competing communications networks. In addition an antitrust suit was filed against AT&T in 1974, the outcome of this being a settlement in which AT&T's local networks were separated from its long-distance services, with all long-distance companies having access to the local networks.

The contribution of economists to this was substantial, there being a much clearer rationale for US deregulation than there was for privatization in the UK. Though the movement towards deregulation started before his work, Baumol's (1982) theory of 'contestable' markets provided a useful framework for working out where regulation was, or was not, appropriate. Baumol and his associates argue that the crucial feature of a market is not the number of firms operating in it, but the ease with which potential competitors could enter it (compare with Clark's arguments, quoted on p. 76). To analyse this they have introduced the concept of a 'perfectly contestable' market: one in which 'entry is absolutely free, *and exit is absolutely costless*' (Baumol, 1982, p. 3, Baumol's italics). Free entry requires that potential entrants must be able to produce goods that are perceived as being of equal quality to those of the existing producers, and that they can produce goods just as cheaply. These conditions imply that a perfectly contestable market is vulnerable to 'hit and run' entry, for should prices rise above cost a new entrant could enter the market, make a profit, and leave the market (without incurring any cost) should the incumbent firms respond by lowering their prices. It follows that in a perfectly contestable market no firm will be able to make more than normal profits, even if the number of firms is very small. In addition, Baumol argued, price will always equal marginal cost in a perfectly contestable market, provided that there are at least two firms in the industry. The implication of this for regulation is that it is freedom of entry and the costs of exit that determine whether or not a market should be regulated. Regulation is required only where markets are not perfectly contestable: where either entry is difficult, or firms have to incur sunk costs (costs which cannot be recovered should the firm quit the industry). For example, if it is expensive to leave an industry, perhaps because of equipment that cannot be re-sold or put to any other use, firms may be deterred from entering it if they believe that existing firms will retaliate: if exit were costless, they would have nothing to lose by entry.

Such arguments about the importance of potential competition suggested that many industries were being subjected to unnecessary regulations and ought to be deregulated. In the airline industry, for example, entry is very free and exit is costless in so far as an airline can use its aircraft on other routes, or sell them, suggesting a case for deregulation. This conclusion was reinforced by work which suggested that industries where, for example, the rate of return was regulated (i.e. the authorities impose a maximum on the rate of profit that an industry is allowed to earn), costs would not be minimized. Empirical studies supported the idea that inefficiencies of this type did exist in certain industries, such as air and road transport. Once deregulation had become established, economists were able to analyse its effects. It has been shown that costs have been reduced in many industries, and that a greater diversity of products and prices has emerged, both of these resulting in benefits for consumers.

In Britain, on the other hand, though there have been significant moves towards deregulation (notably of bus and coach transport), the movement has not gone so far. Part of the reason for this is that the issue has become entangled with that of privatization. As mentioned above, the objectives of privatization and deregulation are, to a certain extent, in conflict with each other. Deregulating an industry in order to introduce greater competition reduces the value of a nationalized industry. In addition it may make it harder to get the co-operation of the managers in that industry, without which the process of returning nationalized industries to private ownership is more difficult. Because of this, the objectives of industrial policy in Britain have been much less clearly defined than in the US. This is illustrated by the fact that in the UK the term 'privatization' has been used very loosely to cover not only the sale of state assets (the sense in which we have been using the term) but also deregulation and the contracting out of work previously done by local authorities or government departments (such as refuse collection and hospital cleaning).

The European Economic Community

The post-war period has seen the formation of several customs unions and free trade areas, the most important of which is the European Economic Community. At the end of the Second World War the economies of Europe were devastated, and international co-operation was seen as part of the process of recovery. During the 1940s a number of initiatives were undertaken towards greater co-operation, but, for political reasons, none of them progresses very far. The first step towards the formation of the EEC came in 1951 with the formation of the European Coal and Steel Community. This involved France, Germany, Italy and the Benelux countries, and established a single market for coal and steel. The motives for this were political, not economic: if a single market were established for these key commodities, it was argued, French and German industry would become so inter-dependent that war between them would be impossible. Over the following years there were a number of initiatives in the direction of political union and greater military co-operation but these came to nothing until, in 1955, it was proposed to establish a customs union. This was to have internal free trade and a common external tariff. This led to the formation of the EEC with the Treaty of Rome in 1958.

Although the motives for the formation of the EEC were largely political, there was nonetheless a belief that free trade within Europe would produce economic benefits. A number of governments (including Britain, the Scandinavian countries, Austria and Switzerland) wished, however, to have these economic benefits without the supra-national institutions of the EEC. The result was the formation of the European Free Trade Association (EFTA), which established free trade between these six countries (later joined by Portugal). This free trade area was much more limited in scope than the EEC, for there was no common external tariff. It thus required a much smaller administrative machinery than did the EEC.

The modern theory of how a customs union would affect trade was laid down by Jacob Viner in 1950. Viner argued that the formation of a customs union had two main effects: 'trade creation' and 'trade diversion'. To understand this consider an example (Meade, 1956, pp. 48–51). Suppose that we are considering the effects of a customs union between Belgium and the Netherlands and that before the union the Netherlands has a tax of 100 per cent on steel from all sources. Suppose further that Dutch steel costs $250 per ton to produce, Belgian steel $150 per ton, and German steel $100. With a 100 per cent tariff, German steel costs $200 in the Netherlands, and Belgian steel $300. The result is that the Netherlands will import steel from Germany, the cheapest supplier. When a customs union is introduced, however, Belgian steel will cost only $150 in the Netherlands, so the Netherlands will import it from Belgium rather than Germany. This is trade diversion: there is a diversion of output from the low-cost German to the high-cost Belgian steel industry. This reduces world output and is inefficient.

To illustrate trade creation, suppose that the initial tariff had been 200 per cent. In this case Belgian steel would have cost $450 in the Netherlands, and German steel $300. The Dutch steel industry would be protected from all foreign competition, and would be able to sell steel at $250 per ton. Given this starting point, the removal of the duty on Belgian steel will 'create' trade, for the Netherlands will import steel from Belgium at $150 per ton, rather than produce it domestically. Production is switched from a high-cost producer to a lower cost producer, thus increasing world output. This is trade creation. The lesson from this is that whether or not the creation of a customs union is beneficial depends on the relative importance of trade creation and trade diversion. Furthermore, world production, and hence welfare, is more likely to be raised, the higher is the initial tariff.

Though Viner's work was extensively criticized as neglecting important aspects of the problem (for example, each country's production costs might vary with the level of its output, or consumption might rise as prices were reduced by the removal of tariff barriers) his approach determined the way the subject was approached in the ensuing years. In Meade's words, 'the way in which any economic theorist now handles this problem is totally different from the way in which he would have handled it if Viner had not written those dozen pages' (Meade, 1956, p. 51).

Some economists attempted to go beyond this type of argument to work out the changes in trade that would occur as a result of specific tariff reductions. The main problem here was in estimating the extent to which (1) consumers would switch from domestic goods to imports as the price of imports fell; and (2) consumers would switch from one country's imports to another's as prices changed. Making one set of assumptions, for example, Verdoorn (1954) claimed that the elimination of West European tariffs would increase trade within Europe by 19 per cent, whilst imports from outsiders would fall by 6 per cent. Another study, by Janssen (1961), concluded that internal trade within the EEC would rise by anything between 64 per cent and 161 per cent if tariff barriers were removed, with external trade falling by only about 5 per cent. These very different results are only partly explained by the fact that one study was for the EEC, and the other for Western Europe as a whole. The rest of the difference arises because Janssen made different assumptions about how imports would respond to changes in prices, something for which empirical evidence was very difficult to obtain.

Such studies simply estimated the effects of tariff reductions on trade flows, whereas what we are really interested in is their effects on national income. When estimates such as Verdoorn's and Janssen's were translated into estimates of national income, as was done by a number of economists, the results suggested that national income would be changed by very small amounts: 1 per cent or less, sometimes much less. The reason for this is that if you start with a tariff of, say, 10 per cent, the maximum by which tariff reduction can reduce costs is 10 per cent. If imports account for 20 per cent of national income then a tariff reduction will release resources amounting, *at most* to only 2 per cent of national income. If the share of total production that is traded internationally is smaller, then the potential gains from a customs union will be smaller.

Why did such figures not undermine the case for customs unions? One reason is that the figures were based on too many arbitrary assumptions for them to be taken too seriously. However, even if the figures were accepted as indicating approximate orders of magnitude, there was the problem that the analysis was wholly static. The architects of the EEC hoped that European integration would increase competition, improve business attitudes, and increase efficiency, resulting in a higher rate of growth. None of these dynamic factors are considered in the above arguments.

3.7 CONCLUSIONS

When considering government policy towards industry and trade it is tempting to focus simply on whether economists supported or opposed *laissez-faire*. To do this, however, would be very misleading because the way such terms have been understood has changed substantially over time. Though seventeenth- and eighteenth-century writers were concerned, as are present-day economists, with free trade and monopoly, the background against which they were writing was so different that they were concerned with very different issues. 'Free trade', for example, had in the mid-seventeenth century a meaning very different from the meaning it has today. Similarly for Adam Smith and the other eighteenth-century writers who used the term *laissez-faire* it meant opposition to regulations which hampered business activity. It did not imply opposition to state intervention *per se*, as is the case for many economists and politicians who use the term today. It is thus dangerous to take conclusions reached a long time ago and to apply them to today's problems without taking account of how the economic environment has changed since then.

Despite the enormous changes which have taken place in the problems economists have tackled, there has nonetheless been substantial continuity. Even though problems have changed, some things have remained much the same. In particular, problems concerning the regulation of trade and industry have always involved dynamic issues as well as questions of static resource allocation. Over the past two centuries there has been much progress in analysing the latter, but relatively little in analysing the former. This is well illustrated by discussions of tariff policy where the development of international trade theory has led to much clearer understanding of the case for free trade in terms of allocating resources efficiently. The arguments about the effects of the EEC on trade were much clearer and more precise than were the arguments of those who discussed the Zollverein or nineteenth-century commercial treaties. On the other hand, we are now no nearer to finding an adequate way to measure the dynamic effects of imposing or removing trade barriers. We cannot predict when reducing tariff barriers will encourage industry by increasing competition and improving business attitudes, and when it will ruin it by exposing it to ruinous competition. Thus although we should not underestimate the very real progress that has been made in analysing these problems, there remain, for the moment at least, important issues about which economists can say little.

4

Money and Inflation

4.1 SIXTEENTH-CENTURY INFLATION

One of the main challenges to the mediaeval economic order was that of rising prices. Throughout the fifteenth century prices, though fluctuating by as much as 30 per cent from one year to the next, had on average changed little. Prices in 1500 were little different from those of a century before. Over the following century, however, prices rose fourfold, the exact course of prices being shown in figure 4.1. Though mild by modern standards, this unprecedented inflation caused alarm, and men sought to explain it. A sustained rise in prices was a puzzle, for whilst the notion that scarcity could cause a price rise was well understood in the mediaeval world, a general price rise unaccompanied by scarcity was something for which no-one had a satisfactory explanation.

Most modern historians see sixteenth-century inflation as a complex phenomenon involving a number of different factors, none of them being satisfactory on their own. In addition the importance of these factors varied from country to country, and over time. The most obvious explanations of inflation are monetary. From the middle of the century South American gold and silver flowed into Spain in vast quantities (see table 4.1), and from Spain it flowed abroad, to Holland, France and England. Though on a much smaller scale, there were also significant discoveries of silver in eastern Europe earlier in the century. In addition to the changes in the quantities of the precious metals, virtually all European currencies suffered from debasement at some stage during the period. More coins were minted from given quantities of gold and silver. The fate of the English coinage, for example, is shown in figure 4.2. Especially between 1544 and 1551, the 'Great Debasement', the amount of currency in circulation was increased through debasement. In addition, the currency increased due to an increase in the amount of silver in circulation. This picture is typical of European currencies, though most were debased by more than were the English coins. Only the maravedi, the currency of New Castille, the country through which most American treasure entered Europe, had the same silver content in 1600 as a century before.

The link between the supply of currency and prices is, however, far from simple: we have no reason to assume that the speed with which money circulated did not change, and supply may have responded to

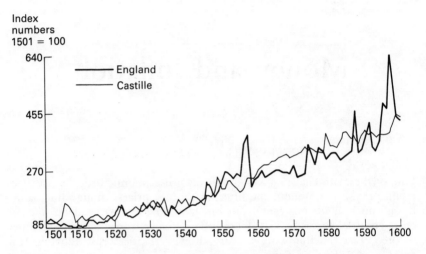

FIGURE 4.1   *Sixteenth-century inflation*
Source: Hamilton (1923), p. 403 and Phelps-Brown and Hopkins (1956), pp. 311–2.

Table 4.1   Spanish bullion imports from America

1503–10	1.2	1571–80	29.2
1511–20	2.2	1581–90	53.2
1521–30	1.2	1591–1600	69.6
1531–40	5.6	1601–10	55.8
1541–50	10.5	1611–20	54.6
1551–60	17.9	1621–30	52.0
1561–70	25.3	1631–40	33.4

million pesos
Source: Hamilton (1923), p. 34.

demand (debasement could occur as a response to a shortage of currency).
Historians have thus been able to justify turning to alternative, non-
monetary explanations of inflation. The sixteenth century appears to have
been a time of relatively rapid population growth, and of a persistent
scarcity of food. Prices of agricultural products rose more rapidly than
those of industrial products, a phenomenon which is hard to explain
simply in terms of monetary factors. War, government expenditures and
poor harvests have also been suggested as important reasons why prices
may have risen.
   It is against this background of persistent and unprecedented inflation
that we find the beginnings of the quantity theory of money. One of the

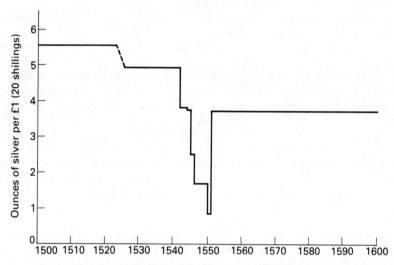

FIGURE 4.2   *English silver coinage in the sixteenth century.*
Source: Challis (1978), pp. 305–6.

earliest writers to suggest a link between the inflow of American treasure
and European inflation was, not surprisingly, a Spaniard, Martin de
Azpilcueta Navarro. Navarrus, as he is often known, was one of an
influential group of scholars at the University of Salamanca, in Castille,
to which so much treasure was coming. His main argument was that

all merchandise becomes dearer when it is in great demand and short supply, and
that money, in so far as it may be sold, bartered or exchanged by some other
form of contract, is merchandise and therefore becomes dearer when it is in great
demand and short supply.

It followed that

(other things being equal) in countries where there is a great scarcity of money
all other saleable goods, and even the hands and labour of men, are given for less
money than where it is abundant. . . . a general shortage of money produces a
general rise in its value. (Navarrus, 1556, pp. 94–6)

Similar arguments were used 12 years later by a French political philosopher,
Jean Bodin. Bodin argued that high prices could arise for a variety of
reasons: abundance of gold and silver; monopolies; scarcity; purchases by
kings and great lords; and debasement. Of these, he argued, abundance
of gold and silver was much the most important. It was the abundance
of gold and silver in Spain and Italy which was the main reason for prices
being higher there than in France, though even France was affected,
treasure being brought into France through trade.

Turning to England we find the quantity theory of money being used as an explanation of high prices by Sir Thomas Smith, though this is only in the second edition of the *Discourse on the Common Weal*, dating from 1581. In 1549 Smith had located the cause of high prices in debasement of the coinage, hardly surprising when we note that he was writing in the midst of the Great Debasement of 1544–51. His argument here had been that because the currency contained less silver after debasement, foreigners would require more of it in payment for imports, and that prices were therefore raised. When the *Discourse* was re-published in 1581 Smith was forced to recognize that if debasement had been the main cause of rising prices, restoring the coinage to its former quality, as had been achieved by the beginning of Elizabeth's reign, should have restored prices to their former levels. This had not happened. Smith suggested two reasons for prices remaining high, one of these being imports of gold and silver from Spanish America:

the greatest store and plenty of treasure, which is walking in these partes of the world, far more in these our dayes, than ever our forefathers have sene in times past. Who doth not understand of the infinite sums of gold and silver, whych are gathered from the Indes and other countries, and so yearely transported unto these costes? (Quoted in Palliser, 1982, p. 143)

The explanations of inflation proposed by sixteenth-century writers such as Navarrus, Bodin and Smith were all based on the well-understood notion that the price of anything depends on scarcity. Prices were seen as relative prices, with money prices depending on the relative abundance of money and goods. A general rise in prices was therefore the result of money's becoming more abundant relative to goods. As statements of the quantity theory of money, therefore, they were deficient in two respects. There was no real analysis of the demand for money, linking demand for money to the volume of spending. In addition, the notion that changes in the quantity of money might bear a certain proportion to changes in the price level was not there. A more complete quantity theory was not developed till the end of the seventeenth century, by John Locke. Before coming to Locke's work, however, we need to consider another very important development, the so-called balance of trade doctrine (see also p. 50).

4.2 ENGLISH MONETARY PROBLEMS IN THE SEVENTEENTH CENTURY

The commercial crisis of the 1620s

During the seventeenth century England was subject to a number of severe economic crises. Of particular importance was the crisis of 1620–1, for it was in response to it that the Balance of Trade doctrine was developed. This crisis involved both high corn prices and a decline in textile exports, probably due to currency manipulations elsewhere in Europe which rendered English exports uncompetitive. For contemporaries the most obvious aspect of the depression was a scarcity of currency. Though everyone agreed, however, that this was England's principal economic weakness, there were divisions of opinion as to the cause and the appropriate remedy.

The traditional view, espoused by Gerard de Malynes, was that silver had left England because the English coin was undervalued: a low exchange rate meant that goods were being sold cheap and bought dear, with the result that trade was 'overballanced' (the value of exports exceeded that of imports). The remedy, he argued, was to regulate foreign exchange transactions so as to restore the exchange rate to its proper level, raising the value of exports relative to imports. Against this, the so-called balance of trade theorists, notably Edward Misselden and Thomas Mun, argued that it was flows of goods that governed the exchange rate and flows of bullion, not the other way round. To stem the outflow of treasure it was necessary to increase the balance of trade, exports minus imports. This required a low exchange rate to make exports more competitive, not a high one.

The difference of opinion between Malynes on the one hand, and Misselden and Mun on the other, involved more than merely different assumptions about the responsiveness of trade flows to prices (if exports and imports do not respond at all to prices, Malynes's position can be sustained; if they respond a lot then that of Misselden and Mun is stronger), for the two positions were based on different views as to how the economy worked. In Malynes's world, coins had an intrinsic value, dependent on their gold or silver content, which it was the sovereign's prerogative to establish. The Royal Exchange was thus necessary to provide merchants with information on the true value of the coinage, so that exchange transactions could reflect this value. In contrast, for Misselden and Mun the buying and selling of goods was fundamental: supply and demand, not the sovereign, determined values, including the value of the currency.

The work of the balance of trade theorists was also important for establishing a link between money and economic activity. They viewed money not as wealth to be accumulated but as working capital. For Mun, the clearest exponent of this view, money was needed to drive trade. The way to accumulate treasure was to allow it to be used in trade. In a chapter entitled 'The Exportation of our Moneys in Trade of Merchandize is a means to encrease our Treasure,' Mun argues that the purpose of exporting money is

to enlarge our trade by enabling us to bring in more forraign wares, which being sent our again will in due time much encrease our Treasure. For although in this manner wee do yearly multiply our importations to the maintenance of more Shipping and Mariners, improvment of His Majesties Customs and other benefits: yet our consumption of those forraign wares is no more than it was before; so that all the said encrease of commodities . . . doth in the end become an exportation unto us of a far greater value. (Quoted in Monroe, 1965, p. 180)

Mun's theory of the balance of trade was important for several reasons. It was a theory of growth centred on foreign trade: as such it embodied a particular conception of economic activity, increasingly challenged in the seventeenth century, in which production was fundamental (see p. 50). In addition it provided a justification for the East India Company, of which Mun was a director, being allowed to export bullion to India, necessary because the company could not find suitable goods for export. Finally, it contained many elements of the price–specie–flow mechanism of Hume and Cantillon, which has formed the basis for most subsequent writing on the balance of payments. Before we come to this, however, we have to consider some important developments in the quantity theory of money.

Locke and the recoinage of 1696

By the mid-1690s the silver coinage had become very debased through clipping. It had become necessary to do something to improve the state of the coins in circulation, and the problem was how to do this. This involved not only the mechanics of how any recoinage should be undertaken (should old coins be accepted at their face value, or according to their weight), but also the question of whether new coins should be minted with a silver content equal to what they used to have, or with a silver content that matched that of the clipped coins currently in circulation. If the former course were adopted the quantity of coins in circulation would have to fall, for new coins would contain more silver than the old ones.

In arguing that the coinage should be restored to its former silver content Locke provided a much more thorough statement of a quantity theory of money than had any of his predecessors. Rather than simply assuming that scarcity raised the price of money he argued that there was of necessity 'a certain proportion of money to trade': 'Every man must have at least so much money, or so timely recruits, as may in hand, or in a short distance of time, satisfy his creditor who supplies him with the necessaries of life, or of his trade' (Locke, 1691, p. 23). The amount of money necessary to carry on a given volume of trade, however, could not be determined exactly, for it depended on 'the quickness of its circulation'. Quickness of circulation depended on how much money people had to hold in order to be able to carry on their trade, something which varied across occupations, and with the timing of payments. Locke observed, for example, that if rents were paid quarterly rather than half-yearly the amount of money needed to pay rents would be halved. Money would circulate more quickly.

Locke thus had a theory of what determined the demand for money, something that his predecessors did not have. He used this to assert a clear-cut relationship between money and economic activity:

If in any country they use for money any lasting material, whereof there is not any more to be got and so cannot be increased, or being of no other use, and the rest of the world does not value it, and so it is not likely to be diminished, this also would be a steady, standing measure of the value of other commodities. . . . [In such a country] any quantity of that money (if it were but so much that every body might have some) would serve to drive any proportion of trade, whether more or less, there being counters enough to reckon by, and the value of pledges still being sufficient, as constantly increasing with the plenty of the commodity. (Locke, 1691, p. 48)

Providing that prices increase in the same proportion as the money supply, the quantity of money does not affect the volume of trade. In a country which uses money in international trade, on the other hand, there must be a certain proportion between money and trade in order to ensure that prices correspond to prices in other countries. If our money supply were to be halved, for example, writes Locke,

it is certain that either half our rents should not be paid, half our commodities not vented, and half our labourers not employed, and so half the trade be clearly lost; or else, that every one of these must receive but half the money for their commodities – labour as they did before. (Locke, 1691, p. 49)

The latter, Locke argued, would be undesirable, for it would mean that exports were sold more cheaply and imports more dearly, turning the terms of trade in England's favour. This argument, however, overlooked the effects of the resulting loss of competitiveness on the volume of exports and imports.

Although Locke's economics marked, in some respects, an enormous advance on earlier writings, containing a clear account of a quantity theory of money, his work was in another respect backward-looking. An important part of Locke's argument rested not on his quantity theory of money, but on his notion that money had an intrinsic value, equal to the weight of the gold or silver contained in it. Money afforded security to its holders, he argued, because of its bullion content, this being the reason why silver was used for commerce. Such a view was, however, out of date by the seventeenth century. Coins were, for most internal transactions, accepted at face value, despite the fact that their bullion content had been reduced by clipping.

This view that a currency's intrinsic value equalled the weight of gold or silver it contained was the basis for Locke's recommendation that England's silver coinage be restored to its former standard. To alter the standard to reflect the amount of silver present in coins actually circulating would be to endorse fraud, for people would be being forced to accept payment in coin which was worth less than the value they were entitled to receive. Between 1696 and 1699 Locke's recommendations were implemented, the old clipped coins being recoined at the old standard. Men who owed money to the government could pay in the old coin, whilst others had to sell their clipped coins for whatever they could get for them. The result of this decision to increase the silver content of the coinage was that silver was undervalued, the silver in the new, full-weight

Table 4.2　The English money supply, 1693–8

		Silver coins			Gold coins	Notes	Money in banks	Money in circulation
		Full	*Old*	*Total*				
1693	Dec	2.5	11.0	13.5	6.5	2.0	0.5	21.5
1694	Jun	2.0	11.0	13.0	6.7	2.0	0.4	21.5
	Dec	1.5	11.0	12.5	7.1	3.6	0.9	22.3
1695	Jun	1.0	11.0	12.0	10.3	3.9	0.9	25.3
	Dec	1.0	11.0	12.0	11.3	4.0	0.8	26.5
1696	Jun	2.2	2.0	4.2	9.1	3.8	0.2	16.9
	Dec	4.2	2.0	6.2	9.1	3.6	0.4	18.5
1697	Jun	6.4	1.5	7.9	9.2	4.1	0.7	20.5
	Dec	7.5	1.5	9.0	9.2	4.1	0.7	21.3
1698	Jun	7.8	1.1	8.9	9.3	4.1	1.0	21.3
	Dec	8.1	0.9	9.0	9.5	4.3	1.1	21.7

£m
Source:　Horsefield (1960), p. 14.

coins being worth more than the coin's face value. Full-weight coins were hoarded or melted down for export. Thus although new coins to the value of £7m. were produced few of these remained in circulation. The result was that the money supply fell dramatically, as shown in table 4.2, and a severe depression followed. The longer-term consequence, again not intended by Locke, was that silver virtually disappeared from circulation: because silver was undervalued relative to gold (i.e. the face value of silver coins was less than the value of the silver they contained) people chose to hoard them and to pass gold coin into circulation. This is an example of Gresham's Law, that bad money drives out good, named after Sir Thomas Gresham sixteenth-century financier. This is the origin of the gold standard, for England came to rely on gold coins and paper currency. It was not until 1774, however, that the fact of a gold standard was officially recognized.

4.3　PAPER MONEY AND THE GOLD STANDARD IN THE EIGHTEENTH CENTURY

Experiments with paper currency

The period from 1690 to 1720 saw a number of important banking experiments. These ventures formed part of a more widespread boom in company promotion: hitherto joint stock companies had on the whole been confined to overseas trade, the Dutch and English East India

Companies (founded in 1600 and 1602 respectively) being the most notable examples. In England companies were formed in the 1690s for purposes ranging from water supply and mining to providing insurance and salvaging sunken treasure ships. Against this background, together with the desperate state of the government's finances as it attempted to finance war with France, it is hardly surprising that attention was turned to banking.

During the period there were many proposals for 'land banks'. The idea was to issue notes against the security of land. Because they were backed by land, it was argued, such notes would circulate at their face value. Though such ideas had a long history, it was only in the 1690s that they came to fruition. Attempts to set up land banks were, however, unsuccessful. For example, the attempt in 1696, to set up a government land bank, failed due to lack of support.

In contrast, a French land bank, the Banque Générale, was successfully set up in 1716, by John Law. The theory underlying this venture had been expounded by Law in his *Money and Trade Considered* (1705). Land, he claimed, 'has a better and more certain value than silver money. . . . Land is what is most valuable, and what encreases in value more than other goods; so the paper money issued from it, will in all appearance not only keep equal to other goods, but rise above them' (Law, 1705, p. 97). The establishment of a land bank which issued paper currency would make it possible to increase the money supply and hence to increase the level of economic activity. After failing to get his ideas accepted in Scotland Law had turned to France, persuading the Regent to help him set up the Banque Générale with a view to putting his ideas into practice.

Law's objective in setting up the Banque Générale was thus to use monetary, fiscal and exchange rate policy to increase the level of economic activity in France. However, he faced the problem that given its small capital (effectively only about 825,000 livres) and the enormous volume of government debt (probably over 450m. livres, much of this being a legacy of the recent war) the bank had little control over interest rates. This led Law into the area of debt management through his Compagnie d'Occident (Company of the West), set up in 1817. This was granted exclusive trading rights to Louisiana (still owned by France) in return for the company agreeing to take over a large quantity of government debt. The Compagnie d'Occident and the Banque Générale became tied up with each other as Law used newly created banknotes to support the price of shares in the Compagnie d'Occident. Notes were issued in very large quantities, and both concerns became the subject of intense speculative activity, share prices rising 36-fold. In 1720 this speculative bubble burst and Law's bank collapsed: it had issued far too many notes.

Though not involving land banks a similar speculative boom, the 'South Sea Bubble', took place in England from 1719 to 1720. When this bubble collapsed, taking many companies with it, joint stock organization became severely discredited, and legislation was introduced making it very difficult to create new companies.

Though Law's ideas on this contained valuable insights, and could be seen as building on the earlier work of men such as Mun, they contained crucial flaws. Law failed, for example, to explain what would prevent notes from being over-issued, and as a result he failed to explain how confidence in the bank's notes, necessary if they were to retain their value, was to be maintained. It has been argued that the failure of Law's venture arose not because the scheme was inherently flawed but because Law was overambitious. There is probably some truth in this but it remains true that the constraint that notes be issued against land does not provide any guarantee that they will retain their value: if notes are over-issued the value of land will be raised, providing the basis for further note issue, as was clearly illustrated by the fate of the 'assignats', the land-based currency issued during the early years of the French Revolution. Once prudential considerations, such as the need for a land bank to maintain metallic reserves, are introduced, land banks become much more like conventional banks.

More significant than any attempt to create a land bank was another banking experiment: the establishment, in 1694, of the Bank of England. This was a joint stock company, established for the purpose of lending to the government. It was unique in that not only did it take deposits and lend both to the government and the private sector, but it also issued notes. Though it was forced to suspend the convertibility of its notes during the recoinage crisis of 1696, its policy was such that the public retained confidence in its notes.

The English gold standard

A gold standard was effectively established in England by the recoinage of 1696 which undervalued silver and caused silver coins to disappear from circulation (see p. 95). The English monetary system in the eighteenth century was, however, still very complicated. We are used to dividing currencies into neat categories: monometallic standards (currencies convertible into a single metal, either gold or silver); bimetallic currencies (where silver and gold are both used); and paper currencies (convertible into neither gold nor silver). The English situation in the eighteenth century, however, fitted into none of these categories. Though there was in principle a bimetallic standard, silver had long since ceased to be a standard of value: silver coins, often very worn or clipped, circulated only as small change. In addition there was a prohibition on the export of English gold coin or of bullion obtained from melting such coin. Foreign coins, however, and bullion obtained from other sources, could be freely exported. The enforcement of this prohibition on the export of English coin was loose: gold obtained from melting guineas could, for example, be exported if the merchant swore that it was obtained from foreign coin. Thus though the prohibition on the export of coin meant that in principle the sterling exchange rate ought to be free to fluctuate by any amount, in practice it behaved much as though gold were freely exportable. On either side of the par value (£3 17s. 10½d., or £3.89 per ounce) were the gold export and import points: the values of sterling at which it became profitable to incur the transport and insurance costs involved in exporting or importing bullion. The actual value of sterling fluctuated between these limits. In times of war risks were greater and these limits were further apart than in peacetime.

The quantity theory and the price–specie–flow mechanism

By the end of the eighteenth century a well-formulated quantity theory of money, going significantly beyond that of Locke, had been established. Two writers are important here: Richard Cantillon, an Irish banker associated with Law's Banque Générale who had got out early enough to leave with a fortune, and David Hume. Cantillon's main contribution (not published until 1755, though probably written as early as 1734) was to build on the arguments of Law and others who had argued that an increase in the money supply could lead to an increase in employment, and to reconcile such ideas with the quantity theory. He approached this by examining in detail the way in which money was introduced into the economy, and the way in which it raised prices, his criticism of Locke being that 'he has clearly seen that the abundance of money makes everything dear, but he has not considered how it does so' (Cantillon, 1755, p. 161). Cantillon considered two ways money might enter the economy, namely from mines and through foreign trade. If new silver came from mines the first effect would be to raise the incomes of mine owners and those who worked for them. Their spending would in turn increase the prices of goods they purchased, at the same time creating extra income for farmers and manufacturers. These would in turn spend their extra income, and so on. In this way money would gradually spread throughout the economy, raising prices as it did so. Eventually all prices will be raised, but in the meantime production will be stimulated. The process through which money earned in foreign trade enters the economy is essentially the same, but the channels through which it passes will be different: merchants will buy different goods from mine owners and different parts of the economy will be affected.

Hume's theory (1752) has much in common with Cantillon's, for he argued that increases in the money supply would have significant but temporary effects on production and employment. In addition, Hume provided the classical version of the price–specie–flow mechanism, a theory that is in Cantillon's *Essai* but entangled with 'mercantilist' elements. The idea underlying the price–specie–flow mechanism is that when sterling falls sufficiently far below its par value in terms of gold to cover the shipping costs (the gold export point) gold will be shipped abroad. England's money supply will then be reduced and the money supply in its trading partners will increase. The process is, of course, reversed when sterling reaches the gold import point. When we combine this idea with the quantity theory and assume changes in the money supply lead to price changes, we obtain the price–specie–flow mechanism. To see how it works, suppose that England has a disproportionately large stock of bullion. Its price level will be high relative to overseas prices and the result will be a balance of payments deficit. The exchange rate will fall: sterling will fall in value relative to gold. When the gold export point is reached gold will be exported, reducing England's money supply and raising the rest of the world's money supply. English prices will therefore fall and prices in the rest of the world will rise. This process will continue until the precious metals are distributed in such a way as to make prices (allowing for transport costs) the same in all countries. When this occurs the balance of payments will be in equilibrium and sterling will be at par.

It is hard to exaggerate the importance of Hume's price–specie–flow mechanism. Not only has it provided the starting point for most subsequent discussions of the balance of payments, but it provided a powerful argument against policies aimed at achieving a balance of payments surplus in order to produce an inflow of bullion and thereby increase the level of economic activity. For such a policy to work it is necessary that any inflows of specie circulate as currency. This will raise prices, thereby affecting the balance of payments and setting in motion an outflow of bullion. Attempts to generate prosperity by increasing the stock of money will, therefore, be self-defeating.

It is worth noting that although Hume's theory (in particular its stress on the response of trade to relative price levels) marked a major advance in our understanding of the balance of payments, most elements of the theory were present in earlier writings: the link between the balance of trade and the money supply; the quantity theory; and the link between prices and trade flows. There was nothing to prevent Locke (who came very close to it) or even Mun from deducing the mechanism, but they did not. As a result their policy proposals, aimed amongst other things at a balance of trade surplus and the accumulation of treasure, were seriously flawed.

Because of his central role in classical economics, it is worth noting that Adam Smith was aware of Hume's monetary theory but made little use of it in his *Wealth of Nations*. Indeed, he emphasized the so-called 'real bills doctrine', according which banknotes could never be over-issued, provided merely that banks followed the rule that they lend only for genuine commercial purposes (that is lending against 'real bills'). If this rule were followed, it was argued, the banks would create no more money than was needed to meet the genuine needs of trade, and banknotes would retain their value. Though some economists, such as Thomas Tooke continued to support the real bills doctrine, it was undermined by Thornton, to whose work we now turn.

4.4   BRITISH WARTIME MONETARY PROBLEMS, 1793–1815

Money and prices after 1793

The years following the outbreak of war with France, in 1793, provide the classic example of economists' theories about the economy changing in response to the evolution of the economy itself. The monetary economics of Smith and Hume had been rendered out of date by changing circumstances in a number of important respects.

Of particular importance was the enormous growth which had taken place in the number of country banks, banks outside London. Though Bank of England notes circulated within London, the note circulation outside London was provided almost exclusively by country banks. Because the law prohibited joint stock banking, all banks except the Bank of England being owned by partnerships of no more than six partners, these country banks were all very small, each serving a limited area. They relied on their connections with London banks for supplies of coin. These London banks in turn had come to rely on the Bank of England. Through these links, the credit system of the whole country depended on the Bank of England. The Bank of England, though established a century before as a means of financing the government, had thus come to perform many of the functions of a central bank. These functions, however, were not yet fully understood.

The role of the Bank of England in the British financial system was brought into prominence in a series of financial crises, particularly important being the crisis of 1793. Though there is evidence that a crisis had started to develop in the preceding months, a major factor was the loss of confidence which followed the outbreak, in February 1793, of war with France. The problem was that there was, following the failure of a number of banks, a loss of confidence in country banks' notes, and as a result there was increased demand for coin (although there was no loss of confidence in Bank of England notes, these were rarely held outside London). This led to the country banks' demanding more coin from their agents in London, who in turn relied on the Bank of England.

There were thus several aspects to this 'internal drain' of gold. There was a need for an alternative circulating medium to replace the notes of the country banks which had failed. In addition, many of the country banks which did survive reduced their note issue to reduce the dangers of their becoming insolvent through a sudden demand for coin. Finally, there was an increased demand for money, as businessmen, because of the greater uncertainty, held a greater amount of cash. The crisis raised the issue of the responsibility of the Bank of England in such a situation. If the Bank was like any other bank it should respond to the loss of coin by reducing its note issue. Many people argued, however, that because the entire banking system depended on the Bank of England for liquidity, it should respond to the loss of coin by *increasing* its note issue. The advocates of this latter view were proved right, for the crisis was averted when the government announced that it was issuing £5m in exchequer bills. These could be discounted at the Bank of England, providing the financial system with the currency it needed. Far from leading to a loss of bullion, the resulting increase in the Bank of England's note issue was accompanied by an increase in its holdings of bullion. The increased note issue restored confidence, reducing demand for gold coin. Furthermore, the number of Bank of England notes in circulation soon fell back to its level before the crisis.

The crisis of 1793 has been considered in some detail because it illustrates the complexity of the British financial system, and the fact that institutional developments had rendered earlier ways of thinking about money out of date. Of far greater importance, however, was the crisis of 1797. In the years leading up to 1797 there had been drain of gold abroad: in addition to expenditure on the war, which forced the government to turn to the Bank of England for gold, there was probably a loss of gold when France returned to a metallic currency after the collapse of the 'assignats', the paper currency issued in the early years of the French revolution. The main factor in the crisis, however, was once again an internal drain of gold caused by a loss of confidence in country bank notes, this loss of confidence being caused by rumours that the French were about to invade. In 1797, following the landing of a small number of French troops in Pembrokeshire, the government ordered the Bank of England not to redeem its notes in gold until Parliament's views on the matter could be obtained. This 'temporary' suspension of convertibility lasted for over 20 years.

The suspension of convertibility provides the background to the monetary controversies of the next 20 years. It was not until 1800, however, when the value of sterling, as measured both by the exchange rate and the price of gold, first fell significantly below its par value (see figure 4.3), that the question of how an inconvertible paper currency works was tackled. This is the background to what is arguably the period's, if not the century's, greatest contribution to monetary economics: Henry Thornton's *An Enquiry into Nature and Effects of the Paper Credit of Great Britain* (1802). The fall in the value of sterling around 1800 was short-lived, the exchange returning to par for several years. Theoretical discussion revived, however, when sterling depreciated once again, in 1809, remaining below par for the rest of the war.

In addition to the price of gold, figure 4.3 shows three other measures of the value of sterling: the prices of gold and silver, and the exchange rate at Hamburg (measured as the price of foreign exchange). These measures of the external value of sterling are shown together with an index of the price level. This shows that the years when sterling was below par were also years of high prices. In interpreting this evidence, however, it is important to remember that, though they were of course very much aware of rising prices, they did not use price indices as measures of the value of money. The value of money was generally taken to be measured in terms of gold, not of commodities.

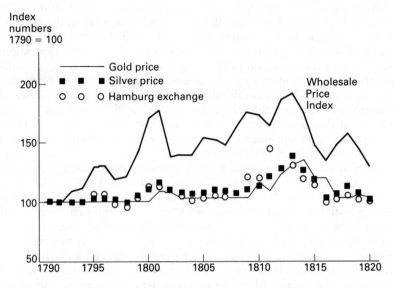

FIGURE 4.3   *The value of sterling, 1790–1820*
Source: Viner (1937), p. 144; Mitchell (1978), p. 388.

Figure 4.4 shows the extent of the expansion of Bank of England credit. In the years after 1797 the volume of Bank of England notes and deposits increased enormously, whilst holdings of bullion fell to very low levels. The period from 1797 to 1815, when the currency supplied by the Bank of England rose rapidly, was the time when, with the exception of 1802 when prices fell sharply, there were rising prices.

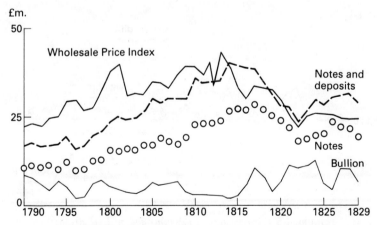

FIGURE 4.4   *The money supply, 1790–1829*
Source: Mitchell and Deane (1962), pp. 442–3; Mitchell (1978), p. 388.

Over-issue of currency was, however, only one explanation of the rise in the price of gold. The main alternative explanation lay in the abnormal payments abroad (extraordinary remittances) which had to be made in several years. One reason for these payments was military expenditure, together with subsidies paid to Britain's allies against Napoleon. The other was the need to import large quantities of corn in several years when harvests were bad. These are shown in figure 4.5, which shows the apparent link between them and the price of gold, considered the main measure of the value of sterling. If the level of extraordinary remittances is compared with the price of silver, or the exchange on Hamburg, an even closer correlation can be found.

The wartime experience of a paper currency thus raised a variety of issues. The responsibility of the Bank of England for the stability of the financial system has already been mentioned. In addition to this and the obvious issues of whether, how, and how soon should convertibility be restored, the important questions were: how far was over-issue of currency responsible for the fall in the value of sterling? What was the connection between the issue of currency, the value of sterling, and commodity prices? What would be the consequences of reducing the Bank of England's note issue? To answer these questions it was necessary to construct a theory of how an economy with a paper currency actually worked, something not provided by the monetary theories of Smith and Hume.

Henry Thornton's Paper Credit

Though the so-called 'bullion controversy' continued for two decades, Henry Thornton's *Enquiry into the Nature and Effects of the Paper Credit of Great Britain* came as early as 1802, having been written during the period immediately after the suspension of cash payments in 1797. The nature of

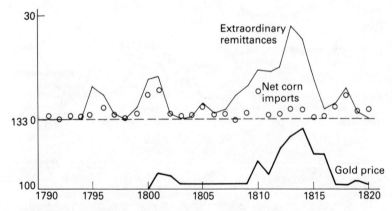

FIGURE 4.5　*The balance of payments and gold, 1790–1820*
Source:　Viner (1937), p. 144; Mitchell and Deane (1962), p. 94.

this book is indicated in its opening paragraph where Thornton points out that whilst his first intention was 'merely to expose some popular errors which related chiefly to the suspension of cash payments of the Bank of England, and to the influence of our paper currency on the price of provisions' (Thornton, 1802, p. 67), he was forced, in order to expose these errors, to discuss more general questions. Thus the book was prompted by topical issues and it was in order to address these that Thornton turned to more fundamental, theoretical issues.

Thornton's work will be explained in two stages. The first stage will be to outline his answers to three important questions. (1) What policy should the Bank of England follow in a financial crisis? (2) What is the link between the supply of currency and the price of bullion? (3) Is it possible for the Bank of England to issue too much currency? The main aspects of his monetary theory are covered in the answers to these questions. The second stage will be to examine the framework underlying his answers to these questions, and to explain why his ideas are so important.

(1) Thornton made use of his knowledge, as a banker, of the way the British financial system worked to argue that the situation of the Bank of England was very different from that of any other bank. If a country bank reduced its note issue this made the bank more secure: its notes would circulate less widely, and it would be less likely to face a sudden demand for gold coin. The reason why the situation of the Bank of England was so different was that whereas country banks might lose coin because of a loss of confidence in their notes, perhaps due to the failure of a bank, this was not the case with the Bank of England. The public did not lose confidence in Bank of England notes, for everyone recognized these and they were never confused with notes issued by weak or failed banks. When the Bank of England experienced a demand for gold coin this was not because the public had lost confidence in its notes, but because country banks were losing coin and had to turn to the Bank of England to get it.

Thornton argued that in a time of crisis, when the Bank of England was losing gold, the way to protect its gold reserves was to *increase* its note issue: the opposite of what a country bank should do. The reason was that in such a crisis coin was being drained out of London, leading to a shortage of circulating medium there. In addition, the shortage of currency would lead to hoarding: people would wish to hold more cash because they would not be confident that they could obtain it when they required it. If the Bank of England were to increase its note issue confidence would be restored, and demand for currency would be reduced.

(2) Thornton argued that it was through raising the prices of goods that an increase in note issue affected the price of bullion. The sale or purchase of a commodity is a two-sided transaction, in that money is exchanged for the commodity. Prices will thus depend not only on supply and demand for the good in question, but also on supply and demand for money. If money is plentiful, people will be prepared to give more of it

in exchange for a good. When prices rise this will lead to a balance of payments deficit, for exports will become more expensive, and importing will become more attractive. The result of the balance of payments deficit will be a fall in the value of sterling, whether measured by the exchange rate or the price of bullion.

It is important to note, however, that Thornton did not see over-issue of currency as the only factor which could lower the value of sterling. Balance of payments deficits could be brought about by other factors, such as bad harvests, or remittances abroad. Thus a fall in the value of sterling did not necessarily mean that the Bank of England ought to reduce its note issue, for to do so might cause depression at home. If the factors underlying the deficit were temporary it might be best to let the Bank of England's gold reserves be reduced, replenishing them when the balance of payments became more favourable. A sustained high price of bullion, however, was seen as a sure sign that notes had been over-issued.

(3) A number of economists, including Adam Smith who was, of course, assuming a currency convertible into gold, had argued that it was impossible for banks to over-issue notes, provided that these were issued against so-called 'real bills'. A real bill was one issued in order to purchase a specified quantity of goods already in existence. The idea behind this was that if notes were issued only by discounting real bills they could never be over-issued, for notes would be issued only to meet the genuine needs of trade. Over-issue of notes was blamed on issuing against fictitious bills: as the currency issued was not needed for normal commercial transactions it could be used speculatively, raising prices.

The real bills doctrine assumes that there is a definite limit to the amount that businessmen will wish to borrow from the Bank of England. Thornton argued that this doctrine was erroneous on the grounds that it took no account of the rate of interest at which bills were discounted (the rate of interest at which the Bank lent money). Suppose that, perhaps as a result of war and increased economic activity, the normal rate of profit to be obtained on commercial transactions were to rise to 6 per cent, but that, because Usury Laws prohibited the Bank from raising it any higher, the Bank continued to lend at 5 per cent. It would become profitable for people to borrow indefinitely from the Bank, and so lending, and the note issue, would increase.

Would there be any limit to this increase in lending? Thornton argued that whilst, in his words, 'a large extension of bank loans may give a temporary check to the eagerness of general demand for them' (Thornton, 1802, p. 255), such a check would be only temporary. The increase in note issue does not correspond to any increase in real capital, and it is on this that the normal rate of profit earned in business depends. The rate of discount at the Bank will therefore remain below the normal rate of profit, and it will remain profitable for people to increase their borrowing. Furthermore, the increased circulation of notes will have to be held by someone. Because notes, which bear no interest, are held to finance transactions, this means that either the volume of transactions or the price level must increase. Demand for notes will thus rise to accommodate the increased supply. The result is that there is no tendency for the note issue to limit itself: the quantity of notes in circulation will continually rise, the resulting increases in the price level raising the demand. This will occur for as long as the Bank of England's discount rate is below the normal rate of profit.

These are the main elements of Thornton's monetary theory. What makes them so important is that they were more than a series of *ad hoc* pieces of theorizing, but they all formed part of a coherent approach to economic problems, based on a set of basic underlying principles. Four aspects of Thornton's theoretical framework are worth pointing out. (1) He sees the phenomenon of credit as fundamental, viewing money, whether coin or notes, as merely one form of credit. This means that he does not look at money in isolation but sees, for example, the possibilities for substituting different forms of credit for each other. (2) Assets, whether notes, coin or any other asset, have to be held by someone. Thus, although he does consider the circulation of currency, he never loses track of the fact that there must always be people who are willing to hold it. This means that the circulation of money cannot be seen as a mechanical process, but depends on attitudes, particularly important being confidence: both confidence in the value of the currency, and confidence that sufficient supplies of currency will be available.

In addition to these points, relevant specifically to monetary economics, there are two aspects of Thornton's work of more general importance. (3) Thornton is continually looking at the way markets interact with each other: the effects of note issue on the price of bullion, for example, are indirect; a shortage of coin may require an increase in the supply of some other asset. Because of his awareness of the links between different financial markets he is always looking at the equilibrium of the financial system as a whole. (4) Finally, Thornton assumes that people are motivated by self-interest, looking for sources of profit, and responding to changes in prices. Businessmen will borrow from the Bank of England whenever it is profitable for them to do so; traders will increase their exports or imports only if it becomes profitable for them to do so; demand for notes and other assets will depend on the costs and benefits of holding them, and so on.

Like Smith, therefore, Thornton is explaining the behaviour of the economy by making the assumption that people pursue their own self-interest, and that their actions are linked through a series of markets. He reaches different conclusions from those reached by Smith, however, for two reasons. Firstly, he applies these principles more consistently than Smith. For example, he criticizes Smith for neglecting the fact that exporters will not increase their exports without an incentive to do so; and for neglecting the fact that different circulating media (such as coin, notes or bills) may circulate at different speeds, because the costs of holding on to each of them differ. Secondly, Thornton brings to his analysis a detailed knowledge of financial institutions, and the way the financial system is constructed. To create a useful economic theory it is not enough to make general assumptions about behaviour: it is necessary to take account of the institutions which exist, and to work out how people will behave given these institutions.

The bullion controversy

For several years after 1802 the value of sterling remained reasonably close to par, and interest in monetary questions subsided. It revived again, however, with the depreciation which occurred from 1809 onwards (see figure 4.3). This depreciation was accompanied by an increase in the Bank of England's note issue (see figure 4.4), raising the issues of how far the Bank of England was responsible for sterling's decline, and what should be done about it.

The most extreme position in this controversy was that taken by Ricardo, who in 1810 published a pamphlet *The High Price of Bullion a Proof of the Depreciation of Bank Notes.* Though his analysis had much in common with Thornton's, he reached a much simpler, more clear-cut conclusion. There was one reason why the value of bank notes had fallen (or equivalently that the price of bullion had risen): too many notes had been issued. The adverse balance of payments was simply a consequence of this.

The main reason Ricardo reached such different conclusions from Thornton was that, as in all his work, he stressed the long run. As one example of this consider his use of Hume's price–specie–flow mechanism. When considering the effects of an increase in the money supply Ricardo jumps straight to a situation where Hume's mechanism (see p. 99) has had time to work itself out: where the distribution of the precious metals between countries is such that each country's balance of payments is in equilibrium. Ricardo thus derives his policy conclusions from a comparison of two situations, in both of which international price levels are equalised. In contrast, Thornton derived his policy conclusions from analysing a situation where exporters had not necessarily had time to respond completely to international price differences.

Ricardo's approach is revealed particularly clearly in his explanation of why he felt able to argue that changes in the money supply did not affect interest rates. Ricardo accepted Thornton's view that an increase in note issue would depress the interest rate, but Ricardo went on to argue that

It is *only during the issues of the bank,* and their effect on prices, that we should be sensible of an abundance of money; interest would, during that interval, be under its natural level; but as soon as the additional sum of notes or of money became absorbed in the general circulation, the rate of interest would be high, and new loans would be demanded with as much eagerness as before the additional issues. (Bullion Committee, 1810, paragraph 22)

Thus although Ricardo accepted Thornton's theory, he stressed the long run. It is because he ignores the short run, transitory situation where the interest rate differed from its natural rate, that he could conclude that the interest rate was independent of the quantity of circulating medium.

In 1810 a committee of the House of Commons, chaired by Francis Horner, and including amongst its members Henry Thornton and William Huskisson (later President of the Board of Trade), published the 'Bullion Report'. The position taken in the report was fundamentally the same as that taken by Thornton in his *Paper Credit*. It was argued that the Bank of England's note issue should be regulated in the light of the balance of payments:

so long as the suspension of Cash Payments is permitted to subsist, the price of Gold Bullion and the general Course of Exchange with Foreign Countries, taken for any considerable period of time, form the best general criterion from which any inference can be drawn as to the sufficiency or excess of paper currency in circulation. (Bullion Committee, 1810, p. 45)

The committee saw the note issue as large and increasing, and in view of the dangers associated with inflation it wished the note issue to be brought under control. To bring this about they recommended that Parliament require the Bank of England to restore convertibility within a period of two years.

Three points are worth noting here. (1) As the quotation above makes clear, it was only over a long period of time that the exchange rate provided a measure of over- or under-issue of currency. Over short periods of time other factors could cause the exchange rate to deviate from par. (2) Demand for currency was seen as varying in response to changes in confidence. This meant that looking simply at the number of notes issued could not show whether too much or too little currency had been issued. (3) Alarm at home, with the resultant high demand for coin, was seen as a legitimate reason for delaying the restoration of convertibility. For convertibility to work it was necessary that confidence be sufficiently strong for the banking system to be able to meet the domestic demand for circulating medium.

The anti-bullionist case was put forward by the Bank of England, which argued that there was no connection between the number of notes issued and the the value of sterling, claiming that it was not possible to observe any correlation between them. The Governor of the Bank of England argued that notes would never be over-issued because 'the public will never call for more than is absolutely necessary for their wants' (quoted in Bullion Committee, 1810, p. 47). He further denied that the interest rate at which bills were discounted could have any effect on the amount of notes issued. As notes yielded no interest, he argued, people would borrow no more than they had to. This argument is one which would make sense only if people were borrowing from the Bank in order simply to hoard notes. If they use the notes they borrow to finance business, then they will have an incentive to minimize borrowing only when the discount rate exceeds the rate of profit they can earn, not whenever it is positive.

Parliament rejected the conclusions of the Bullion Report. Its opponents argued that cash payments should be resumed, not at a definite future date, but only when peace and the political environment permitted it. Whatever the merits of the bullionist case, and by 1827 even the Bank of England had accepted it, it can be argued that the opponents of a rapid resumption of cash payments were probably right in the circumstances. Britain was at war, and to resume cash payments would have created enormous financial problems for the government at a time when it was needing to undertake enormous expenditures abroad. If the war against Napoleon was to be continued, inconvertibility of sterling had to be maintained, whatever the implications for inflation. Whether the anti-bullionist case was fallacious or not was beside the point.

After 1815, however, with the coming of peace, the bullionist case became generally accepted. Even the Bank of England came to accept that convertibility had to be maintained and that if this were to be achieved the Bank could not simply 'meet the needs of trade'. A stricter rule was needed. Discussion thus centred not on whether sterling should be linked to gold but on the rules required if this were to be achieved. Because these debates were, because of the changed economic situation, concerned more with stabilization than with inflation, they are discussed elsewhere (see pp. 133–5).

4.5 MONEY AND PRICES IN THE NINETEENTH CENTURY

The course of prices

The nineteenth century was, on the whole, an age of falling prices. Consider the British price level, shown in figure 4.6. After the end of the Napoleonic wars prices fell, apart from cyclical rises, to 1850. A period of price stability followed until prices again began to decline from the 1870s. This decline lasted until the mid-1890s, after which prices rose. Prices in France and the US followed a similar pattern, the main difference being that there were very high prices in the US during the Civil War.

To a great extent the secular decline in prices shown in figure 4.6 can be explained in terms of 'real' factors. Industrialization and mechanization were reducing manufacturing costs, whilst the opening up of the American west was reducing grain prices. The spread of railways and the advent of steamships reduced transportation costs, especially from the 1870s. Monetary factors were, however, important. The price rises of the early 1850s followed discoveries of gold in California and Australia. In the 1870s the decline in prices and the 'great depression' were blamed by many on a shortage of gold relative to the demand for it, demand being increased as country after country adopted a gold standard rather than a silver one. From the mid-1890s this situation changed, due to further discoveries of gold in California which increased the supply of gold. In the US further monetary disturbances arose as a result of the Civil War: an inconvertible currency, the 'Greenbacks', was issued, convertibility into gold being achieved only in 1879.

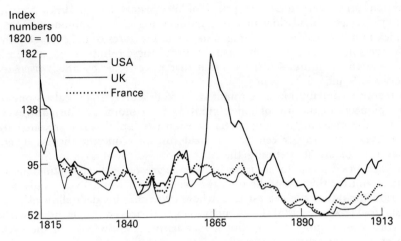

FIGURE 4.6 *Prices in the nineteenth century*

Source: Mitchell (1978), pp. 388–90 and (1983), p. 835.

The mid-century gold discoveries

The gold discoveries in California (1849), Victoria (1851) and New South Wales (1853) and the consequent price rises attracted the attention of economists. Cairnes, for example, developed the theory of Hume and Cantillon to explain why gold discoveries should cause different countries' prices to rise at different rates. He argued that prices would rise most in countries close to the new sources of gold, these regions experiencing an increase in demand; and that the closer a country was to the sources of gold the more would its prices rise. He thus predicted that Australian and US prices would rise most, followed by European prices, Europe being the main destination to which these countries', gold flowed, with Asian prices rising the least. This prediction turned out to be wrong; the reason, Cairnes argued, being that much gold flowed directly from Australia to India.

More significant than Cairnes's extension of the classical theory were statistical investigations into the problem, for these clearly distinguish the period's economics from that of previous generations. The most notable performance here is probably that of Jevons, in his pamphlet 'A serious fall in the value of gold ascertained, and its social effects set forth' (1863). It was, Jevons argued, 'a familiar fact' that 'an article tends to fall in value as it is supplied more abundantly and easily than before' (Jevons, 1863, p. 15), and in view of this many economists had predicted that the Californian gold discoveries would lower the value of gold. Despite over a decade of writing on the subject, Jevons continued, there remained doubt about whether gold was actually depreciating.

Jevons's solution was to *define* a fall in the value of gold as the average rise in prices. He took the prices of 39 'major' commodities and 79 'minor' ones, calculating an index number for each commodity. These index numbers were then averaged to obtain measures of the average price change since 1845–50, his base period. From these results, some of which are shown in figure 4.7, he deduced that prices had, by 1862, risen by between 9 and 15 per cent.

Jevons's contribution here might seem to be purely statistical: as one of the pioneers in the use of index numbers in economics. This, however, is not the case. In reaching the conclusion that gold had depreciated by between 9 and 15 per cent Jevons made use of economic theory. There was first of all his defining the depreciation of gold as the rise in the average price level. In addition he was aware of cyclical fluctuations in prices and for this reason he took the average of a whole cycle as his base period (or rather the nearest to a whole cycle that his data allowed him, data for 1844 and 1851 being unavailable). Prices were, in 1863 when Jevons was writing, falling, but Jevons used his knowledge of the cycle to argue, correctly as it turned out, that prices were at their minimum and that they would rise again. Thus the conclusion that the price rise would prove permanent required a certain amount of economic theory. Even more theory was required to predict the future course of prices: he argued that this would depend on the level of gold production, which in turn would depend on the profitability of mining, itself dependent on the relative price of gold and commodities.

The greenbacks, silver and bimetallism

The principle that currencies should be linked to silver or gold was generally accepted in the nineteenth century. In Britain the gold standard

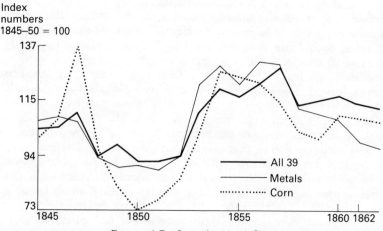

FIGURE 4.7 *Jevons's price indices*

Source: Jevons (1863), p. 46.

was generally accepted from the resumption of specie payments in 1819 until the First World War. In the US inconvertible notes, the greenbacks, were issued during the Civil War, but this was a temporary expedient. Greenbacks were not convertible into specie until 1879, but they were nonetheless convertible into government bonds, the interest on which was payable in gold. Though conceived as temporary, however, the greenbacks were the subject of controversy, for whilst some economists argued that they had to be redeemed in gold as soon as was feasible, others saw them as an integral part of the currency. The crucial issue here was that inflation benefited debtors, and deflation creditors. There was thus pressure from debtors, notably farmers and some manufacturers, in favour of policies that would maintain prices. As a result of this pressure Congress placed limitations on the retirement of greenbacks, the treasury being forced to keep large numbers in circulation.

By the 1880s, however, the attention of those groups wanting an expansion of the currency had shifted away from greenbacks to the issue of silver. By 1873, because the mint ratio undervalued silver (the silver required for a silver dollar was worth $1.02 in gold) silver dollars had disappeared from circulation (Gresham's Law, see p. 96). Similarly there was no incentive to coin silver. Legislation was passed to end the coining of silver dollars. The situation changed during the 1870s when the price of silver fell. There were a number of reasons for this: not only were there large discoveries of silver in Nevada, but also the demand for silver fell as more and more countries switched from silver or bimetallic currencies to gold. Had it still been possible to have silver coined into dollars at the former rate the result would have been that silver would have been brought to the mint for coining, and silver would have replaced gold, possibly increasing the supply of currency. There was thus pressure from both debtors and from silver-producing states for the coining of silver at the old rate, the legislation ending this being described as 'the crime of 1873'. This pressure resulted in the Bland–Allison Act (1878) and the Sherman Silver Purchase Act (1890), which provided for limited coinage of silver, and for the issue of notes backed by silver. Though the silver purchased was limited, it covered, after 1890, virtually the whole US production of silver.

Despite these concessions, pressure for unlimited coinage of silver at the ratio of 16:1 (i.e. an ounce of gold being valued as equal to 16 ounces of silver) continued, reaching its culmination in the Presidential election of 1896, where silver was a major plank in the platform of the Democratic candidate, William Jennings Bryan. The issue was settled by two factors: Cleveland's victory over Bryan in 1896 and new discoveries of gold in the Yukon and in South Africa, together with new processes for extracting gold from the ore. From the mid-1890s gold produced the inflation that was intended to be produced by silver.

The silver issue was perhaps most intense in the US, but other countries did not escape it. The question of bimetallism, the using of gold and silver alongside each other, was widely debated in many countries. Two advantages were seen for bimetallism. It was argued that a currency based on two metals would be more elastic than one based simply on gold. In addition, it was hoped that price fluctuations would be lower under a bimetallic system than under a monometallic one. In the British Empire there was also the problem of India's currency, for the rupee was based on silver, and sterling on gold. This led to controversy, for a number of writers, especially in India, claimed that the value of the rupee was being kept unreasonably low so as to make the terms of trade between Britain and India more favourable to Britain.

The quantity theory

The main analytical tool used to analyse these problems was the quantity theory of money, much of the debate being conducted within the classical framework established by Cantillon and Hume. In the long run prices would, other things being equal, rise in proportion to increases in the quantity of money, but in the short run monetary expansion would stimulate production, for wages would lag behind prices. On top of this there was the specie–flow mechanism linking price levels in different countries. As for the effects of inflation on creditors and debtors, little economic theory was required: the effects were immediately apparent. The role of economic theory was further limited by the ethical character of some of the arguments used. It was argued, for example, that the US government had a moral duty to redeem the greenbacks in gold.

It is against this background that we find the classic statements of the quantity theory of money. Best known is Irving Fisher's theory, based on the equation $MV = PT$ (money stock multiplied by the velocity of circulation equals the price level multiplied by the volume of transactions). Equally important was the Cambridge version of this equation, expounded by Alfred Marshall and his successors, notably Pigou and Keynes, $M = kPY$ (money stock equals a constant times money income, P denoting the price level and Y the level of real income). Though Fisher focused on the circulation of money through the economy, whereas Marshall and his pupils concentrated on the amount of money people wished to hold, these theories were substantially the same.

These versions of the quantity theory of money were more formal and more refined statements of the theory of Cantillon and Hume. This does not mean, however, that they contributed nothing to discussions of practical policy issues. The more formal statement of the theory, together with the attempts to test it statistically, directed attention towards a number of important issues. In particular it was necessary to define both the money supply (bank deposits were by now as important as currency) and the appropriate measure of the volume of transactions (should it be National Income, or should transactions in financial assets and in intermediate goods also be included). Introducing bank deposits led to more complicated versions of the quantity equation, for different types of money would circulate at different speeds. Thus Fisher modified his equation to become $MV + M'V'' = PT$, where M is now the stock of currency and M' the stock of bank deposits, with V and V' denoting their respective velocities of circulation.

Irving Fisher

Irving Fisher was the economist who did most to test the quantity theory statistically. In *The Purchasing Power of Money* (1911) he estimated the terms in the equation $MV + M'V'' = PT$. Statistics on M and M' were easily obtained. He then used figures on total checks deposited on two days (one in 1896, the other in 1909) together with annual statistics on bank clearings to estimate $M'V''$ (transactions settled using bank deposits) and hence calculated V'. MV (transactions settled using currency) was estimated from statistics on the money deposited in banks and total money wages paid, together with a 'small miscellaneous item'. V could then be calculated. Because he wanted to include all transactions, he calculated figures for P and T which covered wages and stock market transactions as well as internal and external trade in goods and services. Defining his index numbers so that the quantity equation was satisfied exactly for 1909, he obtained the results shown in figure 4.8. He concluded that these two, independently derived, sets of figures agreed closely with each other, though not so closely as the correlation coefficient of 98 per cent suggested.

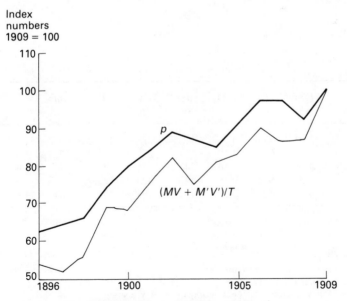

FIGURE 4.8 *Fisher's test of the quantity theory*

Source: Fisher (1911), p. 293

Whatever the limitations of Fisher's figures, they were markedly better than anything available to his predecessors.

The late nineteenth-century quantity theorists also made significant contributions towards understanding the role of the rate of interest. Fisher is renowned for his work on the real rate of interest and his argument that if there is inflation, interest rates will rise to reflect this. Periods of high inflation will thus be periods of high interest rates, the real cost of borrowing (equivalently the return to lending) being unaffected by inflation. Though the notion can be found, as can so much else, in Thornton's *Paper Credit*, it was Fisher who saw its significance. Furthermore, by testing it statistically he did much to establish the idea.

As an example consider his analysis of the financial crisis of 1907, his statistics on which are given in table 4.3. Before the crisis we see rapidly rising deposits, with the banks' reserve ratio falling. The money interest rate was high, but the real rate was negative in the two years before the crisis, all this being consistent with a rising volume of transactions (both $M'V'$ and bank clearings) and a rising price level. After the crisis money interest rates rose, banks increased their reserve ratios and deposits stopped rising. The volume of transactions and prices began to fall. The rise in the money rate of interest combined with the fall in the inflation rate caused the real interest rate to rise dramatically, from -0.9 to 8.1 per cent. 'No wonder', Fisher remarked, 'that borrowing enterprisers often found it hard to make both ends meet' (Fisher, 1911, p. 273). He saw the rise in the real interest rate as the main reason for the recession which ensued.

Table 4.3   Fisher's statistics on the crisis of 1907

	Dep $b.	Res $m.	R/D	Clear $b.	M'V' $b.	P	Inf %	r %	Real r %
1904	3.31	658	0.20	113	228	113.2	0.7	4.2	3.5
1905	3.78	649	0.17	144	279	114.0	5.3	4.3	−1.0
1906	4.06	651	0.16	145	323	127.9	−1.7	6.4	8.1
1907	4.32	692	0.16	145	323	127.9	−1.7	6.4	8.1
1908	4.38	849	0.20	132	294	125.7	na	4.4	na

Dep: Deposits of National Banks
Res: Reserves of National Banks
R/D: Ratio of column 1 to column 2
Clear: Clearings
P: Price index number (January)
Inf: Inflation rate during year
r: Money interest rate (New York) on 60-day loans ·
Real r: Interest rate minus inflation rate

Source: Fisher (1911), p. 271.

Knut Wicksell

Thornton also anticipated important elements of the other major contribution of late nineteenth-century writers on monetary economics: Knut Wicksell's theory of the cumulative-process. Wicksell accepted the quantity theory of money as the only scientific theory of the price level, but was dissatisfied, for it provided no explanation of *how* prices changed in response to a change in the money supply. His response was to distinguish two rates of interest: the money rate of interest (the rate of interest charged on bank loans) and what he called the natural rate of interest. The natural rate of interest is the rate of interest at which savings and investment are equal, or, in other words, at which demand and supply of loans are equal. This is shown in figure 4.9. If the money rate equals the natural rate, the supply of savings will be exactly enough to finance investment, and there will be no inflation. If, on the other hand, banking policy is such that the money rate falls below the natural rate, demand for loans will exceed the supply of savings, the difference being met by the banking system. In figure 4.9 this is $I - S$. This extra lending will result in an increase in the

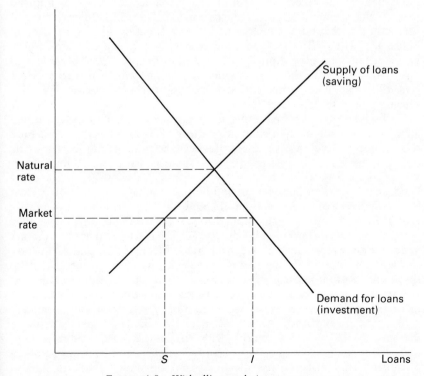

FIGURE 4.9   *Wicksell's cumulative process*

money supply. In addition, because investment exceeds the amount people
wish to save, demand for goods and services will exceed the supply, and
prices will rise. The mechanism whereby an increase in the money supply
raises prices is, therefore, through increasing investment relative to saving,
thus raising the aggregate demand for goods.

Wicksell went on to argue that such a process might continue indefinitely,
because savings and investment would remain unequal as long as the
money rate of interest remained below the natural rate. In addition,
inflation would raise the demand for money, ensuring that the newly
created money remained in circulation. This 'cumulative process' would
come to a halt only if the banking system ran out of reserves. In a pure
credit economy, with no need for gold reserves, this need never happen.

Wicksell concluded that because the interest rate was unobservable,
direct, positive support for his theory was 'almost impossible' to obtain.
He found some evidence for his ideas, however, in price movements
during the nineteenth century. His first piece of evidence was Jevons's
indices of prices during and after the Napoleonic wars (figures 4.3 and
4.6 are not based on Jevons's figures but they cover the period). Inflation
occurred, Wicksell claimed, because wartime expenditures involved a
massive sacrifice of liquid capital, raising the natural rate of interest, whilst
the issuing of inconvertible paper currency enabled the Bank of England
to keep the money rate of interest down to 5 per cent. Unlimited credit
was issued at this rate of interest, creating a situation like that shown in
figure 4.9. After 1815 the natural rate of interest was depressed by 'a very
heavy accumulation of capital' (i.e. savings rose and the supply curve in
figure 4.9 shifted to the right), whilst the money rate remained at 5 per
cent till 1836. The result was that savings exceeded investment, this
causing prices to fall sharply.

Wicksell's other evidence came from the period after 1873 (see figure
4.10). He argued that the rise in prices from 1850 to 1873 was due mainly
to a very high level of investment: this was the time when the major part
of the European railway network was being constructed. A number of
wars also contributed to the demand for capital. After 1873, on the other
hand, there was continuous peace and massive capital accumulation pushed
the natural rate of interest down. Though interest rates (as measured by
central bank discount rates) appeared higher from 1850 to 1873 than after,
which appeared to contradict his theory, Wicksell claimed that open market
interest rates were often above bank rates before 1873, and frequently
above them after 1873, suggesting that bank rates were being pulled up
(by a high natural rate) in the earlier period, and pushed down later on.

Variations in the inflation rate were thus explained in terms of variations
in the natural rate of interest, with the money rate remaining relatively
constant. This explained the puzzle noted by Thomas Tooke, a critic of
the quantity theory writing in the 1840s, that interest rates tend to be high
in times of inflation and to be low in periods of depression. This explanation
of inflation and deflation has much in common with Fisher, for he also

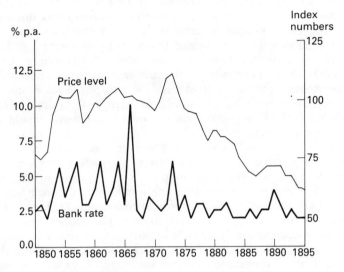

FIGURE 4.10 *Interest and prices, 1850–95*

Source: Mitchell and Deane (1962), pp. 456–8 and 474.

explained fluctuations in terms of an unresponsive rate of interest (see p. 116).

Though the evidence cited by Wicksell may seem thin by modern standards, it marks a notable advance on work undertaken even half a century earlier. Price index numbers were available covering long periods of time and these were routinely used in conjunction with economic theory. The need to test theories against statistical data was accepted and, though they attempted to do this, economists clearly recognized the limitations of the data they were using.

The theory of bimetallism

The advantage of a more formal treatment of monetary questions is shown very clearly in Walras's analysis of bimetallism. Discussion of this issue was plagued by disputes as to whether the government had the power to fix the value of gold in terms of silver, and disputes about whether it was possible for gold or silver to have different values as coin and as bullion. Walras's analysis provided a clear way of settling such issues conclusively by writing down supply and demand equations for a bimetallic system. There was the non-monetary demand for each commodity, which depended on prices, and there was the monetary demand determined by the quantity theory. Against this were the stocks of the two metals. This left six unknowns to be determined (the quantities of gold and silver in monetary and non-monetary uses, and the prices of gold and silver), but only five equations. This meant that the government was free to fix one variable, such as the value of gold in terms of silver. Provided that both metals were in circulation it could impose this ratio by its minting policy, and the precious metals would have the same value either as coin or as bullion. On the other hand, once either of the metals ceased to be presented at the mint for coinage, the government would lose its power to enforce a fixed ratio, and the price of bullion would differ from the price of coin, the latter being of little importance as the overvalued metal would neither circulate nor be coined.

To reach these conclusions it was not necessary to use any formal equations to describe supply and demand. Marshall, for example, in his evidence to a Royal Commission inquiring into the issue in 1888, reached substantially the same conclusions using methods no different from those of Mill, if not those of Hume. A more formal treatment, however, made it possible to take the argument much further. The issue of whether prices will be more stable under a bimetallic system, for example, is a complicated one, the answer to which depends on the exact form of the demand functions for non-monetary gold and silver, and it cannot be answered satisfactorily using informal arguments. Though Walras's analysis of such questions remained limited, he established the method by which they could be settled.

4.6 POST-WAR INFLATION

Background

Though there were clearly exceptions (notably the hyper-inflation in the Weimar Republic) monetary economists in the inter-war period were concerned more with the business cycle and mass unemployment than with inflation (see Chapter 5). Since 1945, however, inflation has become a major issue, stimulating an enormous amount of economic research. Though post-war discussions have clearly owed much to earlier generations, the background to these discussions has, for a number of reasons, been very different. Many of these, such as the increased involvement of government in the economy and the greater availability of statistics, affect all areas of economics. Others are relevant specifically to discussions of money and inflation. Particularly important has been the development of international monetary institutions such as the International Monetary Fund (IMF) and greater co-operation between different countries' central banks, because this has made it possible to dispense with gold for international payments to an extent not possible before. Thus where nineteenth-century writers might have compared an inconvertible currency with a currency based on a metallic standard, recent writers focus on the issue of flexible versus fixed exchange rates. Though many of the issues involved are very similar, there are nonetheless important differences.

The quantity theory of money

In the 1940s the quantity theory came to be eclipsed, stress being placed on the flow of spending rather than on the stock of money. Keynes applied the ideas contained in the *General Theory* (see p. 154) to the problem of inflation in his pamphlet *How to Pay for the War* (1940) in which he addressed the issue of how wartime expenditure should be financed. His argument depended on the assumption that whilst an increase in spending would produce a rise in output as long as the economy was operating at less than full capacity, once full capacity was reached any increase in spending would result in inflation. This was the origin of what came to be called 'inflation gap' theories: they explained inflation in terms of the gap between the level of spending and the quantity of goods available to be purchased. The gap could be reduced through raising taxation, cutting government spending or by measures to increase the level of saving, any of which would reduce inflation.

In addition to these 'demand-pull' theories of inflation, it was argued that inflation could arise through costs rising for reasons unconnected with the level of demand in the economy. Market power, it was argued, might be used by firms to raise their profit margins, or by unions to raise wages, either of which would cause prices to rise. This led to the view, common in the 1950s, that inflation could be explained in terms of a combination of 'demand-pull' and 'cost-push', the relative importance of these two factors varying over time. Given the circumstances of the 1940s and early 1950s such a view was understandable. The main periods of inflation (see figure 4.11) were clearly due to high demand (the Second World War and the Korean War), and high demand could easily be explained in terms of high government spending. It was not clear that the quantity of money was particularly important. Such a view was reinforced by the notion that it was the availability of credit and liquidity, rather than money *per se*, that was important in determining the level of private sector spending, and that such factors could not adequately be measured by a single number. Most important, however, was the fact that whilst cost-push theories were never really very satisfactory explanations of inflation, inflation was, as figure 4.11 shows, in most years not a very pressing problem. The few years of high inflation could be explained in terms of high demand.

Though his most important ideas on the subject were worked out earlier, it was in 1956 that Milton Friedman attracted attention with his 'restatement' of the quantity theory of money. Friedman's problem was that of how to defend the quantity theory in the face of clear evidence that the velocity of circulation was not constant, for there was clear statistical evidence that it changed enormously. If the velocity of circulation was very variable, this could be taken as supporting the generally held view that there was no strong connection between money and inflation. His answer was to argue that the essence of the quantity theory of money was the stability of the demand function for money. Demand for money, he argued, depended on a number of factors, notably income, interest rates, share yields and the rate of inflation. For Friedman therefore, changes in the velocity of circulation (the ratio of money to income) were not inconsistent with the quantity theory: they were simply evidence that there had been changes in interest rates or some of the other factors affecting the demand for money.

Such an approach left open the issue of whether it was prices or the level of output that would be affected when a change in the money supply caused the level of income to change. Friedman produced statistical evidence which suggested that in the short run monetary changes would have powerful effects on output, whilst in the long run only prices would be affected. He claimed, however, that the lags involved in this process were long and variable, which meant that it would be difficult to use monetary policy as a way of controlling the level of output. The optimal policy was, he argued, to fix the growth rate of the money supply so as to ensure that money was not a source of disturbances.

The first phase in the debate between 'Keynesians' and 'monetarists' thus focused on the stability of the demand for money function. Friedman and his associates attempted to show how observed fluctuations in velocity could be explained without compromising the hypothesis that the money demand function was stable. In addition, there were attempts to test the quantity theory directly against the Keynesian theory. If the Keynesian theory were correct, it was argued, there ought to be a stable relationship between 'autonomous spending' (government spending, investment,

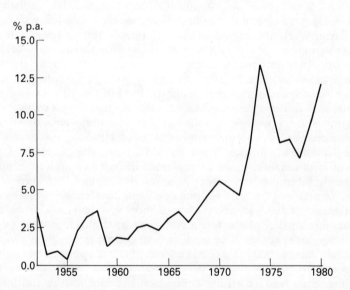

FIGURE 4.11   *Inflation in industrial countries, 1952–80*

Source: IMF *Financial Statistics* Yearbook 1982, p. 62.

exports) and the level of income. If the quantity theory were a better account of the world, on the other hand, there ought to be a closer relationship between the stock of money and the level of income.

Although it might seem that this provided a straightforward way to test the theories against each other, this proved not to be the case. It came to be accepted that neither the simple quantity theory model nor the simple Keynesian model could describe the economy sufficiently accurately for such a test to be conclusive. The economy was too complicated. Theoretical arguments, not simply statistical tests, had to be used to decide in favour of one theory rather than the other. The impossibility of settling arguments with purely empirical evidence was also illustrated by Milton Friedman's *Monetary History of the United States, 1867–1960* (1963, written jointly with Anna Schwarz). In this volume Friedman attempted to establish that money had a strong influence on the economy and that the supply of money was an important variable in its own right, not simply a reflection of demand. The problem was that it was impossible, without suitable theoretical arguments, which Friedman did not provide, to prove that any causation ran from money to demand rather than vice-versa.

The labour market and inflation

A new line of inquiry into the problem of inflation was opened up in 1958 when A. W. Phillips published his famous curve showing that the rate of change of money wages was inversely related to the unemployment rate. This curve was an empirical relationship he had discovered, with which he tried to show that, despite all the changes which had taken place since the nineteenth century, the relationship between wage inflation and the unemployment rate had not changed. The Phillips curve became so popular, however, for a number of other reasons, the main one being that it opened up an extremely fruitful line of inquiry, to which both economic theory and econometric techniques could be applied. As an empirical relationship the Phillips curve needed explaining, and it proved easy to explain it in terms consistent with the conventional notion of how markets operated: if supply of labour exceeded the demand wages would fall, and if demand exceeded supply they would rise. The peculiar shape of the curve could be accounted for by invoking frictional unemployment (unemployment which arises because of the time it takes newly unemployed workers to find a suitable new job).

In addition, once the notion of the Phillips curve had become established, a process which took only a couple of years, there was the task of measuring it using better techniques than Phillips had employed. Time series data on inflation and unemployment rates were readily available, and there were numerous other variables (such as union power, measured by the percentage of workers belonging to a union) that could be introduced into the equation in order to test different hypotheses about the labour market. The Phillips curve, therefore, proved a wonderful concept on which to base econometric research.

This phase in the theory of inflation dominated the 1960s, but towards the end of the 1960s the focus of attention shifted. One reason was that Phillips curves began to break down: they could no longer predict the inflation rate as accurately as in the past. A reason for this was suggested by Milton Friedman in 1967: he argued that wage bargains were concerned with real wages, for it is real wages that are relevant to both the employer and the employee. From this he concluded that if the Phillips curve described the operation of the labour market, unemployment should affect the growth rate of real wages and that the inflation rate should depend not only on the unemployment rate, but also on the expected rate of inflation.

This hypothesis provoked an enormous amount of econometric research. The problem was that because inflationary expectations are not directly measurable it was necessary to test hypotheses about the Phillips curve (e.g. did people take full account of inflation?) together with a hypothesis about how inflationary expectations were formed (e.g. that people used the previous period's inflation rate to predict inflation in the current period). Such tests were inevitably inconclusive, though it soon became apparent that some variable such as inflationary expectations had to be included.

Friedman's argument about the Phillips curve was also important because it had profound consequences for economic policy. The reason for this was his conclusion that there was only one unemployment rate, the 'natural rate of unemployment' that was consistent with a stable inflation rate. There was no permanent trade-off between inflation and unemployment. His argument is that the only way the government can cause the unemployment rate to fall below the natural rate is by causing an unexpected increase in the inflation rate. After a while, however, people will realize what has happened and will revise their expectations upwards. To maintain the low level of unemployment the government will therefore have to raise the inflation rate again and again. The result is that unemployment can be kept below the natural rate only at the cost of a continuously *rising* rate of inflation.

The consequence of this was that the nature of the debate between Monetarists and Keynesians changed substantially. The emphasis was no longer on the demand for money, or the velocity of circulation, but on whether and for how long it was possible to use monetary and fiscal policy to prevent unemployment from rising above the natural rate. James Tobin, for example, a leading American Keynesian, has argued that the Monetarist policy of targeting the growth rate of the money supply will lead to prolonged spells of high unemployment which could be avoided by an appropriate use of monetary and fiscal policy. Friedman and his followers, on the other hand, stress both the difficulties involved in such a strategy and the inflationary dangers implicit in allowing politicians to take decisions about the money supply

Though his policy prescriptions and the techniques he employed were relatively new, Friedman's monetarism had much in common with the views of the classical quantity theorists. For Friedman, as for Cantillon, Hume, Fisher and Marshall, monetary changes have short-lived effects on output, and permanent effects on the price level. Frictions, rigidities and lags are brought in to explain the short-run effects of monetary changes on output. In the 1970s, however, there arose a more extreme form of monetarism, which has come to be called the 'New Classical Macroeconomics' (not to be confused with 'neoclassical economics'). The New Classical Macroeconomics is based on the assumption that individuals take up all the opportunities for profit open to them. Markets must be in equilibrium, with supply equal to demand, otherwise there would be unexploited opportunities for profit. Similarly, when people form their expectations they will take account of all the available information, using it in the most efficient manner possible. Taken together these two assumptions, of continuous market clearing and rational expectations, are very powerful for, given certain other assumptions, they can be used to show that monetary policy can *never* be made systematically to affect unemployment. All the government can do is to alter unemployment in a random way. Not only, therefore, are governments very unlikely to have any success in stabilizing the economy but it may be completely impossible for them to do so. Though the policy conclusions usually drawn from such models can be labelled 'Monetarist', they are clearly a long way from the quantity theory of Friedman, let alone that of Fisher, Wicksell or Thornton, all of whom saw an important role for monetary policy in stabilizing the economy.

4.7 CONCLUSIONS

There has been an enormous degree of continuity in the development of ideas on money and inflation. Money and inflation began to be linked in the sixteenth century when the extent of the inflation men experienced led them to seek new explanations. Theories were gradually refined until by the middle of the eighteenth century there existed a well-developed quantity theory of money. Though it needed modifying to reflect institutional changes such as the development of the financial system and the move towards an economy based on credit rather than on metallic currency, and though it has been expounded more rigorously, the quantity theory has remained essentially the same from Hume to Friedman.

In the development of the quantity theory, empirical evidence has always been of limited importance compared with theoretical arguments. In the eighteenth century and earlier, statistics were few, and unreliable, and there was no question of using them to settle disagreements. Throughout the nineteenth and twentieth centuries statistics became increasingly available, but even with the resulting profusion of statistical information it was still theoretical arguments that were decisive. It is very difficult to use statistics to demonstrate causation: even if monetary changes always came before changes in income we could not be certain that causation ran from money to income. In addition, there is the problem that the economy is too complicated to be fully described by a relatively simple theory, and on top of this it is changing all the time. When inflation accelerated at the end of the 1960s, for example, theories which had previously fitted the data tolerably well began to fail.

This is not to say that monetary economics proceeded without any reference to the real world: far from it. Empirical data have been vital in two respects. Firstly, economists have had to keep abreast of the enormous institutional changes which have taken place. A good example of this is provided by a comparison of Thornton's work with that of Hume or Cantillon: by the end of the eighteenth century there were new monetary problems to be tackled, and the structure of the British financial system had changed enormously, and as a result theory had to change. Secondly, empirical data have also been important in providing a check on theoretical developments. For example, in their work on the quantity theory both Fisher and Wicksell were constrained by empirical evidence which ruled out certain explanations of price fluctuations. The solution of Tooke's empirical puzzles was one of Wicksell's major concerns. Similarly, although statistical testing did not provide conclusive evidence as to the validity of Friedman's quantity theory, for example, it did make it clear that very simple versions of the quantity theory could not be made to work. Throughout the history of the quantity theory statistical data have constrained the way economists have been able to use it, even though they have neither proved nor disproved the theory itself.

5

Employment and Economic Fluctuations

5.1 COMMERCIAL CRISES IN BRITAIN BEFORE 1850

Prior to the industrial revolution

At the beginning of the sixteenth century the English economy was backward in comparison with the economies of many parts of continental Europe. From around 1540, however, there was a slow but significant industrial expansion, many new industries being established, and others being developed on a larger scale. Of these the most important was the woollen textile industry, which exported a large proportion of its output, mainly to Eastern Europe, Holland and Germany. At the same time, internal commerce was increasing, and regional specialization was growing. Not only London (the population of which had reached about 200,000 by 1600), but also the regions specializing in wool production contained large numbers of people dependent for their livelihood on exports of cloth. By the seventeenth century, therefore, the majority of contemporary observers saw trade as the main prop of the economy. When exports fell, unemployment rose, for in certain regions (notably the West, East Anglia and the West Riding of Yorkshire) employment in the woollen industry was so large that when it contracted there was no possibility of everyone finding work elsewhere.

Exports might be reduced for a number of reasons: new manufacturers might be set up, often by the state, elsewhere in Europe, competing for markets; wars on the continent, or political problems, might lead to trade being stopped; foreign purchasing power might be destroyed; or currency manipulations might disrupt trade. The currency was a particular problem in an age when money was primarily metallic, and when gold and silver circulated together.

The dynamics of economic activity in the seventeenth century were very different from those of the nineteenth- or twentieth-century economy. One of the major differences was that fixed capital (investment in buildings, machinery and so on) was relatively unimportant, labour being the major factor of production. Production depended on the availability of circulating capital, for stocks of raw materials had to be purchased and held while they were being worked up into finished goods. This meant that capital was very mobile. If demand for cloth rose, manufacturers could very quickly increase the number of people they employed; and when demand fell they could easily withdraw their capital, simply by not re-investing the money they obtained when they sold their stocks of finished goods. This mobility of capital had two consequences. One was that production could fluctuate very rapidly, falls in production leading to periods of unemployment. The other was that industry was very dependent on a continuous supply of liquid capital. This contributed to the dependence of the economy on trade, for trade was the only source of gold and silver.

Another major source of instability was the state of the harvest. Grain prices clearly affected the standard of living of textile workers. In addition, when grain prices were high people had to spend a much higher fraction of their income on food, thus reducing demand for other goods, including textiles. It was only a small minority who benefited from bad harvests. Being wealthier this minority was not likely to increase its spending by nearly as much as those who suffered had to reduce theirs. Finally, poor harvests often led to imports of grain, resulting in a loss of gold and silver. Because credit techniques were still rudimentary, the supply of finance would be reduced, and industry would be disrupted. Though major economic crises in the seventeenth century were rarely, if ever, caused by bad harvests alone, the weather was an important factor underlying commercial fluctuations. The worst crises occurred, as in 1621–2 and 1629–31, when bad harvests coincided with a trade-induced slump in the textile industry.

These features of the early seventeenth-century English economy explain why the period's economic theories emphasize, almost to the exclusion of everything else, trade and money. Mun's *England's Treasure* (see pp. 50 and 166), for example, was written in response to the crisis of 1621. Though such writers made important contributions to economic thought, however, they did not even attempt to construct any theory of the cycle, for economic fluctuations were not part of a regular pattern, but were caused primarily by outside events, mostly in continental Europe. Specialization was sufficiently far developed that disruption to trade, and bad harvests, caused considerable unemployment, this unemployment taking some time to be eliminated. The flexibility of the economy meant not only that such crises could develop very rapidly, but also that when trade recovered the economy could respond quickly. When a crisis developed, whether it was due to problems with cloth exports or to a bad harvest, the main symptom was a shortage of money. The result was that those who wrote on these problems focused their attention on money. Unemployment and commercial crises, were, right through to the early nineteenth century, an aspect of monetary economics.

Though the economy developed significantly over the following century, the underlying causes of economic fluctuations remained much the same. For the eighteenth century we have the advantage of statistics on overseas trade. As figure 5.1 shows, these suggest random fluctuations rather than any regular cyclical pattern. Harvest crises came at irregular intervals:

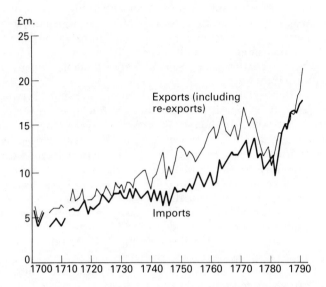

FIGURE 5.1   *English trade in the eighteenth century*

Source and note: Mitchell and Deane (1962), pp. 279–81. Figures are in £m. at (constant) official prices.

1710, 1725, 1767, 1783, 1792–3 and 1795–6. In addition war had serious effects on trade: trade rose after the Treaty of Utrecht in 1713; there followed war-induced depressions from 1718 to 1721, and from 1744 to 1748; in the 1760s opposition to first the Stamp Act, and later Townshend's duties, disrupted exports to the American colonies; trade was further disrupted by the War of American Independence, ending in 1783. From 1783 onwards we have the surge of exports associated with the mechanization and expansion of the cotton industry (see p. 15).

The emergence of the business cycle

In the eighteenth century, as in the seventeenth, outside factors were the main determinants of the level of economic activity, and fluctuations were, to a great extent, random. At the same time, however, there were factors making for more systematic variations in the level of economic activity.

In the eighteenth and early nineteenth centuries the dominant pattern was the 'trade', or 'inventory' cycle. The reason for this cycle was that merchants sent goods abroad speculatively, on the basis of limited information about market conditions in export markets. If inventories (stocks of goods) in an export market fell, prices would rise, and word would reach Britain that it was profitable to ship more goods. Exports would rise, and prices in the foreign country would fall. However, because of the time it took for information about this to reach Britain, the movement would go too far: inventories would rise sufficiently high, and prices fall so low, that exporting would become unprofitable. There would thus be a reduction in exports until, eventually, inventories would fall to the point where exporting once again became profitable, whereupon the process would repeat itself.

This 'trade' cycle was of fairly short duration, normally between four and seven years. The time it took for information to reach London was never, even before the introduction of telegraphs, very long. In addition, the level of exports could be altered very quickly: within months if not weeks. Very different was the 'investment' cycle which came to dominate the British economy by the second half of the nineteenth century. This was of much longer duration (nearer nine years), for investment projects were much less flexible. Once canals, railways, or even domestic housing projects had been started, they could not easily be curtailed. Demand for investment tended to be concentrated at the peak of the trade cycle: profits and sales were buoyant, and confidence high. In addition, investment depended critically on the availability of credit and the state of the stock exchange. Speculation in financial markets, and the crises which ensued, thus had a strong influence on economic activity.

At the end of the eighteenth century the shorter trade cycle was still the dominant pattern, but over time the importance of the investment cycle increased substantially. This is shown in Figures 5.2 and 5.3. Figure 5.2 shows the growth of industrial production over the nineteenth century

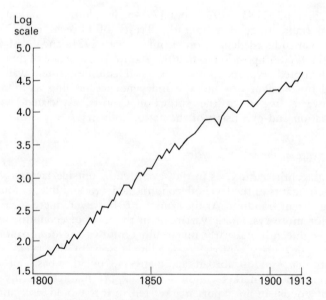

FIGURE 5.2   *British industrial production, 1815–1913*

Source: Hoffmann index, in Mitchell and Deane (1962), pp. 271–2.

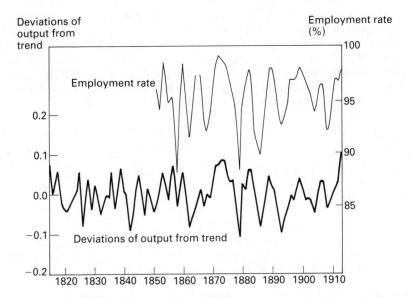

FIGURE 5.3   *British industrial fluctuations, 1815–1913*

Source and note: Deviations of Hoffmann index of industrial production (Mitchell and Deane, 1962, pp. 271–2) from trend, where the trend is given by $0.046\,T - 0.00015\,T^2 + 1.28$, where T is the date minus 1800. The coefficients were estimated by least squares. The T squared term was introduced because the trend growth rate was clearly not constant throughout the period.

and makes the point that any cycles must be seen against the background of a rising trend. Although cycles can be seen in figure 5.2, they are shown much more clearly in figure 5.3, which shows the deviations of industrial production from the underlying trend. The change which took place around 1860 is evident from this graph: cycles become longer and more regular, corresponding to the increased importance of the investment cycle *vis-à-vis* the trade cycle. From 1800 to 1860 there were 14 cycles, averaging 4.3 years in length, whereas between 1860 and 1913 there were only seven cycles, with an average length of 7.6 years. Also shown in figure 5.3 are data on the percentage of the labour force employed. Though these figures have to be treated with extreme caution (they are based on returns by a very small number of trade unions, and do not indicate the level of employment in the economy as a whole) they do provide some evidence that the series on industrial production is providing a reasonable indication of fluctuations in the level of economic activity.

Early writings on the cycle

The years after 1815 were ones of deflation, with periods of severe depression, with falling prices and high unemployment (see figures 4.6

and 5.3), with severe crises occurring in 1816 and 1825. Economists approached these problems from two points of view: the controversy over 'gluts', and debates over monetary policy.

The dominant position on gluts was that of Ricardo, who took his ideas from Jean-Baptiste Say and James Mill. Say, in his *Traité d'economie politique* (1803) had argued that supply creates its own demand: people sell goods in order to be able to purchase other goods. This rather loose doctrine was tightened up by James Mill, who argued that

if a nation's power of purchasing is exactly measured by its annual produce, as it undoubtedly is, the more you increase the annual produce, the more by that very act you extend the national market, the power of purchasing and the actual purchases of the nation. (Mill, 1808, p. 135)

He concluded from this that

Whatever the additional quantity of goods therefore which is at any time created in any country, an additional power of purchasing, exactly equivalent, is at the same instant created; so that a nation can never be naturally overstocked either with capital or with commodities.

A general glut of commodities, Mill argued, was impossible. If there is a glut of one commodity, there must be a shortage of some other commodity. Using such arguments Ricardo was able to blame the post-war depression on the problems involved in adjusting from war to peace. Unemployment arose, he argued, not because too many goods were being produced, but because the wrong goods were being produced.

This position was challenged by Malthus, the best known of Ricardo's critics, who argued that general gluts could, and did, occur. He claimed that the distress of the working classes could not be explained in terms of the transition from war to peace: such adjustment could be effected within a year or so. In addition, he could find no evidence of any 'understocked' employments balancing those where demand was insufficient.

Malthus's ideas were very loosely formulated (Ricardo had no problem in finding flaws in them), but his main argument was valid. It was that if supply and demand are to grow in a balanced fashion, neither growing faster than the other, there must be an appropriate balance between consumption and investment. This is the notion underlying the following passage, where Malthus is discussing the post-war depression.

If, at the very time that the supply of commodities compared with the demand for them, clearly admonishes us that the proportion of capital to revenue is already too great, we go on saving from our revenue to add still further to our capital, all general principles concur in shewing that we must of necessity be aggravating instead of alleviating our distress. (Malthus, 1836, p. 435)

Malthus is assuming that savings get invested, increasing the supply of goods, thus aggravating the glut.

In his discussion of gluts Malthus claimed, many times, that there might be a lack of effective demand. This is compatible with the theory outlined above, for he nearly always added the qualification 'relative to supply'. What he failed to do, despite many passages which suggest he was close to such an explanation of unemployment, was to analyse what determined the level of effective demand for commodities and how a shortage of effective demand might keep production below its potential level. The main reason for this was probably his acceptance of the notion that savings would automatically be invested, and hence spent: along with Smith, Say, James Mill and Ricardo, he dismissed the idea that savings might be hoarded, thereby reducing the demand for commodities.

A very different interpretation of post-war problems was provided by those economists who, in the tradition of eighteenth-century writers such as John Law (see p. 97), advocated using the issue of paper money to maintain full employment. Prominent amongst these was Thomas Attwood. Like many eighteenth-century economists, Attwood argued that declines in the flow of expenditure would depress prices, and that falling prices would lead to depression, with low levels of both production and employment. Such depressions would be made worse in that price falls and reductions in the money supply would reinforce each other. Falling prices would make it harder for merchants to borrow from banks, and the money supply would fall. Reductions in the money supply would lead to further falls in spending, and hence further price falls. Fluctuations will be further exacerbated by speculation: when prices are falling, for example, people will tend to hoard more, thus reducing spending still further.

Attwood provided a clear account of the way falling expenditure and falling income interact with each other.

When prices fall, production is arrested until the expenses of production [costs] fall in an equal degree; and whilst production is thus arrested, *consumption* is also diminished; . . . the inducements to employ labour . . . are diminished, and the prices of labour fall. The consumption of labour [i.e. by labourers] is thus diminished, and the prices of property again fall, and again act in depressing labour, and in crippling production. (Attwood, quoted in Link, 1959, p. 28)

This process was reversible, rising expenditure and prices leading to rising production and employment.

In parts of his writing Attwood went further towards a theory of the cycle, by suggesting 'natural remedies' for expansion and contraction. A contraction may turn into expansion when, for reasons he did not explain, production falls by more than spending, resulting in a rise in prices. Similarly, an expansion may come to an end when accumulated stocks are excessive in relation to demand. However, although he recognized that there might be such 'natural remedies' for economic fluctuations, Attwood stressed the role of monetary policy. The Bank of England should, he argued, create sufficient currency to ensure prosperity, his goal being full employment, defined as 'a greater demand for labour than labour can possibly supply' (quoted in Link, 1959, p. 28). Attwood conceded that his plans for achieving full employment were incompatible with the gold standard, for they would lead to rising prices, something he favoured. He was thus going against the dominant view, which was that it was important to maintain the convertibility of sterling into gold at a fixed price (see p. 110).

It was between 1815 and 1850 that economists started to devote attention to the problem of the cycle. The major contribution here was that of Samuel Jones Loyd, later Lord Overstone, with his well-known 'cycle of trade'. In 1837 he distinguished 10 stages of a cycle:

We find [the state of trade] subject to various conditions which are periodically returning; it revolves apparently in an established cycle. First we find it in a state of quiescence, – next improvement, – growing confidence, – prosperity, – excitement, – overtrading, – convulsion, – pressure, – stagnation, – distress, – ending again in quiescence. (Overstone, 1857, p. 44)

Though they were rarely the original cause of fluctuations, fluctuations in credit accentuated the cycle. The role of monetary policy, therefore, was to restrain the cycle, preventing credit from fluctuating excessively. The way this was to be achieved was through linking the supply of banknotes to the Bank of England's stock of gold: the so-called 'currency principle', embodied in the Bank Charter Act of 1844. Allowing the supply of banknotes to fluctuate with the needs of trade (the 'banking principle', advocated by economists such as Thomas Tooke) would, claimed Overstone, lead to excessive fluctuations in the money supply.

Between 1815 and 1850, economists confronted the problem of unemployment (though they did not use this term) and they started to relate it to the problem of the trade cycle. The economist who, more than any other, managed to synthesize all these strands of thought, was John Stuart Mill (not to be confused with his father, James Mill, discussed above). He solved the apparent paradox of Say's Law by pointing out that whilst it was true for a barter economy (where goods are exchanged directly for each other) it was not true of an economy in which money was used.

Now the effect of the employment of money . . . is that it enables this one act of interchange [barter] to be divided into two separate acts or operations; one of which may be performed now, and the other a year hence, or whenever it shall be most convenient.

It follows that it is possible that there may be

at some time, a very general inclination to sell with as little delay as possible, accompanied with an equally general inclination to defer all purchases as long as possible. (Mill, 1844, p. 70)

In other words, people may wish, albeit temporarily, to hoard money, simply in order to be able to buy commodities at a later date. It is thus quite possible that unemployment may arise through deficient demand.

When it came to the role of monetary policy in alleviating problems of unemployment and the cycle, Mill followed the Banking School. His theory of the cycle was based on speculation: when people expect profits they use credit to increase their purchases of commodities, thus raising prices and profits. The original expectation of higher profits thus becomes self-fulfilling, and prices rise too far. When people realize that prices have risen too far, they start to sell, and contraction begins.

It might be thought that, with such a view of the cycle, Mill would subscribe, like Overstone, to the currency principle as a means of reducing fluctuations. There were two reasons why he did not. The first was that not all fluctuations were caused by speculative activity. Sometimes crises could be alleviated by credit expansion beyond the limits imposed by the stock of gold. In 1847, for example, a crisis arose because the high price of cotton and large food imports led to a loss of gold and a contraction of credit. Had banking principles been followed, the crisis could have been averted. The second reason was that periods of expansion were not normally fuelled by an expansion of the note issue. The time when the Bank of England increased its note issue was, Mill claimed, just after prices had begun to fall, for it was when businessmen started to face financial problems that they turned to the Bank of England for support. Expansion of the note issue, he argued, was an appropriate way to alleviate depressions.

5.2 BUSINESS CYCLES AND UNEMPLOYMENT, 1860–1914

Theories of the cycle in the 1860s and 1870s

Though earlier writers, such as Overstone, had recognized the existence of a cycle, the economists who were most responsible for establishing the notion of a cycle were Juglar and, to a lesser extent, Jevons. They were both important, not so much for their ideas on what caused cycles, but for their statistical work, which did much to establish the idea that there was a regular cycle, of about 8–10 years duration. Beyond this, their ideas and approaches were very different.

Clement Juglar, in *Des crises commerciales et leur retour périodique, en France, en Angleterre et aux Etats-Unis* (1862) concentrated on a group of monetary statistics (discounts and advances, bullion reserves, notes issued and current account deposits) to establish the cyclical pattern that had prevailed from 1800 to 1860. As his title indicates, he concentrated on crises, arguing that the symptom of an impending crisis was that discounts and advances were rising, but metallic reserves falling. After the crisis, metallic reserves rose. The table he used to summarize the history of crises is reproduced as table 5.1. This shows a regular series of crises, each followed by a period of liquidation (the trough of a recession). Crisis years are clearly characterized by a high level of deposits (D) and low bullion

Table 5.1 Juglar's table of commercial crises

		France				England				US		
		D	RM	C		D	RM	C		D	RM	C
1800	L	111	25	8	L	6	6	15				
1801												
1802												
1803					C	10	3	17				
1804	C	630	1	79	L	9	7	17				
1805	L	255	83	48								
1806												
1807												
1808												
1809												
1810	C	715	32	117	C	20	3	24				
1811	L	591	124	54								
1812					L	12		23				
1813	C	640		133								
1814	L	84	5	10								
1815					C	14	2	28				
1816												
1817					L	3	11	29				
1818	C	615	34	126								
1819					C	6	3					
1820	L	253	218	79								
1821					L	2	11	23				
1822												
1823												
1824												
1825												
1826	C	688	86	254	C	4	2	25				
1827					L	1	10					
1828	L	427	238	156								
1829					C	3	6	19				
1830	C	617	104	238	L	1						
1831												
1832	L	150	281	192								
1833												
1834												
1835												
1836	C	760	89	241						457	43	
1837		756	248	190	C	15	4	18	C	525	37	149
1838						8	10	19		485	35	116
1839	C	1047	249	234	C	12	2	17	C	492	45	135

	France				England				US		
	D	RM	C		D	RM	C		D	RM	C
1840											
1841	L	885	169	169	L	7	16	22	L	386	49	75
1842											
1843											
1844											
1845											
1846											
1847	C	1327	57	311	C	38	8	17			
1848									344	35	128
1849	L	256	626		L	4	22	23	332		114
1850											
1851											
1852											
1853											
1854											
1855											
1856									634	59	204
1857	C	2085	72	649	C	49	6	22	C	684	58	214
1858									583	74	155
1859	L	1414	287								

France in million francs, England in £ million, USA in $ million.
D   — Discounts
RM — Bullion reserves (réserves métallique)
C   — Circulation

Source: Juglar (1862), p. 8.

reserves (RM), whilst in a year of liquidation the reverse is true. As well as noting that the figures generally support Juglar's conclusions about the movement of discounts and metallic reserves, it is worth noting the paucity of the data with which he had to work (table 5.1 contains most of his statistical data).

More important, however, than Juglar's theory of how crises developed was his insistence, backed up with statistical evidence, that the cycle was a regular feature, inherent in industrial societies.

It is necessary to get used to the idea of the periodic return of these commercial upheavals, which, at least up to now, seems to be one of the conditions for the development of large scale industry. (Translated from Juglar, 1862, p. 6)

Crises appear only amongst peoples whose commerce is highly developed. Where there is no division of labour, no external trade, more rigid internal trade and in addition credit is limited, they are less likely. (Translated from Juglar, 1862, p. 5)

In the second edition of his book (1889), Juglar found that the cycle had repeated itself after 1860 much as it had done before. He argued that the cycle was fundamentally independent of outside events, though these would aggravate it and would explain why observed cycles were so irregular. For example, he had no problem in explaining the irregular, and unsynchronized, fluctuations between 1800 and 1815 in terms of the war and its effects on trade.

Jevons, too, established a statistical picture of the cycle, but he concentrated first on thirteenth- and fourteenth-century grain prices and later on trade between England and India in the eighteenth century. He viewed the cycle not as something inherent in the nature of industrial society, but as determined by an outside cause: the weather. In the late nineteenth century the view was widely held that there was a connection between sunspots and the weather. Jevons linked the weather to harvests, and hence to the level of economic activity. It thus made sense to look for cycles over as long a period as possible and to look at data on grain prices, one of the few things for which such long runs of statistical data existed.

Important though it was, the work of Juglar and Jevons contained no real theory of how cycles might arise out of the normal working of a capitalist economy. The economist who did suggest such a theory, albeit a very vaguely formulated one, was Karl Marx (the main source of Marx's views on the cycle is volume III of *Capital*, and although this was published in 1893, Engels gives 1864–7 as the time when it was written). Marx saw capital accumulation as the driving force behind the cycle. Capitalists were assumed to be motivated by a desire to accumulate capital as rapidly as possible, with the result that from time to time too much capital·would be produced. This would lead to a sudden fall in the rate of profit, and a part of the capital stock would lie idle. At the same time there would be unemployment of the labour force, and production would stagnate. Eventually, however, capital depreciates sufficiently to raise the rate of profit, and accumulation increases once more. The cycle repeats itself.

In Marx's theory, crises arise because capital accumulates to the point where capitalists run out of markets: because capital is used to produce commodities, over-production of capital implies over-production of commodities. This problem of potential over-production was particularly important to Russian Marxists during the 1890s, a period when, under the Tsarist regime, the Russian economy was becoming industrialized, and growing very rapidly, for they were concerned with whether Russian capitalism could create a market sufficient for its own development, or whether it would inevitably collapse. Though these debates were, together with Marx's own writing on the subject, neglected by most non-Marxist economists, one book arising out of them was particularly influential: Tugan-Baranovsky's *Industrial Crises in England*, published in Russian in 1894, and in German in 1901. Between 1901 and 1913 many writers addressed the problem of the cycle, many of them building on Tugan-Baranovsky's work. It was thus through Tugan-Baranovsky that Marx's ideas filtered through into orthodox economics.

The world economy

During the 40 years leading up to the First World War there was a clear business cycle in the world's major economies, as is shown by the estimates of industrial production shown in figure 5.4. In the US there were two periods of very severe depression, in the 1870s and the 1890s. The 1880s were a period of prosperity, the recession after 1882 being but a minor setback. Like the US, Germany grew rapidly, but with no severe recessions, merely periods when growth slowed down slightly. In Britain, on the other hand, though the depressions of the 1870s and the 1890s were less severe than their equivalents in the US, the whole period after 1873 was one of sluggish growth. In the late 1880s, when the US was growing rapidly, Britain was experiencing a severe recession. Despite these important differences, however, there was a clear cyclical pattern common to all these countries. There were clear cyclical peaks in all four countries in 1873, 1882 and 1890–3, with less clear ones in 1899–1900 and 1907. The extent of the fluctuations made the cycle an important problem. In addition, the evidence seemed consistent with the contention made by Juglar and Jevons (and Marx) that there was a regular cycle of approximately ten years' duration.

Unemployment

Unemployment was an aspect of the capitalist system on which Marx laid great emphasis. The 'industrial reserve army', as he called it, was necessary if capitalism was to be able to provide labour for the periodic, sudden expansions of industry characteristic of capitalism. In contrast, most classical economists, though they recognized that unemployment could be wasteful (workers might lose their skills), regarded irregularity of employment as a social problem caused by the normal working of the economic system. The New Poor Law of 1834 was based on the assumption that unemployment was, at least for the able-bodied, an inevitable occurrence which men should anticipate and provide for out of their earnings whilst employed. Unemployment was, on the whole, simply not seen as an economic problem.

This attitude changed towards the end of the nineteenth century, with unemployment coming to be seen as one of the most harmful consequences of trade depressions. In England, for example, the term 'unemployment' came into use in the 1880s. J. A. Hobson, whose ideas on the cause of unemployment are considered below, argued that the word was generally

(a) Industrial production in the UK and the US

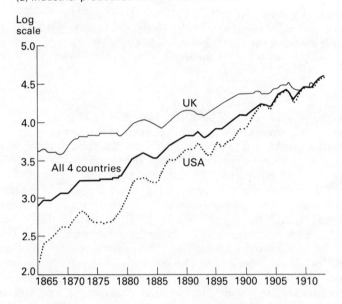

(b) Industrial production in France and Germany

FIGURE 5.4 *Industrial production, 1865–1913*

Source: Lewis (1978), pp. 248–75.

used to denote 'all forms of involuntary leisure suffered by the working classes'. He linked unemployment explicitly to waste, arguing that 'the more scientific definition would . . . identify unemployment with the total quantity of human labour power not employed in the production of social wealth, which would rank . . . as superfluity or waste' (Hobson, 1896, pp. 9–10).

It was at this time that the first statistics on unemployment were collected. The example was set by the UK Board of Trade, which from 1888 published figures for the percentage of trade union members receiving unemployment benefits (these were paid by the unions) at the end of each month. These figures covered only a small fraction of the workforce, for only a limited number of unions made returns to the Board of Trade, these covering mainly skilled manual workers. There are figures for earlier years but these are even less reliable. Similar statistics were collected in France from 1895, in Germany from 1903 and in the US (for example figures for the state of New York begin in 1902). Because of their limited coverage these figures do not indicate the overall level of unemployment, but they probably do show how unemployment fluctuated over the cycle. Comprehensive unemployment statistics were not collected until after 1914.

J. A. Hobson

Before 1914 it was the less orthodox economists, frequently outsiders to the economics profession, who paid greatest attention to the problem of unemployment. In Britain the most important such 'heretic' was undoubtedly J. A. Hobson. Hobson argued that unemployment was the result of 'over-production', defined as 'the production of commodities in excess . . . of the demand for export at remunerative prices, and of the amount of income or earnings available for their purchase in the home market' (Hobson, 1896, p. 62). The reason for this over-production was, he claimed, that saving was too high, and consumption too low, the result being that the level of spending was too low to sustain a high level of production. If savings were invested (used to purchase new capital goods) this would exacerbate the problem by raising productive capacity without doing anything to raise demand.

Hobson claimed that the cause of low consumption was a very unequal distribution of income, for the existence of a limit to what any individual could consume meant that the receivers of very high incomes had no choice but to save a high proportion of their income. Unemployment could thus be remedied by introducing measures to make the distribution of income more equal: by taxing 'unearned' income (including capital gains on land), rents and monopoly profits; or by raising the share of wages in national income. Not only would such a redistribution, by raising spending, reduce unemployment, but it would also provide greater opportunities for using savings profitably.

In Britain, as was pointed out earlier, industry was, despite cyclical fluctuations, persistently depressed after 1873. In contrast, in the US the pattern was one of strong expansion interrupted by sometimes severe, but relatively brief, periods of depression, notably in the 1870s and the 1890s. There were nonetheless several American economists who addressed the problem of unemployment. Frank Hawley and Uriel Crocker, for example, put forward underconsumptionist arguments similar to Hobson's. Amongst more orthodox economists, Francis A. Walker, the first president of the American Economic Association, argued that because demand for one industry's products depends on incomes earned in other industries, it would be possible for production to get stuck at a very low level with as much as a third or half the country's productive capacity lying idle (Walker, 1879). Industries would be locked in a vicious circle: no industry would be able to raise production without other industries increasing their purchases; purchases could not be raised until production and hence incomes had been raised. Such a situation, Walker argued, characterized the depression from 1874 to 1877 in the US when, he claimed, as much as 25 per cent of productive capacity lay idle (recent estimates of industrial production such as those discussed above suggest that this estimate may not have been very far out).

Alfred Marshall

On the whole, however, orthodox economists focused on the cycle rather than unemployment. For Alfred Marshall, Knut Wicksell and Irving Fisher, for example, the main policy problem was not reducing unemployment, but minimizing fluctuations. As an example of this consider Marshall's account of the cycle. He starts by explaining what we would now term the 'real' rate of interest: that the real rate of interest is the nominal rate minus the rate of inflation. This introduces an element of speculation into business life, for though firms know the interest rate they are paying when they take out a loan, they cannot know what the inflation rate is going to be.

The consequence of this uncertainty is that, when prices are likely to rise, people rush to borrow money and buy goods, and thus help prices to rise; business is inflated, it is managed recklessly and wastefully; those working on borrowed capital pay back less real value than they borrowed, and enrich themselves at the expense of the community.

Salaries and wages generally retain their nominal value, which means that when prices rise their real value falls. This means that

the employer pays smaller real salaries and wages than usual, at the very time when his profits are largest in other ways, and is thus prompted to over-estimate his strength, and engage in ventures which he will not be able to pull through after the tide begins to turn.

When afterwards credit is shaken and prices begin to fall, everyone wants to get rid of commodities and get hold of money which is rapidly rising in value; this makes prices fall all the faster, and the further fall makes credit shrink even more, and thus for a long time prices fall because prices have fallen. At such a time employers cease their production because they fear that when they come to sell their finished product general prices will be even lower than when they buy their materials . . .

Workers resist cuts in nominal wages for fear that if they agree to them it will be hard to raise wages again later:

they are inclined to stop work rather than accept a nominal reduction even though it would not be a real one. The employer, on his part, finds a stoppage his easiest course; at all events, by diminishing production he will help to improve the market for his own goods. He may not happen to remember that every stoppage of work in any one trade diminishes the demand for the work of others; and that, if all trades tried to improve the market by stopping their work together, the only result would be that everyone would have less of everything to consume.

Marshall sums up the situation by saying

The fluctuations in the value of what we use as our standard are ever either flurrying up business into unwholesome fever, or else closing factories and workshops by the thousand in businesses that have nothing fundamentally wrong with them, but in which whoever buys raw material and hires labour is likely to sell when general prices have fallen further. (Marshall, 1887, pp. 191–2)

For Marshall, therefore, the major cause of fluctuations, and hence unemployment, was fluctuating prices. If prices could be stabilized through reforming the monetary system, then unemployment would automatically be relieved. Similar views were held by Fisher and Wicksell (see pp. 115–19).

Business cycle theory by 1914

By 1914 economists had made enormous advances in their understanding of the business cycle. Between 1900 and 1914 there was a proliferation of theories of the business cycle. Though this did not result in any consensus as to what caused the cycle, it produced many new ideas capable of development. More important than this, however, was the advance in empirical knowledge about unemployment and the business cycle. The progress that had been made compared with a generation earlier can be seen by looking at two works: Wesley Clair Mitchell's *Business Cycles* (1913), and Gustav Cassel's *Theory of Social Economy* (written by 1914, though the war delayed its publication till 1918).

As regards the range of statistical material, Mitchell's *Business Cycles* is unrivalled, preparing the way for the quantitative research that Mitchell, as director of the newly formed National Bureau for Economic Research, was to organize from 1920 to 1945. Mitchell's weakness, however, was his aversion to theory. He regarded the business cycle as too complex a phenomenon to be analysed in terms of a simple theory. He found merit in virtually all current theories of the cycle, arguing that they all had something to contribute. Where people went wrong was in looking for a single cause of business cycles. Mitchell thus concentrated on investigating in great detail what actually happened during business cycles. The main problems with such an eclectic approach are that without a well-specified theory it is virtually impossible to ascertain what causes what, or to explain why an economy behaves as it does. It also makes it virtually impossible to test theories of the cycle.

In contrast, Cassel, whose ideas were very influential in the inter-war period (though written by 1914, his *Theory of Social Economy* was not published till after the war), provides a much better illustration of how the disparate lines of research instigated by Juglar and Tugan-Baranovsky could be brought together. Like Juglar, Cassel started by identifying a series of crisis years, or turning-points, when economies moved from a period of advance to one of decline. These (1873, 1882, 1890, 1900 and 1907) were years when interest rates were at their highest, as shown in figure 5.5. Comparing Britain, Germany and the US he found few significant differences in either the number of cycles or their timing. Cassel then went on to show the connection between these crisis years and fluctuations in industrial production. He defined the cycle in terms of the production of fixed capital: 'A period of advance is one of special increase in the production of fixed capital; a period of decline, or a depression, is one in which this production falls below the point it had reached' (Cassel, 1923, pp. 520–1). His reason for this was that it was primarily production of capital goods which fluctuated over the cycle, production of other goods growing much more steadily. Cassel did not have access to measures of industrial production such as we have today, so he used pig iron production as a proxy for production of capital goods, and consumption of coal as a measure of production as a whole. Given that fluctuations in coal consumption could be accounted for by fluctuations in the output of capital goods (pig iron) he deduced that production of consumption goods fluctuated little.

Cassel then went on to examine the behaviour of prices, wages and unemployment over the cycle. Prices and wages rose during a period of advance, with the greatest rises being in the prices of minerals, which rose dramatically before a crisis, and fell equally dramatically afterwards. Associated with the rise in wages during a period of advance was a rise in the share of income going to labour, and a fall in the share going to business. Unemployment was shown to fluctuate as we would expect, the greatest fluctuations occurring in capital goods industries.

On the basis of this information Cassel was able to present a theory of the cycle. The stimulus to investment comes from low interest rates, for the lower the rate of interest, the greater the number of projects that will be profitable. Low interest rates, therefore, lead to increased production of capital goods, and to a period of advance. This rise in investment,

(a) The London bank discount rate and price levels

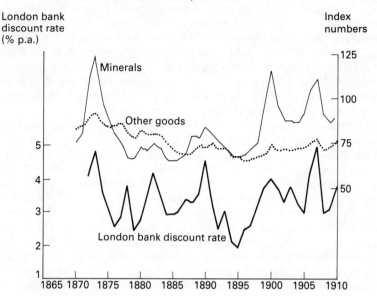

(b) World iron and coal production

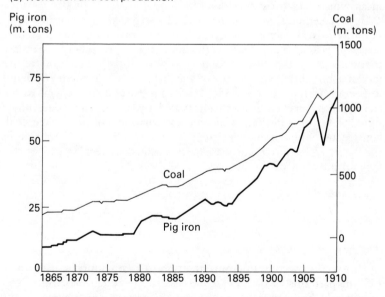

FIGURE 5.5 *Cassel's data on the cycle, 1865–1910*

Source: Cassel (1923), p. 642.

however, is not accompanied by any increase in savings: indeed rises in wages will tend to reduce business income and hence saving. This means that a shortage of finance will emerge and interest rates will rise. At the same time, shortages of materials and labour will raise materials prices and wage rates, reducing profitability. The result will be a fall in investment and the economy will move, through a crisis, into a period of decline. During the decline these processes will be put into reverse. Demand for finance will fall relative to savings, and so interest rates will fall. Falling material prices and wage rates will raise profitability and eventually a rise in investment will bring the depression to an end.

Though this process seems quite plausible, and is consistent with the empirical evidence outlined above, it leaves open the question of why there should be fluctuations rather than simply a steady advance. Here Cassel took up a number of suggestions made by earlier writers.(1) Investment takes time to respond to changes in interest rates, which means that by the time investment starts to fall in response to a rise in the interest rate, the shortage of funds will have become very acute, and interest rates will have risen too far. (2) Lags in the response of interest rates to changes in investment will result in investment fluctuating excessively. (3) The lag between the start of an investment project and its completion will mean that productive capacity continues to increase even after output prices have started to fall as a result of excess capacity. (4) Periodic disturbances may arise from either advances in technology (e.g. the introduction of railways, automobiles or electricity) or the opening of new markets. These were all ideas which had been developed in the period since 1900.

By 1914, therefore, economists had succeeded in constructing a fairly good statistical picture of cyclical fluctuations over the preceding half century. Their data were very limited by present-day standards (in particular they did not have measures of total production or national income) but their statistics were adequate to enable them to identify the important features of the cycle. Cassel's picture of the general pattern, for example, is very close to that revealed by the modern data underlying figure 5.4. In addition, coherent explanations of the cycle had been constructed which were consistent with a wide range of empirical data on the cycle. Unemployment was, quite reasonably, seen as part of the more general problem of the business cycle.

5.3   THE INTER-WAR PERIOD

The historical record

In this section we confine our attention to two countries: Britain and the US. In part this is because to discuss the experience of other countries would take too long (Germany and the rest of continental Europe, for example, suffered enormous upheaval during the war and after), but the main reason is that most of the economic ideas we need to consider originated in these two countries.

The main features of the interwar business cycle are shown in figures 5.6 and 5.7. The figures for both Britain and the US are, of course, dominated by the crash of 1929 and the ensuing depression, more severe than any depression before or after. By 1932 unemployment had risen to over 20 per cent in both countries, this rise in unemployment being accompanied, especially in the US, by a massive fall in output. After 1932

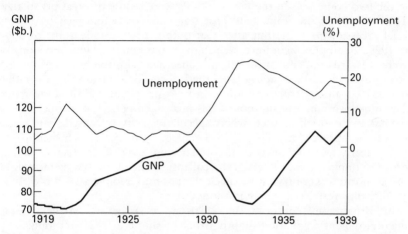

FIGURE 5.6 *National income and unemployment in the US, 1919–39*

Source and note: US Bureau of the Census (1960), pp. 73 and 139. Real GNP in $billion. Unemployment as percentage of labour force.

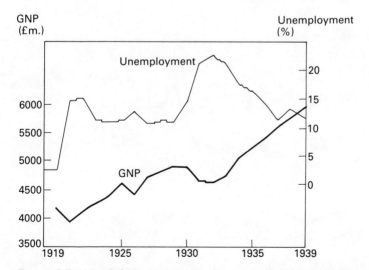

FIGURE 5.7 *National income and unemployment in the UK, 1919–39*

Source and note: Mitchell (1978), pp. 66 and 416. Real GNP in £million. Unemployment as percentage of the labour force.

there was a steady recovery which continued until 1938. Also evident from figures 5.6 and 5.7 is the post-war boom, which affected both countries in 1919–20. This was a worldwide phenomenon which occurred as a result of restocking after the war. Output rose sharply, but once stocks were restored demand fell, and recession followed.

Beyond this, however, the story is very different in the Britain and the US, as a result of which discussions of economic policy were very different in the two countries. In the US the 1920s were a time of great prosperity. The collapse of the immediate post-war boom was followed by a very brief recession in 1921, but after that output rose steadily right through to 1929. Unemployment fluctuated slightly, but remained low. Economists were, towards the end of the 1920s, concerned with the health of the US economy, but this was not because the US was doing badly. It was rather that they realized that the boom had to come to an end at some stage. The most prominent symptom of this prolonged period of prosperity was the rise in the stock market, where speculative activity caused share prices to rise to unprecedented heights by 1929 (see figure 5.8). Such share prices were clearly out of line with the underlying level of production and in order to minimize the effects of the collapse (which they saw as inevitable) the authorities were trying to check the boom. Credit was, from early in 1928, being restricted, but with little effect.

In Britain, in contrast, the 1920s were a period of depression, unemployment recovering slightly from the slump of 1921, but remaining at just over 10 per cent. The major problem was depression in the export industries (textiles, shipbuilding, iron and steel, and coal). To a great extent this depression has to be seen in the context of Britain's long-term

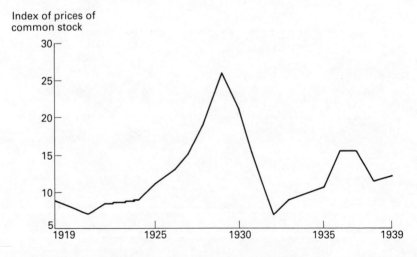

FIGURE 5.8   *Share prices in the US, 1919–39*

Source: US Bureau of the Census (1960), p. 657.

decline, but there were important short-term factors involved as well. Many contemporaries were concerned about the British government's decision to return to the gold standard. During the war, the government had been forced to suspend the convertibility of sterling into gold, and the decision was taken after the war to return to gold at the pre-war exchange rate of £1 = $4.86. By the time this was achieved, in 1925, British prices had risen more than US prices, which meant that British costs had to be reduced if industry was to remain competitive. Wages had to be reduced. This problem of lowering wage rates in order to increase competitiveness proved very difficult, dominating economic policy in the late 1920s. One consequence of this policy was the General Strike of 1926.

The behaviour of prices and wages in the US and Britain is shown in figures 5.9 and 5.10. In both countries prices and wages rose sharply during the boom of 1920, falling equally sharply in the ensuing recession. Thereafter experiences differ. In the UK prices and wages fell slightly, and at nearly the same rate, through most of the 1920s. In the US prices were nearly static, with wages rising gradually for most of the 1920s, rising sharply in 1928. After 1928, wages were halved by 1932, with a smaller, but nonetheless very substantial, fall in prices. In contrast, wages and prices fell only slightly during the depression in Britain.

The problem of Keynesian economics

The inter-war period saw the emergence, with the publication of Keynes's *General Theory of Employment, Interest and Money* in 1936, of Keynesian economics which, in one way or another, has dominated thinking about

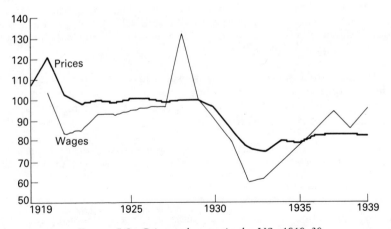

FIGURE 5.9 *Prices and wages in the US, 1919–39*

Source and note: US Bureau of the Census (1960), pp. 92 and 139. Wages are an index of average weekly earnings by production workers in manufacturing, 1929=100. Prices are GNP deflator, 1929=100.

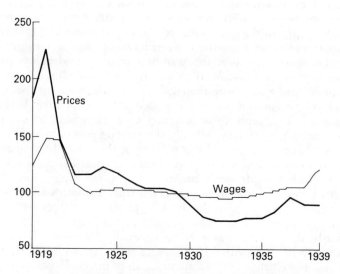

FIGURE 5.10 *Prices and wages in the UK, 1919–39*

Source and note: Mitchell (1978), pp. 76 and 416. Wages are in industry, 1938=100. Prices are implicit GNP deflator, 1929=100.

unemployment and the business cycle for the past 50 years. In his first chapter, a single page, Keynes wrote that his object was

to contrast the character of my arguments and conclusions with those of the *classical* theory of the subject, upon which I was brought up and which dominates the economic thought, both practical and theoretical, of the governing and academic classes of this generation, as it has done for a hundred years past. (Keynes, 1936, p. 3; Keynes's italics)

Keynes argued that in classical economics the question of what determined the level of output as a whole was not addressed. The postulates of classical economics were applicable only to the special case where resources were fully utilized. He concluded from this that

the characteristics of the special case assumed by the classical theory happen not to be those of the economic society in which we actually live, with the result that its teaching is misleading and disastrous if we attempt to apply it to the facts of experience. (Keynes, 1936, p. 3)

Classical economics, he argued, was based on the related assumptions that there is no such thing as involuntary unemployment, and that supply creates its own demand.

With the triumph of Keynesian ideas there developed a number of myths about what, very quickly, came to be called 'the Keynesian revolution'. One myth was that Keynes's account of 'classical economics' provided an adequate description of economics before the *General Theory*. If this were true, there would be no problem in evaluating Keynes's contribution to economics: the replacement of a hopelessly inappropriate theory with something far superior. Another was the myth that Keynes was responsible, almost single-handed, for changing government policy: that prior to Keynes's influence wage-cutting was seen as the remedy for unemployment, whereas after the *General Theory* governments turned to demand management and in particular control of government spending, in order to maintain full employment. Though there is an element of truth underlying both these myths, however, they are both *very* misleading accounts of what happened, for the real picture is much more complicated, and to understand what happened we need to look at discussions of the business cycle and unemployment policy in the period before the *General Theory*.

Unemployment policy in the US

During the 1920s American economists were keenly interested in the problem of the business cycle. Business cycle theory came to be seen as a distinct branch of economics. Students took courses on the business cycle, and textbooks appeared. There was widespread debate over the nature of the cycle, one of the major disagreements being whether cycles were primarily monetary in origin (caused by irregular growth in the money supply) or whether they were caused by 'real' factors (such as new inventions, new resources or factors such as the harvest). Though the main ideas put forward during the 1920s were developments of ideas that had been put forward before 1914, these discussions of the business cycle are important because they provide the context in which economists discussed the problem of unemployment policy.

One of the earliest official statements on unemployment policy was that of the President's Conference on Unemployment in 1921, set up and chaired by Herbert Hoover, then Secretary for Commerce. This proposed setting aside 10 per cent of normal spending on public works as a reserve which could be used when recession came. It was argued that the spending of these funds would raise incomes in the construction industry, and that when these incomes were spent on consumer goods there would be a further stimulus to activity. Incomes in the consumer goods industry would then be raised, raising spending still further. The result of this would be that a given level of public works spending would, through this 'multiplying effect', sustain a much larger level of industrial activity and employment. Furthermore, because public works projects had been set aside over the rest of the cycle, the projects undertaken during a recession would all be necessary, commercially viable, ones.

These notions underlay Herbert Hoover's response, as President, to the recession after 1929. He attempted to increase spending plans and to keep wages high, arguing that cutting wages (as many employers wished to do) would simply reduce demand, making the slump worse. These measures to increase spending were supported by many economists, including Irving Fisher, the main proponent of the quantity theory of money. Between 1929 and 1930 this policy had some measure of success, new construction being raised by about 20 per cent in the public sector, and by about 7 per cent in regulated industries in the private sector (railroads, telephones, gas and electricity), but unemployment rose nonetheless.

After 1930, however, the policy failed, the main reason being that it proved impossible to sustain the high level of public works expenditure, let alone to increase it. A rise in interest rates in 1931 made it harder for both private businesses and state governments to maintain their spending plans. In addition, many firms which till then had managed to resist the pressure to cut wages were forced to do so. There was thus pressure on the Federal government to raise its public works programmes. This was resisted by the administration on a number of grounds. One, entirely compatible with the attitude towards stabilization policy outlined above, was that there were no appropriate public works projects to be undertaken. Another, which amounted to a reversal of policy, was that increased spending on construction, far from aiding the rest of the economy through 'multiplying effects', would harm it: the borrowing required to finance federal government spending would raise interest rates, crowding out private business spending, impeding recovery. Hoover argued that public works spending could be used to alleviate unemployment only so long as it did not threaten the government's solvency: by 1931 measures to balance the budget had become more important, as without them business confidence would not be restored.

This move against public works policy was supported by only a small number of economists. In 1930 Senator Wagner reintroduced his bill for an Employment Stabilization Board to plan public works construction so as to relieve unemployment, seeing the main purpose of the bill as being to raise Federal construction spending by $1,000m., financed by selling bonds. He canvassed a large number of economists on the issue, and with very few exceptions his bill had their support.

The New Deal

In 1933 Franklin Roosevelt became President, immediately implementing the 'New Deal'. The main idea underlying this programme was to raise prices, in order to reduce the value of debts. In Roosevelt's own words, written after the event,

We had determined definitely to seek an increase in all values. Two courses were open: to cut down the debts through bankruptcies and foreclosures to such a point that they would be below property values; or else to increase property values until they were greater than the debts. Obviously the latter course was the only legitimate method of putting the country back on its feet without destroying human values. (Quoted in Scheiber *et al.*, 1976, p. 367)

To raise prices a number of measures were introduced. The Farm Relief and Inflation Act (1933) gave the President the power to increase the number of notes in circulation, to devalue the dollar in terms of gold, to accept silver in payment of war debts and to coin unlimited amounts of silver at whatever ratio of gold to silver he considered appropriate. This enabled Roosevelt to increase the money supply so as to raise prices. In addition there was an expansion of Federal spending, this being accompanied by a persistent, large deficit. In 1932, under Hoover, the deficit had risen from $462m. to $2,700m. and it remained high right through the thirties. This expenditure was on a number of programmes all designed to relieve the effects of the depression. There were loans to commerce and industry to save businesses from bankruptcy. Measures were taken to assist agriculture and there were large programmes of public works ranging from conservation (such as planting trees in the 'dust bowl') to flood control and housing schemes.

The New Deal was the first deliberate attempt by government to lift the US economy out of a recession. The measures introduced were not part of an overall plan but were a series of expedients, with the government responding to a series of specific problems. In so far as there was a general macroeconomic theory underlying the New Deal, it was the belief that raising prices was the way to restore economic activity. The rationale for increasing government expenditure was not provided by Keynes. In so far as Keynesian ideas can be linked to the New Deal, this was because such ideas existed in the writings of American economists working independently of Keynes. The derivation of the multiplier by the President's Conference on Unemployment in the 1920s has already been discussed. A position even closer to that of the *General Theory*, very close to what Keynes was thinking in 1933–4, can be found in J. M. Clark's *Strategic Factors in Business Cycles*. Finally, it is important to point out that the New Deal had parallels in several other countries, notably Sweden. It was not an isolated event but was part of a much wider change in attitudes towards government policy.

Employment policy in the UK

In Britain, as explained above, economists were concerned with the problem of persistent unemployment throughout the 1920s. Contra-cyclical relief works had been proposed as early as 1909 in the Minority Report of the Royal Commission on the Poor Laws, and in the early 1920s there was some official support for such schemes. Attitudes hardened, however, after 1925 when it became clear that high unemployment was not going to be a temporary phenomenon. Not surprisingly in view of its concentration in certain industries, unemployment came to be seen as a structural problem, for which the appropriate remedies were industrial reorganization, cost cutting and labour mobility. At the same time, however, there also emerged the so-called 'Treasury view', that whatever money the state borrowed to finance relief works would be taken from funds that would otherwise go to finance private investment. In 1929 Winston Churchill, then Chancellor of the Exchequer, claimed 'It is orthodox treasury dogma, steadfastly held, that whatever might be the political or social advantages, very little additional employment can, in fact, and as a general rule, be created by state borrowing and expenditure' (quoted in Winch, 1969, p. 109).

The most notable opponent of the 'Treasury view' was, of course, Keynes. Though he recognized that the problem did lie with export industries, he accepted that because of the over-valued exchange rate these industries were not going to be in a position to employ as much labour as they had previously done. The answer was schemes of 'national development' involving raising the level of public investment. Such schemes would raise employment directly, but would also lead to employment in the private sector. Keynes thus supported the proposals for public works put forward by Lloyd George and the Liberal Party. The 'Treasury view' was answered with the argument that a large fraction of savings was not being invested productively, but remained hoarded as bank deposits. Public investment could thus be increased without reducing private investment.

Although Keynes may have been the most well-known exponent of such policies, it is important to note that he was not in a minority amongst economists. Keynes remarked, in 1929: 'I know of no British economist of reputation who supports the proposition that schemes of National Development are incapable of curing unemployment' (Keynes, 1971–83, XIX, p. 813). Indeed, the economist who first argued against the 'Treasury view' was not Keynes, but Pigou, Marshall's successor who was singled out for such severe criticism in the *General Theory*, who attacked the argument in his inaugural lecture in 1908.

The challenge of the General Theory

The main argument in the *General Theory* is about effective demand. This is determined by the aggregate demand and supply functions. The aggregate supply function is defined as the aggregate supply price (cost) of the output produced by a given number of men, whilst the aggregate demand function gives the proceeds (revenue) entrepreneurs expect to receive as a result of employing any given number of men. These are shown in figure 5.11. The level of effective demand is the point where aggregate supply and demand are equal: if D were greater than Z, entrepreneurs would have an incentive to increase employment; it it were lower, they would have an incentive to reduce it.

The main factors determining the level of effective demand, Keynes argued, were the propensity to consume and the incentive to invest. He postulated the now-familiar consumption function, with consumption rising as income increases, but at a slower rate (a marginal propensity to consume of less than one). Given the marginal propensity to consume income was related to investment via the multiplier. The level of investment

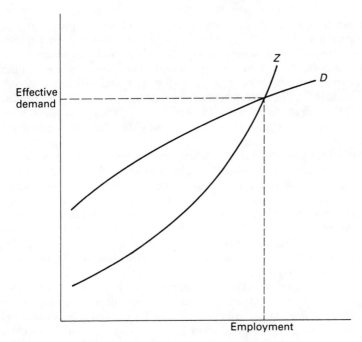

FIGURE 5.11   *Keynes's theory of employment*

in turn depended on expectations and on the rate of interest. This was expressed using the concept of the marginal efficiency of capital, defined as the discount rate which makes the present value of the expected returns from an asset equal to the cost of the asset. Given the marginal efficiency of capital (and hence the state of expectations about the future) a rise in the interest rate will reduce investment, and vice-versa. This left the interest rate to be explained, using the concept of liquidity preference. The speculative motive for holding money (holding cash to avoid a capital loss when the price of bonds is expected to fall) was introduced to explain why it might, under certain circumstances, be perfectly rational for people to hoard.

   In Keynes's theory the level of employment was determined by the state of liquidity preference (which determined the rate of interest), the marginal efficiency of capital (which, together with the rate of interest, determined the level of investment) and the marginal propensity to consume. These three factors determined the level of aggregate demand and hence the level of effective demand, and the level of employment. There was no reason why there should be full employment. The willingness of men to work provided a maximum to the level of employment, but there was no reason why this maximum would be achieved.

Keynes's theory provided both an explanation of how an economy might get into a depression, with persistent high unemployment, and a justification for using fiscal policy as a means of curing such a depression. For employment to be increased, aggregate demand had to be increased and this depended on a rise in investment. This would not take place as long as expectations were depressed: the marginal efficiency of capital would be low. Public investment could raise spending directly, producing a multiplier effect on effective demand, and would also serve to raise entrepreneurs' expectations, possibly raising the marginal efficiency of capital.

In both Britain and the US, as was explained earlier, government spending was generally accepted as an anti-unemployment policy. Furthermore, by 1936, when the *General Theory* was published, there had been four years of recovery. Why then did the *General Theory* have the impact that it did? The conventional answer is that economists had the policies but not the theory to back up those policies: that there was an element of schizophrenia amongst economists, whose theoretical system ruled out the possibility of unemployment but whose policy prescriptions included expanding demand to reduce unemployment. This answer is, however, misleadingly over-simplified. The level at which it is true is that the only formal theory of the labour market involved a demand curve dependent on marginal productivity and a supply curve dependent on the willingness of workers to supply labour (the marginal disutility of labour). Given competition in the labour market supply would equal demand, and there would be no unemployment unless, of course, the wage rate were for some reason too high. At another level, however, as we have already seen, economists did have a theory of unemployment as part of the business cycle. Though the links were never very thoroughly worked out, demand for labour was linked to the level of spending as well as to the marginal product of labour. This was true not only of American writers on the business cycle, such as Mitchell or J. M. Clark (probably the leading authority on the cycle in the early 1930s), but also of Pigou. Though he never formulated his theory precisely, Pigou argued that an increase in spending would raise incomes and produce further increases in spending (this was a commonplace notion by the 1920s). He also recognized that an expansion of demand might under some circumstances be a necessary prerequisite for full employment: if demand were too low, he claimed, full employment might require a negative wage rate.

These theories of unemployment, however, were not formulated very precisely. In addition, there was not even an agreed, commonly understood framework within which theoretical issues could be discussed. The meaning of the terms saving and investment, for example, had not been clearly defined. This lack of agreement even on basic concepts was well illustrated by the controversy which dominated the very early 1930s, between Keynes and Hayek, who put forward very different explanations of the cycle. Not only did they disagree on what caused the cycle, but they could not even agree on definitions, and as a result each accused the other of being completely incoherent. This may be an extreme case, but it illustrates the lack of any agreed framework for discussions of macroeconomic issues.

In the *General Theory* Keynes provided a set of concepts that could be used as a framework for discussing problems of unemployment: aggregate demand was clearly distinguished from income; savings and investment were defined (though there was still some problem here until Myrdal introduced the distinction between *ex ante* and *ex post*); the consumption function and the marginal propensity to consume; the marginal efficiency of capital; liquidity preference, or the demand for money. Using these, Keynes was able to provide a much more formal analysis of the problem of unemployment than had most of his predecessors. J. M. Clark summed up Keynes's contribution in the following way.

It has seemed to me that what I call the 'income–flow analysis', of which yours is the most noted presentation, has done something which has not been done in comparable degree since Ricardo and Marx: namely, constructed a coherent logical theoretical system or formula having the quality of a mechanism, growing directly out of current conditions and problems which are of paramount importance and furnishing a key for working out definite answers in terms of policy. On this a 'school' has grown up. All that has tremendous power; it is also exposed to the dangers of too-undiscriminating application, from which 'classical' economics suffered. (Letter to Keynes; printed in Keynes, 1971–83, XXIII, p. 191)

It was because it provided a simple, but effective theoretical framework on the basis of which further research into macroeconomics could take place that the *General Theory* was such an immediate success. In particular Keynes's theory proved suitable for mathematical treatment, and as a framework for statistical work. National income accounts, for example, came to be organized along Keynesian lines. This possibly accounts for why it was mainly the younger economists who were so enthusiastic about Keynesian economics. Amongst older economists there were many who reacted much more critically, not rejecting Keynes's ideas out of hand (though there were of course some who did this) but questioning whether some of his concepts were oversimplified.

In this section we have concentrated on Keynes. The reason for this is that limitations of space mean that it is necessary to be very selective, and given the way Keynes's ideas have dominated post-war economics Keynes had to be treated fairly thoroughly. This emphasis on Keynes should not, however, be taken as implying that Keynes was alone in arguing such views. Reference has already been made to J. M. Clark and American economists who came close to anticipating the ideas Keynes put forward in his *General Theory*. Mention should also be made of the Swedish economists Erik Lindahl and Gunnar Myrdal who, starting from Wicksell's cumulative process, reached conclusions very similar to those reached by Keynes. Finally there was Michal Kalecki who reached a similar position starting from Marx. Given that the central ideas of the *General Theory*, in particular the multiplier, were ideas which in some form had been around for many years, and given the unprecedented nature of the economic crisis for which a remedy had to be found, it was hardly surprising that similar ideas should emerge in so many places at the same time.

5.4 UNEMPLOYMENT AND THE CYCLE SINCE 1945

The long boom

After the period of reconstruction after the war, both western Europe and the US entered a long period of prosperity and economic growth, from around 1950 until 1973. Unemployment was low and the business cycle was mild. During this period Keynesian ideas were dominant. In the UK full employment was accepted as a goal of economic policy in 1944, and the idea of using the budget to stabilize the economy, with the budget deficit being allowed to rise during a recession, was accepted throughout the 1950s. In so far as there was a business cycle, its timing seemed linked to the timing of general elections: there was expansion during the run-up to an election, with balance of payments problems and the need to contract the economy after the election. Most of the time unemployment was between 1 and 2 per cent, a level that would have seemed unattainable a few years earlier. The contrast between the relative stability of these years, with low inflation and low unemployment, and the 1970s is clearly shown in figure 5.12.

Figure 5.12 *Inflation and unemployment in the UK, 1956–79*

Sources: *Economic Trends Annual Supplement*, 1983; *International Financial Statistics Yearbook*, 1982.

The US also had a goal of full employment, but during the 1950s the commitment to Keynesian ideas was less strong. It was only after 1960, under Kennedy's presidency, that the ideas of the 'New Economics' were really taken to heart. From 1958 to 1962 unemployment was, as is shown in figure 5.13, high relative to the levels achieved for most of the 1950s, and the government responded to this with a tax cut in 1964, even though the budget was in deficit. The result was a period of growth and falling unemployment. By the late 1960s, however, the results of this planned reduction of taxation became confused with the problems of the Vietnam War. Spending on the war was increasing, but there was an unwillingness to raise taxes to finance it. The results were inflationary.

Keynesian economics dominated academic research into macroeconomics during this period. There was theoretical research into Keynesian economics, continuing the attempt to make sense of the *General Theory*, for although the book's main arguments were by now well understood, it had thrown up numerous theoretical puzzles. Had Keynes, for example, shown that an economy might get permanently stuck in a situation of high unemployment, or had he merely shown that unemployment might last a very long time? Was Keynes's consumption function compatible with the traditional theory of consumer behaviour? More important than this theoretical research, however, was the use of Keynesian economics as the basis for empirical work, for the 1950s was the first time when economists had available a large quantity of statistical data and powerful

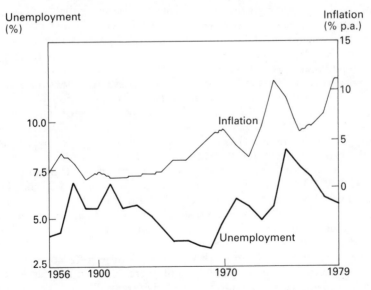

FIGURE 5.13   *Inflation and unemployment in the US, 1956–79*

Sources: OECD *Historical Statistics, 1960–75*; OECD *Main Economic Indicators* (various issues); *International Financial Statistics Yearbook,* 1982.

techniques for analysing it. The aggregate consumption function was investigated very early, and very successfully, with the result that by the end of the 1950s economists knew a lot more about how more consumption behaved, and were able to predict its behaviour quite well. The other major components of the *General Theory*, the investment function and the demand for money function, proved much more difficult.

This was the period when economists started developing economy-wide forecasting models. One of the earliest, and most influential, of such models was the Klein-Goldberger (1955) model. By modern standards this was a small model, containing only a handful of equations, but it nonetheless represented a level of predictive power almost unthinkable 20 or 30 years earlier. During the 1950s and 1960s, as econometric techniques improved and as the cost of computer time fell, more and more models were estimated. Most of these, from the Klein-Goldberger model on, were Keynesian in inspiration in that output was determined by the level of aggregate demand, this comprising consumption, investment, government spending and the trade balance. During the 1970s these models changed, reflecting developments in economic theory, but the Keynesian flavour of many models remained.

The 1970s: new problems and new theories

Keynesian economics was under attack from Monetarists through much of the 1950s and 1960s (see p. 121). Milton Friedman, in particular, challenged very early on the notion that stabilization policy was likely to be effective. It was not, however, until 1967, with the invention of the expectations-augmented Phillips curve (see p. 124) that Friedman had a powerful theoretical argument to offer as to why attempts to maintain full employment were likely to be inflationary. Even then, it was not generally agreed that the long-run Phillips curve was vertical, and if it were not vertical then there was scope for stabilization policy.

It was during the 1970s that, in response to a series of unprecedented events as much as to theoretical challenges, attitudes towards employment policy changed. The major challenge was clearly that posed by the rise in the price of oil which took place in 1973–4 and in 1979. The extent of this rise is shown in figure 5.14: relative to the general US price level the price of oil fell gradually from the mid-1950s to 1970–2, and then it rose fourfold within a year, remaining at this higher level. This had a number of major effects. (1) Because oil exporting countries immediately found themselves with large revenues which they could not spend immediately, there was a massive reduction in world demand. The price rise had redistributed income away from oil importing countries, who were forced to cut their spending, but there was, initially at least, no corresponding rise in spending from oil exporters. (2) Real incomes in oil importing countries were sharply reduced, which meant that standards of living had to fall. This caused adjustment problems in that it proved, in some countries, difficult to lower wages. (3) Because industrial countries

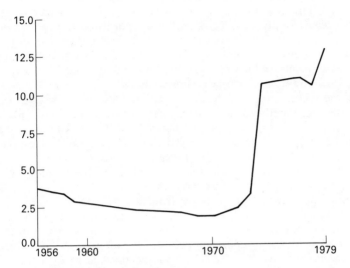

FIGURE 5.14   *The price of oil relative to US consumer prices, 1956–79*
Source: Calculated from figures in *International Financial Statistics Yearbook.*

had to export more in order to pay for their energy imports, domestic production had to be reorganized so as to produce fewer goods for the home market and more for export. (4) The sharp rise in the cost of energy made it necessary to change to more efficient production methods.

The result of the first oil shock of 1973–4 was thus a world recession, but one in which inflation was rising fast (data for the US and the UK are shown in figures 5.13 and 5.12). The traditional remedy of expanding demand could not be applied, because it would have done nothing to alleviate the balance of payments problems to which industrial countries were exposed. Paradoxically, there was a need to impose restrictive policies, firstly in order to control inflation and secondly in order to adjust to the effects of the oil shock. Had economic policy been co-ordinated on an international scale, some other response might have been possible, but this was not possible at the time. In addition, with the move towards flexible exchange rates, probably inevitable given the disturbances to which the world economy was being subjected, there was a need for an alternative approach towards economic policy. It was thus during the second half of the 1970s that most industrial countries moved towards a system of targets for the growth rate of the money supply.

This move towards monetary targets was, of course, something that would have been very unlikely without pressure from Monetarists over a number of years. Friedman had, since the 1940s, been arguing that governments should establish targets for the growth rate of the money supply so as to provide a secure framework within which growth could take place. The growing acceptance of the need for monetary targets did not, however, imply that the Monetarist arguments about the futility of stabilization policy had all been accepted. It was rather that in the new and uncertain environment of the late 1970s, monetary targets provided a framework around which counter-inflation policy could be based.

The 1970s saw enormous developments in macroeconomic theory. In part these were a response to the events of these years: greater concern with inflation, together with an awareness that the traditional explanations were simply inappropriate, meant that old ideas had to be reconsidered. The major impetus, however, was theoretical. A group of economists, the most important of whom was Robert Lucas, argued that the traditional, Keynesian, way of viewing the related problems of the business cycle and unemployment policy was misconceived. It was vital, they argued, to take account of the fact that people learn from what they see going on around them. This is the basis for the much-maligned concept of 'rational expectations': the notion that individuals' expectations of the future will be as good as they could possibly be given the information available when the expectations are formed. Everything that is predictable will be predicted, though mistakes will still be made, for typically there will be completely random events which cannot be predicted correctly.

When combined with the assumption that prices adjust so as to equate supply and demand all the time (that markets 'clear'), the assumption of rational expectations can be used to produce some very strong predictions (this is the New Classical Macroeconomics, also discussed on p. 125). Most important is the result that demand management policy (whether changing government spending or the money supply) will be unable to have any systematic effect on the level of output or unemployment (though as all unemployment is voluntary, it is not clear that the level of unemployment really matters in such models). It has also been argued that Keynesian models, not incorporating rational expectations, will be useless as a guide to policy-making, however well they explain the past experience of the economy. The reason is that if the government changes its policy (as would be the case if the government wished to design an optimal policy on the basis of the macroeconomic model) then the constraints affecting the private sector will change. The private sector will modify its behaviour accordingly, with the result that the original macro model on the basis of which policy was designed will no longer work.

The lesson that Lucas and his associates draw from such ideas is very clear-cut. In a paper provocatively entitled 'After Keynesian macroeconomics', Lucas has, together with Thomas Sargent, outlined his views of what has happened.

For the applied economist, the confident and apparently successful application of Keynesian principles to economic policy which occurred in the 1960s was an event of incomparable significance and satisfaction. These principles led to a set of simple, quantitative relationships between fiscal policy and economic activity generally, the basic logic of which could be (and was) explained to the general public and which could be applied to yield improvements in economic performance benefiting everyone. . . . Understandably and correctly, noneconomists met this promise with skepticism at first; the smoothly growing prosperity of the Kennedy–Johnson years did much to diminish these doubts.

We dwell on these halcyon days of Keynesian economics because without conscious effort they are difficult to recall today. In the present decade [1978], the US economy has undergone its first major depression since the 1930s, to the accompaniment of inflation rates in excess of 10 percent per annum. . . . These events did not arise from a reactionary reversion to outmoded, 'classical' principles of tight money and balanced budgets. On the contrary they were accompanied by massive government budget deficits and high rates of monetary expansion, policies which, although bearing an admitted risk of inflation, promised to modern Keynesian doctrine rapid real growth and low rates of unemployment.

That these predictions were wildly incorrect and that the doctrine on which they were based is fundamentally flawed are now simple matters of fact, involving no novelties in economic theory. The task now facing contemporary students of the business cycle is to sort through the wreckage, determining which features of that remarkable intellectual event called the Keynesian Revolution can be salvaged and put to good use and which others must be discarded. (Lucas and Sargent, 1978, pp. 295–6)

The response of the leading Keynesian economists, such as Franco Modigliani or James Tobin, has been to accept rational expectations as a useful, and possibly indispensable, concept, but to argue that Lucas and his associates have taken the idea too far. New Classical models assume, for example, that everyone holds the same view of how the economy works. In addition, there are many facts that maximizing behaviour and competitive markets cannot explain, notably the persistence of high unemployment. Thus although there were serious limitations inherent in Keynesian economics as it was put forward in the 1960s (notably the neglect of the supply side and of expectations) Tobin and Modigliani would nonetheless strongly defend certain Keynesian ideas. The crisis in Keynesian economics has arisen, Tobin has argued, because Keynesian macroeconomics was never anchored in a satisfactory microeconomic theory: Keynesian macroeconomics can explain many facts about unemployment and the cycle, but its theoretical foundations are weak. The task facing macroeconomists, Tobin and Modigliani would argue, is to strengthen these foundations, not to abandon Keynesian economics in favour of a theory that is even less well equipped to explain the facts.

5.5 CONCLUSIONS

Over the past two centuries there has been enormous progress in our understanding of the problems of employment and the cycle. Particularly important has been the changing nature of the problem: the economic fluctuations to which pre-industrial England was subject were very different from those of the nineteenth-century trade cycle; by the twentieth century, with the increased importance of fixed capital, the nature of the cycle had changed still further. Even after 1945 the nature of the unemployment problem in the 1970s was very different from that of a decade earlier, let alone the 1930s. Economists', theories have had the task of changing very substantially to deal with these changing circumstances.

As with most areas of economics, the main difference between what we know today and what our predecessors knew is that we now have much more information, and in particular statistical information, about the economy. Business cycles and changes in the level of economic activity can be analysed with a degree of precision that was not possible before the war, let alone in the nineteenth century. In addition, for all the limitations of macroeconomic models (and these are many) present-day economists can predict much more confidently than could their predecessors. They face, however, the problem that much more precise predictions are demanded from them.

Advances in economic theory have, however, been fundamental. The basic ideas of Keynesian economics were, in a limited sense, understood early in the nineteenth century by writers such as Attwood and John Stuart Mill, and before them by the eighteenth-century monetary writers, such as John Law, discussed in chapter 4. The notion that changes in one person's spending had repercussions on other people's spending was widespread. It was not, however, until Keynes provided a formal theory of how the level of output was determined in such a system that the idea became completely respectable. As long as the theoretical foundations were thought shaky, the idea was open to persistent doubts, whatever the common sense behind it. The importance of an adequate theory is shown by the recent 'crisis' in Keynesian economics. This has arisen primarily not because recent events have undermined Keynesian theory, for empirical evidence causes as many if not more problems for competing theories, but because the theoretical basis for Keynesian economics is now seen as weak. Intellectual standards in economic theory have changed and important strands of Keynesian economics are now seen as being inadequately explained. There is, of course, a positive reason for wanting to place Keynesian economics on a sounder theoretical basis. As long as economic theories are modified to respond to empirical anomalies in an *ad hoc* way, their power to predict future events is going to be limited. If Keynesian economics can be placed on a sounder theoretical footing, its power to predict successfully in the future will, we hope, be increased.

6

The Theory of a Market Economy

6.1 SIXTEENTH- AND SEVENTEENTH-CENTURY PAMPHLETEERS

Introduction

Previous chapters have been organized around specific economic problems, examining how economists have responded to them, but this chapter adopts a different approach, focusing on more abstract economic theory. There are two reasons for this. The first is that underlying much of the work discussed in previous chapters is the development of an ever more thoroughly worked out theory of supply and demand. It is essential to consider this in more detail. The second reason is that it is abstract economic theory rather than the way economists have tackled particular issues of policy that has attracted so much criticism. If we are to understand and respond to these criticisms it is necessary to consider more carefully what this abstract theory is, and where it has come from.

A theory of economic equilibrium based on supply and demand started to be developed in the sixteenth century, the reason for this being that, before any such theory could emerge, two things were necessary: human behaviour had to be seen in terms of self-interest, and the economy had to be organized, at least to a significant extent, on capitalist lines. In England both of these developments took place in the sixteenth century.

Though the emergence of a capitalist, market-oriented economy was a long and gradual process the sixteenth and seventeenth centuries saw substantial changes in this direction. Associated with this breakdown in the mediaeval economic system were a number of unprecedented economic problems which required explanation. In England, for example, the sixteenth century witnessed not only the inflation that pervaded Europe, but also serious problems of unemployment, both in the countryside where land was being enclosed and turned over to sheep-farming, and in the towns. Such problems came, moreover, at the time when nation states were beginning to be established: men were thus concerned not only with understanding these new problems, but also with policies that would benefit the nation.

At the same time as the mediaeval economic order was breaking down so too was the mediaeval view of the world, the sixteenth century seeing the intellectual developments known as the Renaissance. Thinkers turned away from the idea of a world governed by the rules and moral codes of medieval society towards one where behaviour was governed by self-interest, a change characteristic of political as much as economic thought (this is the time of Machiavelli and Hobbes).

The Discourse of the Commonweal

Against this background the abstractions necessary to analyse economic equilibrium in a competitive economy evolved very gradually. To see this, consider one of the *best* of mid-sixteenth-century writings: *A Discourse of the Commonweal of this Realm of England*. The authorship of this is disputed, but it was probably written in 1549 by Sir Thomas Smith, an important government official during the reign of Elizabeth I. This work addresses the three main economic issues of the day (in addition to the question of why there was division of opinion over religion): (1) rising prices; (2) distress in the countryside, due to land being enclosed and turned over to sheep; (3) distress in towns, due to men buying foreign imports instead of English manufactures.

Though the pamphlet is invaluable as a source of information on mid-Tudor England, what makes it so remarkable is the analysis of the price mechanism that underlies his explanation of the distress in the countryside. Smith argues that the reason for the expansion of sheep-farming at the expense of husbandry is that it is more profitable, and that as long as this situation persists sheep-farming will continue to expand. Only when these two occupations are equally profitable will any balance between them be restored. The reason why sheep-farming is so profitable, Smith argues, is that wool can be exported freely, whereas restrictions on the export of corn depress its price, making husbandry less profitable. The remedy for distress in the countryside is therefore to allow corn to be exported on terms equal to those on which wool can be exported, for this will raise the profitability of husbandry relative to that of sheep-farming.

In addition to this remarkable piece of economic analysis there are insights into many aspects of how a market economy works. Smith sees, for example, the dependence of supply and demand on price, and he recognizes the interdependence of all prices, one trader's price being another's cost. These remain, however, isolated insights. They are not generalized and unified into an overall theory of a market economy.

Mun's England's Treasure

Similar remarks can be made concerning the burgeoning pamphlet literature of early seventeenth-century England. The main stimulus here was a series of crises in which the problem was a collapse in demand for exports (see p. 127). These crises, though not fully understood, were clearly connected with foreign trade. Furthermore, the area of foreign trade was one where government regulation was very great, and where there were strong vested interests to be defended, trade being controlled by a number of large trading companies, each with its own special privileges. As a result many pamphlets were published, interpreting the current situation in a way that suited one interest or another. Numerous pamphlets were written, for example, in support of the East India Company's trading privileges.

As an example of this literature consider Thomas Mun's *England's Treasure by Forraign Trade* (discussed on pp. 50 and 128). As with Sir Thomas Smith's pamphlet nearly a century before, Mun's pamphlet contained valuable economic insights. Though he was not the first to do this, he developed the notion of the balance of trade, allowing for invisible as well as visible trade, and he saw the importance of considering multilateral as well as bilateral trade balances. He was capable, too, of analysing the connections between disparate phenomena, as is illustrated by his explaining the connection between trade, production of woollen textiles, the price of wool and the price of landed property. Though Mun was capable of making generalizations, however, these were still limited in their scope.

6.2   THE EMERGENCE OF SCIENTIFIC ECONOMICS

Sir William Petty

Though many men, ranging from merchants to government officials, wrote on economic matters, and though they succeeded in making notable contributions to economic thought, their analysis remained limited. Seventeenth-century England was, however, a community in which men were passionately interested not only in trade but also in science. Francis Bacon's work belongs to the first half of the century, whilst Restoration England saw the establishment of the Royal Society, dedicated to scientific inquiry along Baconian lines: experimentation and careful observation were seen as the route towards scientific discovery. Given the importance of trade to seventeenth-century England it is hardly surprising that the work of the Royal Society's members included not only the work on the natural sciences for which it is well known (the main examples being Newton's laws of motion and Boyle's laws of gases) but also work on economic matters.

As examples of the work undertaken by these scientists, consider the contributions of Sir William Petty and John Locke. Petty, like his contemporaries, was concerned primarily with concrete issues, his contributions to economic analysis emerging out of his investigations into these issues. Despite this, however, his scientific attitude is very clear. This is made clear by the opening passage of his *The Political Anatomy of Ireland* (1672):

Sir Francis Bacon, in his Advancement of Learning, hath made a judicious Parallel in many particulars, between the Body Natural, and Body Politick, and between the Arts of preserving both in Health and in Strength: And it is as reasonable, that as Anatomy is the best foundation of one, so also of the other; and that to practice upon the Politick without knowing the Symmetry, Fabrick, and Proportion of it, is as casual as the practice of Old-women and Empyricks. (Petty, 1899, p. 129; italics removed)

He chose to examine Ireland on the grounds that its anatomy was very simple and that it was a country with which he was familiar. Petty's method, described in his better known *Political Arithmetick* (1690) was to 'express my self in Terms of *Number, Weight,* or *Measure*; to use only arguments of Sense, and to consider only such Causes, as have visible foundations in nature' (Petty, 1899, p. 244). In his political anatomy, or political arithmetic, Petty provided statistical measures of land use, population, numbers in different occupations, incomes and many other aspects of the economy. Though his methods were, as he himself admitted, very crude, with guesses and rough approximations underlying most of his estimates, his scientific intent is clear enough. In the course of these inquiries Petty made numerous contributions to economic theory, one of the most important of these being his definition of national income as equal to national expenditure, a fundamental feature of modern national income accounting. In his work on Ireland, for example, he estimates total expenditure at £4m. p.a. from which he deduces that, since lands and housing are worth £1m. p.a., the labour of the people must be worth £3m. p.a.

It was as part of his work on taxes that Petty provided what some later economists, notably Marx, took to be the first formulation of the labour theory of value. As with all Petty's work, this was a response to a practical problem: to determine the value of the 'ordinary' rent of land. The value of the corn produced by working on a plot of land, Petty argued, was equal to the amount of silver a man could obtain by devoting the same amount of labour to mining silver. He saw this principle as 'the foundation of equallizing and ballancing of values' (Petty, 1899, p. 44). Although this can be read as containing the basis for a labour theory of value in which the value of a commodity is proportional to the amount of labour required to produce it, however, Petty also used land as a measure of value: if a natural par between land and labour could be found, inputs of land and labour could be reduced to each other 'as easily and certainly as we reduce pence into pounds' (Petty, 1899, p. 85). Petty could be said to have a land *and* labour theory of value as much as a labour theory.

John Locke

By the late seventeenth century there existed a well-developed supply and demand theory of value, as can be seen very clearly in the writings of John Locke. Whereas earlier in the century the main stimulus to thought on the theory of value had come from problems concerning trade and the foreign exchanges, in Locke's time it came from the demand for a legal maximum interest rate and the state of the domestic coinage, both subjects on which Locke wrote.

In late seventeenth-century England people were worried about the commercial success of the Dutch, and a remedy frequently proposed was to lower the legal maximum rate of interest to 4 per cent, the rate prevailing in Holland. Locke's argument against this was that there was a natural rate of interest, determined by supply and demand and that interference with this would be ineffective. Though his earliest defence of this case (1668) had serious shortcomings as a piece of economic reasoning, his pamphlet *Some Considerations of the Lowering of Interest and Raising the Value of Money* (1691) contains some very well developed economic arguments.

One of Locke's concerns in this pamphlet was to explain the value of land, and he started from the premise that the relation between the value of land and the income derived from it was equivalent to that between the price of a loan and the interest paid on it. He thus deduced that land values ought to be inversely related to the market interest rate: when it rose the value of land would fall, and vice-versa. This relationship, however, could be distorted by factors which affected supply and demand, such as a glut of land for sale, or a shortage of funds to invest. Lowering the legal maximum interest rate to 4 per cent could not raise land values because if lending, albeit illegally, yielded 6 per cent, men would be unwilling to use a 4 per cent interest rate when working out land values. Furthermore, restraints on interest would encourage hoarding, reduce the money in circulation and hence prices. Falling prices would depress rents.

The importance of Locke's work, however, lies not in the details of his arguments so much as in his tackling them from the point of view of natural law philosophy. Economic affairs were, for Locke, governed by natural laws, these laws being as inexorable, permanent and reasonable as those governing the physical world. The natural laws governing economic affairs were the following. (1) 'There is no such intrinsic, natural settled value in any thing as to make any assigned quantity of it constantly worth any assigned quantity of another' (Locke, 1691, p. 42). (2) The marketable value of all commodities 'is the proportion of their quantity to their vent'. Vent was defined as 'the passing of commodities from one owner to another, in exchange' (Locke, 1691, p. 43) and comprised consumption, export and the laying up of commodities for private use. In other words, price was determined by supply and demand. (3) Money is governed by the same laws as other commodities. The price of a good is thus determined by the amount of money relative to supply and demand for the good.

Though this attempt to see economic affairs in terms of natural laws was of enormous importance, Locke's use of natural law philosophy was not without its problems. One was the confusion, characteristic of seventeenth-century natural law philosophy, between scientific principles and moral standards. Natural laws were inevitable, and yet certain of them could be violated. If positive laws did not accord with natural laws, then affairs would be mismanaged. This was not, however, a recipe for laissez-faire: men were imperfect and so government was needed to impose the dictates of natural law. Another problem associated with Locke's philosophy concerned his treatment of money (see p. 95).

Dudley North

Despite their importance, natural law philosophy and the Baconian methods of the Royal Society were not the only influences working towards a scientific approach to economics. Another was that of Descartes. Descartes's influence is explicitly recognized in the pamphlet *A Discourse on Trade*, written by Sir Dudley North, and published in 1691 by his brother Roger North. In the preface to this Roger North defended his brother's method in the following terms. 'He begins at the quick, *from principles indisputably true,* and so proceeding with like care comes to a judgement of the nicest disputes and questions concerning trade. . . . And hence it is that knowledge in great measure is become mechanical . . . [which means] built upon clear and evident truths' (North, 1691, p. v). He goes on to stress the importance of being able to abstract, Dudley North's method being to 'reduce things to their extreams, wherein all disputations are most gross and sensible', rather than viewing things 'in the state of ordinary concerns, whereof the terms are scarce distinguishable'.

The 'indisputably true' principles that formed the basis for Dudley North's arguments were fourfold. (1) 'Trade is nothing else but a commutation of superfluities.' Though this might seem a trivial point, it was important in that some of North's contemporaries argued that gold and silver could never be superfluous. (2) North equated wealth with the ability to produce goods rather than with possession of precious metals:

He who is most diligent, and raises most fruits or makes most of manufactory, will abound most in what others make or raise, and consequently be free from want and enjoy most conveniences, which it truly to be rich, although there were no such thing as gold, silver, or the like among them.

(3) The value of gold and silver is determined by the same factors as the value of other metals: they are all useful, with gold and silver simply being more useful than other metals. (4) Prices of all goods are determined by supply and demand (North, 1691, pp. 2–4). Though the language is different, these assumptions clearly have much in common with Locke's natural laws.

The writings of men such as Petty, Locke and North were concerned with practical policy issues just as much as were the writings of their predecessors and contemporaries. In addition, many of their insights into the way the economy operates can be found in earlier writing. The way in which they approached their task, however, was very different, for they were concerned to provide a scientific basis for their claims: they neither appealed to authority, nor used claims of disinterestedness to support their arguments. In their work we can see supply and demand being used as a *general* explanation of the way markets operate. Whereas many of their predecessors used such reasoning in isolated cases, it was in the late seventeenth century that men started to look beyond explanations relevant to particular cases to see supply and demand as a general explanation of economic affairs.

6.3 CANTILLON AND THE PHYSIOCRATS

Richard Cantillon

Though the beginnings of a general economic theory based on supply and demand can be found in late seventeenth-century writings, it was in the eighteenth century that this notion began to be developed in a comprehensive and systematic way. An important figure here is Richard Cantillon, an Irish banker who lived both in London and Paris, and whose most influential work was probably first published in French (see also p. 99). The difference between his work and most of those considered above is evident from its title: *Essay on the Nature of Trade in General* (first published in 1755, though probably written in 1730–4). Though Cantillon is concerned with policy issues, these are secondary to his main task of explaining how the economic system works.

One of Cantillon's main achievements was to provide a much more elaborate analysis of how supply and demand work to determine an equilibrium in the economy as a whole than had any of his predecessors. Two aspects of this are important. The first is that he goes beyond individual markets to analyse the role of the price system in allocating resources in the economy as a whole. Because of its importance it is worth seeing just how he does this. His starting point is to consider a single large isolated estate (we would now say a planned economy). On this estate the allocation of resources between different activities will be determined by the 'fancy' of the owner: part will be used to produce corn, part to produce animals, food and clothing (to provide for both the owner and his servants) and part will be turned into parks and so on. Cantillon then goes on to consider what would happen if production were decentralized, men who had previously been overseers working under the owner's command becoming farmers and entrepreneurs. His conclusion is that,

after this change all the people on this large Estate live just as they did before [i.e. final demand is unchanged], and so all the portions and Farms of this great Estate will be put to the same use as it formerly was.

For if some of the Farmers sowed more corn than usual they must feed fewer Sheep, and have less Wool and Mutton to sell. Then there will be too much Corn and too little Wool for the consumption of the inhabitants. Wool will therefore be dear, which will force the inhabitants to wear their clothes longer than usual, and there will be too much Corn and a surplus for next year. And we suppose the Landowner has stipulated for the payment in silver of the . . . [rent] to be paid to him, the Farmers who have too much Corn and too little Wool, will not be able to pay him his rent. (Cantillon, 1755, p. 61)

Cantillon then goes on to argue that if the farmers are 'excused' they will produce more wool and less corn the following year, for 'Farmers always take care to use their land for the production of those things which they think will fetch the best price at Market.' If this adjustment goes too far and too much wool is produced, then they will readjust back in favour of corn, and so on from year to year.

This equilibrium is of course dependent on the structure of demand, and will change if there are any changes in demand. As it is only those who are better off who have any choice in the way they spend their income, it is the entrepreneurs and, above all others, the owner of the estate, that determine the pattern of economic activity. If the owner's tastes change (say he wants to rear more horses and retain fewer servants) this will lead to price changes (demand for hay will rise, and that for corn will fall), and these price changes will cause resources to be re-allocated.

The second major aspect of Cantillon's general equilibrium theory is his theory of value. He argued that supply and demand will determine market prices, but that in 'well organised societies' the market prices of 'articles whose consumption is tolerably constant and uniform' will never vary very much from what Cantillon, to us very misleadingly, called 'intrinsic values'. The intrinsic value of a commodity was determined by the amount of land and labour that went into its production. The par between land and labour was determined by the amount of land that was needed to produce enough consumption goods to enable a worker to survive and reproduce. Cantillon thus had a land theory of value.

Apart from its providing an explanation of the relative prices around which market prices fluctuated, Cantillon's land theory of value provided the basis for his claim that 'All classes and individuals in a state subsist or are enriched at the expense of the proprietors of land' (Cantillon, 1755, p. 43). This is like Marx's later argument about the exploitation of labour, but applied to landowners.

The Physiocrats

Many of Cantillon's ideas were taken up by a group of men who were the first to describe themselves as 'economists'. Though they described themselves as 'Les Economistes', however, they are more widely known as the 'Physiocrats' on account of their belief that nature should be left to run its course (the literal meaning of 'physiocracy' is 'the rule of nature'). Pre-eminent amongst them was Quesnay, the author of the remarkable 'tableau economique'.

The purpose of the tableau economique (see pp. 9–12) was that of 'displaying expenditure and products in a way which is easy to grasp, and for the purpose of forming a clear opinion about the organization and disorganization which the government can bring about' (Quesnay, quoted in Meek, 1962 p. 108). Discussions of the tableau often focus on some of the assumptions on which it is based, assumptions which today seem peculiar. In particular Quesnay, influenced by Cantillon, saw only agriculture as being productive: it is the contribution of the land which enables agriculture to produce a surplus. In contrast, manufacturing is 'sterile', the value of its product being no greater than the value of the inputs used up. To stress this, however, is to miss the main point, which is that whilst many previous writers had some notion of an economic equilibrium, and whilst they understood that the various parts of an economy interacted with each other, it was Quesnay who first provided a formal model of such an equilibrium. Using Quesnay's *tableau* it is, for example, possible to work out *exactly* how a change in the landlords' spending will affect each of the two sectors, and it is possible to check that consumption is exactly matched by production of the appropriate goods, and each sector has an income sufficient to finance its expenditures. With Quesnay's *tableau*, therefore, there is a sense in which the theory of supply and demand in the economy as a whole is for the first time described sufficiently precisely to see whether or not it is coherent.

6.4 ADAM SMITH

The works discussed so far comprise only a tiny fraction of the economic literature of the sixteenth, seventeenth and early eighteenth centuries. They are enough, however, to establish that, by the time Adam Smith came to publish his celebrated *Inquiry into the Nature and Causes of the Wealth of Nations* (1776), the notion that economic affairs should be analysed in terms of an equilibrium based on supply and demand was well established. Supply and demand were seen as a general explanation of market prices; in addition some economists explained the level about which prices fluctuated in terms of costs. Furthermore, the markets for different goods were recognized to be interdependent, the price system being seen as a means of allocating resources in the economy as a whole. The existence of this literature explains the view of some authorities that there were no really novel ideas in the *Wealth of Nations*.

Of what then did Smith's achievement consist? Three things are worth picking out. (1) As the title of his main work indicates, his subject matter was the nature and causes of the wealth of nations. Smith focused attention on economic growth in a way not true of any of the economists mentioned above, this concern dominating economics for the next century. (2) He provided a systematic appraisal of government policy. (3) He provided a far more systematic account of the operation of the market mechanism than had any of his predecessors.

Smith's theory of the market mechanism is based on the concepts of market and natural price. The former is the price determined by supply and demand, whereas the latter (Cantillon's 'intrinsic' value) was the price about which prices tended to gravitate. Though more elegantly expressed, this was substantially the theory of Locke and Cantillon. Where Smith went beyond any of his predecessors was in providing a more satisfactory account of what determined natural price, and in doing so providing an account of the interdependence of the markets for goods and for factors of production: land, labour and capital.

Smith explained natural price in terms of costs of production, these comprising wages, profits and rents, each paid at the 'ordinary' rate. The rates of wages, profits and rents were determined in similar manner. The natural rate of wages, for example, depended upon the amount necessary for a man to maintain himself and his family, but rose above this rate in an advancing economy, and fell below it in a declining economy. Similarly the natural rate of profits depended on whether society was advancing or declining, though with profits the connection was the other way round: in an advancing economy capital was accumulating and competition kept profits low, whilst in a declining economy capital was scarce and profits high. Smith has been criticized for circular reasoning here, but such a charge is unfounded. What Smith is doing is explaining the interdependence of commodity and factor markets: factor prices depend on factor demands and hence on commodity prices and outputs; commodity prices depend on costs, and hence on factor prices.

6.5   CLASSICAL ECONOMICS

Despite the scope and quality of earlier economic writings it was Smith's *Wealth of Nations* which dominated the economics of the following century, to the exclusion of virtually all earlier writings. This book, however, contained numerous ideas, capable of being developed in a number of directions. For many economists the Smithian theoretical framework was sufficient. They could use it to approach questions of economic policy, or as the basis for empirical research. Others, whilst remaining strongly under Smith's influence, moved in the direction of a subjective, utility-based theory of value. However, the most noticeable development, in England at least, was that associated with David Ricardo. Though Ricardo's influence *never* eclipsed that of Smith, his importance is such that subsequent developments cannot possibly be understood without examining his contribution in some detail.

In the words of a leading authority on Ricardo, 'If economics is essentially an engine of analysis, a method of thinking rather than a body of substantial results, Ricardo literally invented the technique of economics' (Blaug, 1985, pp. 135–6). To see what is meant by this we have to return to Smith's *Wealth of Nations*. This book presented a theory of how a market economy operated, but although the theory was a relatively simple one it remained fairly 'realistic'. The reason for this is not simply, or even primarily, that the book contained much historical, and factual material (though this is true) but rather than the concepts analysed in the theory were easily understood generalizations about a real economy. It was easy, for example, to understand the significance of terms such as the stock of necessaries or division of labour. When we come to Ricardo's work, on the other hand, this is no longer possible, for his theory is made much more precise in that it deals with a hypothetical economy in which many characteristics of the real world are assumed to be absent. Although in one sense anyone who makes any generalizations at all is using a model, it can legitimately be argued that Ricardo argued in terms of an economic 'model' in a way that Smith did not.

The best way to see this is to consider, very briefly, some of the technical problems that arose in Ricardo's theory of growth (see pp. 19 and 63). There were two critical aspects of this theory. (1) There was an inverse relationship between wages and profits (whenever the wage rate rose the rate of profit fell, and vice-versa). (2) The rate of profit depended on 'agricultural' productivity, and was unaffected by what happened in manufacturing. In his first work on the subject, his *Essay on the Influence of a Low Price of Corn on the Profits of Stock* (1815), Ricardo ensures that both these propositions are true by using a 'corn model'. He assumes that there is a single agricultural commodity, corn, which is both input and output. The wage rate can be measured in terms of kilos (of corn) per day; the capital stock can be measured in kilos of corn; and because farmers' revenues and costs can both be measured as quantities of corn, the rate of profit is the ratio of two quantities of corn. There is no need to bring prices into it at all. The rate of profit, therefore, depends simply on agricultural productivity and the wage rate in terms of corn. Ricardo then assumes that competition will ensure that the same rate of profit is earned in industry as in agriculture (otherwise capitalists would move capital from one to the other), which means that the rate of profit in agriculture determines the rate of profit in the economy as a whole.

Given the assumptions of the corn model these conclusions are watertight. In reality, however, workers consume more than simply corn, and in addition agricultural production requires inputs not only of labour and seed-corn, but also machinery. If he wanted his conclusions to apply to the real world, therefore, Ricardo had to show that the real world worked in substantially the same way as his corn model. To do this he needed to aggregate: to add quantities of different commodities together so that he could argue in terms of a single commodity, 'corn'. If commodities were to be added together he needed a set of prices, and hence a theory of value. It is here that the labour theory of value comes into Ricardo's theory.

However, Ricardo discovered that when he considered a more general model the labour theory of value did not hold: the value of a good would not in general be proportional to the amount of labour required to produce it. In addition, the rate of profit in agriculture would depend on the prices of industrial goods. To see this, consider the effects of a rise in industrial productivity (say the costs of producing clothing have fallen). The price of clothing will fall, which means that, if competition forces wages down to subsistence, wages will fall. As nothing has happened to change the price of corn, the rate of profit in agriculture will rise. Ricardo's corn model is undermined.

Because of these problems Ricardo devoted an enormous amount of energy to trying to find a way of measuring prices in such a way that the results of the corn model would be true in a more general model: he was aware of the technical problems that might occur in a world with many commodities and he sought some way of getting round them (his search for an 'invariable measure of value').

The result of all this was that, for all that they had in common, and this was a great deal, Ricardo's method was clearly very different from Smith's. Ricardo was analysing the economy in terms of a highly simplified 'model'. Theoretical problems, arising out of the attempt to achieve logical rigour, impelled Ricardo's analysis in a way not true of Smith's. The main example of this was the theory of value. Where Smith refers to an invariable measure of value his concern is the very down-to-earth one of assessing changes in the standard of living over time. Ricardo, on the other hand, needed an invariable measure of value in order to overcome the problems which arose when his corn model was extended to encompass more than one commodity. Despite the very abstract nature of some of the issues considered (in particular the technicalities of the labour theory of value) this abstract theorizing was relevant to a practical problem of great importance: the validity of the results obtained from Ricardo's corn model. It is this attempt at rigorous economic theory that is the basis for the claim, quoted above, that Ricardo invented the technique of economics.

Ricardo had an enormous influence on English classical economics. His vision of the process of economic growth as dependent on a limited supply of cultivable land was widely shared. His method of 'strong cases' (using simplifying assumptions) could not be ignored. In addition, he made important contributions to a number of areas of economics, most notably the theory of international trade (see p. 59). Despite this, however, classical economics was not simply Ricardian economics. Classical economics was concerned principally not with model-building but with policy, and the usefulness of models for policy-making could be disputed. Additionally, Ricardo's theory was subject to very severe criticism at an early stage, a number of important attempts being made to provide alternatives to his theory of value. Rather than consider these, however, we now turn to the type of economics that, from the 1870s and 1880s, began to displace classical economics.

6.6 NEOCLASSICAL ECONOMICS

Early neoclassical economics

From the 1870s and 1880s economics came to be dominated by a new type of deductive theory, which soon came to be labelled 'neoclassical'. The reason for this label was that, although it differed markedly from the classical economics of Smith and Ricardo, neoclassical economics was, like classical economics, based on deductive reasoning: assumptions were specified, and logical analysis used to work out the implications of these assumptions. This was in sharp contrast to the historical approach, dominant in Germany and very strong in England and the US. The ideas underlying neoclassical economics had a long history, and can be found very clearly expressed in the work of the French engineers such as Dupuit (see p. 67). They took off, however, only after the 1870s, when three economists, William Stanley Jevons (working in England), Carl Menger (in Austria) and Leon Walras (in France) published books in which value was explained in terms of 'marginal utility'. This was the so-called 'marginal revolution'.

Central to neoclassical economics is the notion of general competitive equilibrium. This notion of equilibrium has much in common with Adam Smith's: prices are viewed as being determined by supply and demand in a system of interlinked, competitive markets. The neoclassical economists, the most important of whom were Marshall (1890) and Walras (1874), however, departed from their classical predecessors in describing such an equilibrium in terms of a set of equations. These equations can be divided into four main categories. (1) Demand equations, dependent on consumers' tastes, which describe how demand for each commodity will change when prices change. (2) Equations describing how supplies of commodities will respond to changes in prices and costs. (3) Equations describing demands for factor services (labour and the use of capital goods). These equations, together with those describing commodity supply, are derived from assuming that firms maximize profits. Underlying them are (i) an equation linking the price of each commodity to the cost of producing it, and (ii) production functions, describing the commodities that can be produced using different combinations of inputs. (4) For each factor there will be an equation determining how much will be supplied at different sets of prices. These equations will depend on the preferences of the owners of factors concerned (for example, the value they set on leisure compared with income). This set of equations contains exactly the right number of equations to determine the unknowns, namely the quantity of each commodity produced, the amount of each factor used, the price of each factor, and the relative prices of all commodities (prices have to be measured in terms of something, so we have arbitrarily to set the price of this commodity equal to 1).

A number of points need to be made about this approach to the problem of general equilibrium. The first is that demand is placed alongside supply: neither can be neglected, for they determine prices and quantities together. This is in contrast with the classical approach, for though the classical economists recognized that demand could influence price, they tended to restrict its influence to goods such as paintings by the old masters, the supply of which was fixed. For most of the time the classical economists emphasized cost of production, an aspect of supply, as the determinant of value.

Given this increased role for demand, there was a need to explain how demands were determined. The neoclassical economists explained demand in terms of consumer preferences, which they analysed in terms of 'utility'. Utility in this context did not denote 'usefulness', but rather 'well-being' or 'satisfaction'. Saying that consumers maximized their utility was simply another way of saying that consumers were assumed to make themselves as well off as possible.

Such a set of equations defines an equilibrium which has much in common with Smith's conception of economic equilibrium: prices and the allocation of resources are determined by supply and demand; prices are equal to costs of production, these in turn being dependent on supply and demand in factor markets, this determining the prices of factors and hence costs. It was, however, much more abstract and less realistic. The advantage of this greater abstraction was much greater precision: describing supply and demand in terms of a set of equations made it possible, for the first time, to discover exactly how it worked. The cost was that important issues, of great concern to Smith, were neglected. The neoclassical system is much more static than Smith's. The question of division of labour and increasing returns to scale, so important to Smith, was largely ignored. Where Smith was concerned primarily with increasing the overall level of economic activity, the neoclassical economists were primarily (though by no means exclusively) concerned with the allocation of given resources. A significant exception was Alfred Marshall, who did try to reconcile economies of scale with neoclassical theory, but he ran into difficulties which he solved only at the cost of being rather vague about certain crucial assumptions.

Because of this different emphasis, competition is conceived very differently. For neoclassical economics, competition has two aspects: individual firms and households have no influence over market prices (they are too small) and firms can make no more than the normal rate of profit (the appropriate rate of interest). For Smith, on the other hand, competition was much more of a dynamic phenomenon, causing excess profits to be eliminated: though Smith's competitive economy might be conceived of as moving towards a neoclassical type of equilibrium, he did not analyse it in these terms.

As a result of this new approach to analysing the economy there was a change of emphasis. The classical problem of growth was not neglected, but less emphasis was placed on it, for the new techniques opened up new areas of inquiry. Questions of resource allocation could be analysed far more satisfactorily than the classical economists had been able to do. The bringing in of utility opened up the area known as 'welfare economics', for wealth and welfare could now be distinguished: it was possible to differentiate between the utility of a commodity and its price. In addition, neoclassical techniques, with their emphasis on analysing individual behaviour, made it possible for the first time to provide an analysis of monopoly. Neoclassical theories of monopoly may be inadequate, but monopoly was a subject the classical economists could not even start to investigate.

The development of neoclassical economics

In one sense, once we reach the work of Walras and even more once we reach the second generation of neoclassical economists (Marshall, Pareto, Wicksell, Edgeworth) whose main contributions date from the 1880s and 1890s, we have reached modern economics. Walras's elements have been described as 'the Magna Carta of exact economics' (Blaug, 1985, p. 585), and it has been suggested that 'nearly all economics nowadays [1985] *is* Walrasian economics'. In another sense, however, neoclassical economics has, even when we confine our attention to the theory of economic equilibrium, changed profoundly since the turn of the twentieth century.

The most obvious aspect of this change has been improvements in technique. There is not only the use of much more sophisticated mathematical techniques, one of the main influences here being Paul Samuelson's *Foundations of Economic Analysis* (1947), but also the development of much more precisely. defined economic concepts. These improvements in technique have had two effects. The first is that the theory of how a market economy in which prices are determined by supply and demand has been much more elegantly stated and more thoroughly understood, with many of the loose ends being tied up. The second result of economists' having access to improved analytical techniques is that they have been able to tackle problems their predecessors could never tackle. Both of these need to be considered in more detail, since it is these aspects of contemporary economics that have been criticized for being excessively abstract. Rather than attempt to provide a survey of contemporary economic theory we will consider some examples.

General equilibrium theory since Walras

The process of tying up the loose ends in Walras's general equilibrium theory was started in the 1930s. Gustav Cassel (see also p. 144) had, in 1918, written down a simplified version of Walras's system of equations, and although this was of little value in itself it prompted a number of economists to investigate it more thoroughly. It was found, for example, that when you solved Cassel's equations some of the prices might turn out to be negative, which did not make sense. In addition, it was shown that if there were too few commodities in the model it might be impossible to have an equilibrium with supply equal to demand in every market. To solve these problems the model was modified to allow for the possibility that a market might be in equilibrium with supply greater than demand provided that price was zero. On a beach, for example, there is excess supply of seawater and its price is zero. Though this assumption was introduced to solve the technical problems we have just mentioned, it nonetheless has an economic significance and constitutes an undoubted improvement in the theory.

A related line of inquiry started in the 1930s when two mathematicians, Abraham Wald and John von Neumann, tried to prove rigorously the conditions under which a set of supply and demand equations would have a meaningful solution. This process was continued in the 1950s, leading to what has come to be known as the Arrow–Debreu model, the definitive statement of which is found in Gerard Debreu's *The Theory of Value* (1959). Arrow and Debreu were able to show that if consumers' preferences and the technology available to firms had certain characteristics, and if there were a complete set of markets, an equilibrium would necessarily exist. In addition, it was shown that such an equilibrium would be efficient in the *very limited* sense that, starting from such an equilibrium, it would be impossible to re-allocate resources so as to make one person better off without making someone else worse off: it would be impossible to make *everyone* better off. Such an equilibrium is said to be 'Pareto-efficient' or 'Pareto-optimal'.

No one who understands the Arrow–Debreu model has ever claimed that it describes any actual economy, so why do economists pay any attention to it? There are three main reasons. The first is that supply and demand theory is used to analyse many problems. Proofs of the existence of equilibrium show that this theory is not vacuous: that it is possible for there to be an equilibrium. This is not something that should be taken for granted, despite the apparent simplicity of the theory of supply and demand. The second is that such theory shows how stringent are the conditions for an equilibrium to be optimal, even in the very limited sense defined above. A particularly important condition is that there is a complete set of futures and insurance markets: that it must be possible to insure against *any* eventuality whatsoever and that it must be possible to sign a contract for delivery of *any* commodity at *any* time in the future. Such markets clearly do not exist. Finally, the Arrow–Debreu model provides a framework for thinking about economic problems. When, for example, we find that a model (whether of price stabilization in developing countries or of employment contracts in the US) does not produce an efficient allocation of resources we can approach the problem by trying to work out which markets are missing. This is worthwhile if it leads to new insights that we might otherwise not discover.

The economics of information

In addition to refining already-existing theory economists have applied economic theory to totally new problems. As an example consider the very important area of the economics of information. One of the most well-known papers in this area is George Akerlof's 'The market for "lemons"' (1970). Akerlof analyses the used car market by making the assumption that sellers of used cars know whether or not their car is a bad one (a 'lemon') but that potential buyers do not. To simplify the problem assume that there are simply two qualities of used car (good ones worth $900, mediocre ones worth $500 and bad ones worth $100) and that these exist in equal numbers. If the price is $900 the cars offered for sale will include equal numbers of good, mediocre and bad ones, which means that the average value of cars on sale will thus be $500, which means that buyers will not be prepared to pay $900 (remember that buyers cannot tell which cars are the good ones). If the price is $500, good cars will not be offered for sale and so the average value of cars on the market will be $300. Still no cars will be sold. The only equilibrium price is $100: at this price the value of cars offered for sale will be $100 and buyers will be prepared to buy them. The only possible equilibrium price, therefore, is the price of the worst used car on the market. Trade in higher-quality used cars will not take place.

This example is obviously an extreme one, for in practice buyers will normally have some, possibly limited, information about cars they are buying. In addition, buyers may be willing to take a risk even when the odds are stacked against them. Akerlof's model, however, is nonetheless invaluable in focusing attention on the role of information and on the problems which must be overcome if such a market is to work properly, for similar problems occur in many other markets. The market for insurance is a particularly important example, for insurance companies are faced with the problem that they are frequently unable to distinguish between high- and low-risk customers until after they have sold them a policy. If an insurance company bases the prices of its insurance policies on the average level of risk, it will attract only those customers with a higher than average level of risk. Using such arguments it is possible to show that an equilibrium may not even exist in this market, in the sense that whatever is the price of insurance contracts, companies will want to set a different one.

There are two ways of overcoming the problems which arise in such markets. One is for sellers of high-quality goods and services to find a way of getting this information across to potential buyers. This is referred to as 'signalling'. The best example is probably that of education where, even if education did not make workers more productive, a high level of education might signal a high level of productivity (see Spence, 1973). If it is easier (cheaper) for high-productivity workers to acquire education than for low-productivity ones to do so, then it is possible to have an equilibrium where: (a) employers assume that better-educated workers will be more productive; (b) high-productivity workers decide that it is worth obtaining education; and (c) low-productivity workers decide not to buy education. In such an equilibrium, employers' expectations about the link between education and productivity turn out to be justified, even though education may not raise productivity at all.

It might seem that education and company financial behaviour had nothing in common, but the same arguments about why workers might use education as a signal of ability can be used to provide a reason why companies might choose to pay dividends. The problem with dividends is that if, as is the case in many countries, dividend income is taxed at a higher rate than capital gains, it makes no sense for companies to pay dividends: shareholders would pay less tax if income were retained by companies, raising share values and providing them with capital gains. Shareholders wanting regular income could, provided the cost of selling shares was not too high, obtain it by selling shares. What makes the problem similar to the problem of workers selling their labour is that shareholders have incomplete information about the companies in which they might invest: managers will always wish to present their companies in the best possible light, which means that company reports will not provide an adequate picture of what is going on. It has been shown that if paying dividends is more expensive for less profitable companies (perhaps because paying higher dividends raises the risk that the firm will go bankrupt) it is possible to have an equilibrium where shareholders view dividends as a signal of profitability and where only the more profitable companies find it worth paying dividends. Like education, dividends may be used as a signal.

6.7   THE EVOLUTION OF ECONOMIC THEORY

In this chapter we have traced a number of stages in the evolution of the theory of supply and demand: (1) the emergence of the notion of a market economy, with people responding to profit incentives (Sir Thomas Smith); (2) the attempt to generalize about how prices and the allocation of resources are determined in a market economy (Locke, North); (3) the formulation of a coherent notion of supply and demand equilibrium in the economy as a whole (Adam Smith); (4) abstract modelling of such an equilibrium (Ricardo); (5) the mathematical description of a general equilibrium model (Walras and Marshall); (6) the development of a general equilibrium model to the stage where it can be used to analyse problems beyond the scope of earlier theories (the twentieth century). The story has been told in terms of a gradual refinement of economic ideas, this process leading towards general equilibrium theory. It is important to stress, however, that this is only one of many strands in the evolution of economic ideas, and that whilst this account of the history of economic thought is a defensible one, it is very much simplified. There have been many detours, with economists forgetting, or choosing to ignore, lessons learned by their predecessors.

One point of view, taken by Schumpeter (1954) is that there is one general equilibrium system, and Walras discovered it. Given this perspective, which has an important element of truth in it, accounts of the history of economic thought such as that given here are quite acceptable (though it is important to note that this chapter has *not* been concerned with providing a general history of economic thought, or even of economic theory: merely of the theory of economic equilibrium). To say, however, that there is just one system of general equilibrium is misleading, for the Walrasian model of competitive equilibrium is a very partial account of an economy. It assumes, for example, that consumers' preferences are given outside the model, and it assumes universal price-taking behaviour. Though these may be acceptable simplifications some of the time, neither of them is an accurate description of the real world. Thus although the neoclassical (Walrasian) system of general competitive equilibrium may be the only model of multi-market equilibrium that economists have so far been able completely to understand, it does not follow that this will always remain the case. It is quite possible that economists may come up with a model based on quite different assumptions, and that this will change the way we view both neoclassical economics and the history of economic theory.

Alongside the economics discussed in the preceding chapters there exists a large range of different approaches to economics (post-Keynesian economics, neo-Ricardian economics, Marxist economics, radical economics, institutionalism, 'Austrian' economics) each of which offers an alternative to the neoclassical perspective. The proponents of these approaches have many interesting points to make, ranging from the pervasiveness of uncertainty about the future and the limitations this imposes on the possibilities for rational choice, to the fact that individuals' preferences and tastes are socially conditioned, to the role of class conflict and power in economics. Some of these points will, quite likely, turn out to be very important. These alternatives have not, however, succeeded in displacing neoclassical economics from its central position in the subject. There are no doubt many reasons for this, from professional conservatism and the 'glamour' and prestige attached to the use of advanced mathematics understood only by a few, to the support that neoclassical economics is thought (erroneously) to offer to certain political positions. Above all these reasons, however, is the fact that none of these alternative approaches has yet discovered an investigative logic to parallel that of neoclassical economics. Neoclassical economics has proved capable of illuminating an ever-increasing variety of economic problems and the range of its applicability shows no signs of diminishing.

7

The Discipline of
Economics

7.1 THE CONTRIBUTION OF ECONOMIC THEORY

When we look at the evolution of the discipline of economics over the past four centuries, two things stand out above all others. We now know much more about the economic phenomena we are dealing with than did our predecessors. Particularly notable has been the increased quantity and quality of statistical data: just as the statistics available to Marx and the classical economists were far superior to the intelligent guesses of Petty and his contemporaries, so too are present-day statistics, for all their limitations, far and away superior to those available even at the end of the nineteenth century. The other significant feature of the past few centuries' economic thought is the development and refinement of the theory of supply and demand, discussed in chapter 6, which provided the foundation on which most theoretical advances in applied fields have been based.

Up to the 1870s it is easy to tell the story of the development of economic theory in terms of factors external to the discipline. Though both the classical economists and their predecessors were concerned to develop general principles, practical problems, often very urgent ones, were never far away. Smith's *Wealth of Nations* was centred around the problem of economic growth, and classical economics, dominated by this book, remained overwhelmingly policy-oriented throughout its existence. Even Ricardo's abstractions were used to derive conclusions of direct policy relevance. With the advent of marginalist economics, however, this changed. Although economists continued to be concerned with practical issues, economic theory began to develop a momentum of its own. The calculus of maximizing behaviour provided a wealth of opportunities for abstract speculation, with theoretical puzzles playing an increasing role in setting the agenda for research. After the Second World War, as economists became better trained in mathematics, and hence in formal economic theory, this dominance of theory increased still further.

As we saw in chapter 1, the extent of such theorizing, and the level of abstraction involved, has been widely criticized. Much of this criticism is probably justified. Economists have almost certainly investigated abstract theoretical issues which will have little or no bearing on any real-world problem. The academic system may well give excessive rewards to those proficient in abstract, mathematical theory, at the expense of those who concern themselves with problems such as how to obtain new sources of data. All economists could give examples of research they consider over- or under-rated. To test such propositions is, however, rather difficult, for a number of reasons. For example there is, in the above arguments, a presumption that those currently engaging in 'excessively' abstract speculation would produce more worthwhile results if they were to turn their attention to empirical research. This may well be the case, but it is a proposition that is very hard to test.

How then, can we defend economic theory? The obvious way is to point out that it is impossible to make sense of empirical data without any theory. If we had no explicit, formal economic theories, we would have to rely on what has been described as 'Do it Yourself Economics' (Henderson, 1985). In the words of Walter Heller, an economist involved in policy-making in the US for many years, 'Behind every false dictate of common sense lies a primitive and misbegotten economic theory' (Heller, 1975, p. 5). Contemporary economic theory, it can be argued, provides a more reliable perspective than 'uneducated' common sense, sometimes producing policy conclusions that are contrary to common sense. To quote Heller again,

much of our economic analysis and the uncommon sense growing out of it fly in the face of 'common sense,' for example: that budget deficits need not spell inflation, nor national debt a burden to our grandchildren; that thriftiness can be a mixed virtue; that while exploding oil prices *in*flate costs, they *de*flate demand; that in an overheated economy, greater taxes can be a lesser evil; and so on. (Heller, 1975, p. 5) This is not to say, of course, that economists will always be right. Like anyone else they have made and always will make many mistakes.

In addition to its value in providing a more reliable guide than common sense, economic theory is important because it enables us to answer some much more fundamental questions about the economy. Take the basic notion of an economy regulated by supply and demand in all markets. Economic theory is needed to say whether such a vision of the economy is coherent: only if we can show that an equilibrium will exist in such an economy can we be sure that any theory based on supply and demand is not vacuous, something we should not take for granted. In addition, economic theory can be used to ascertain the conditions under which an economy based on supply and demand will allocate resources efficiently. It has been shown that there are serious limits to what markets can do. For example, it has been shown that unregulated markets will fail to regulate pollution efficiently; that under some circumstances the threat of takeover may not be sufficient to make managers run a firm in the interests of its shareholders; that if information about the quality of a good is limited, market equilibrium may be impossible. By the same token it has been shown that there may also be limitations as to what governments can do: there is not only 'market failure' but also 'government failure'.

Finally, economic theory provides a framework within which we can view economic problems. Inevitably this means adopting a set of blinkers, but the alternative is to adopt a different set of blinkers, not to adopt an 'unblinkered' approach. The idea of a science based solely on empirical data, without any theory, is illusory, as theories are needed before any sense can be made of data. The set of blinkers implicit in mainstream economic theory (the theory we are concerned with in this book) can be justified in two ways. We can argue that the assumption of rational behaviour, for all its limitations, provides the best foundation for economic theory that we can hope to have. Alternatively, we can defend the theory by arguing that it works when confronted with empirical data. This is the subject of the following section.

By way of conclusion to this section, consider the following statement by Frank Hahn, a leading British economic theorist:

At the end of it all I want to praise theorizing in economics because it is one of the highways to understanding and because it has already provided a good deal of it. I want to praise it for its modesty and honesty and also for the occasional excitement and beauty which it provides. Above all I want to praise it for this: no-one who has seriously theorized can be enslaved by the slogans and shibboleths of practical men and women who have not. No-one accustomed to the discipline of coherence and proof will fall a victim to such people. If we were all theorists it might just be a better world. (Hahn, 1985, p. 20)

Hahn is right in claiming that economic theory provides not only beauty and excitement but also a great deal of understanding. The rest of the passage, however, if taken as an description of economics as it exists today, would seem to contain a large element of wishful thinking. Theorists are often far from modest in their claims (Ricardo, Keynes and Lucas are examples of outstanding economic theorists whose claims have been anything but modest). Theorists, like anyone else, have been trapped by over-simple 'slogans and shibboleths'. Furthermore, theory on its own is as sterile as unthinking data collection. If, on the other hand, we take Hahn's words as describing what ought to be, they make a great deal of sense. 'The discipline of coherence and proof', as he calls it, should lead us to question simple solutions to economic problems. Theorizing should not only provide understanding but it should also make us aware of the limits of our knowledge.

7.2 ECONOMIC THEORY AND EMPIRICAL EVIDENCE

The problem

It is abundantly clear that, whether or not they exist in the natural sciences (and this is a debated point), 'crucial experiments' do not exist in economics. Theories have rarely, if ever, been rejected after a statistical test has shown them to be inconsistent with the data. Theories have been abandoned, but this has been a much more gradual process. For example, structuralist development economics was abandoned not because it was refuted by specific statistical tests, but because economists found better ways of making sense of what was happening in poor countries (see p. 41). In addition, empirical evidence seems incapable of settling many issues, the controversy between Monetarists and Keynesians being the prime example. How should we respond to this?

The rhetoric of economics

One response to this problem is that offered by Donald McCloskey (1985). He has claimed that many misunderstandings arise because economists have no official rhetoric to describe what it is that they find persuasive in economic arguments. The 'official rhetoric' of economics (what is taught about methodology in elementary textbooks, and what most economists would say if pressed) emphasizes the testing of economic theories against empirical data, with theories being rejected when they are inconsistent with the data. Such a methodology can be described as simple (some would say naive) falsificationism, for it is based on the belief that good theories are falsifiable, and that the major function of empirical work is the weeding out of false theories through showing that they are inconsistent with empirical evidence. This viewpoint is reinforced by Milton Friedman's 'Methodology of positive economics' (1953), an article which most economists have probably read at some stage in their careers. Friedman's main thesis in this article is that the *only* valid test of a theory is the comparison of its predictions with empirical data. Whether or not a theory's assumptions are realistic, Friedman claims, is beside the point, for predictive power is all that matters. However, although economists speak as though they choose between theories according to their predictive power, this is not in fact the case. In practice, McCloskey argues, the things that persuade economists to take ideas seriously are very different, and as a result the process whereby certain theories are rejected in favour of others is much more complicated.

To demonstrate this, McCloskey considers the example of Samuelson's *Foundations of Economic Analysis* (1947), a book which laid the foundations for most post-war economic theory. This book is replete with references to empirical testing. Samuelson defends his approach to economic theory as being directed at deriving what he calls 'operationally meaningful theorems', theorems which could, if only under ideal conditions, be tested. He did not, however, test any of his theorems. Why, then, did so many economists find his arguments persuasive? McCloskey suggests a number of reasons. (1) Samuelson cites many authorities in support of his arguments. (2) He exhibits an effortless familiarity with complex mathematics, his language implying that mathematical results are both easy and certain, whilst the economics is more uncertain. For example, when expounding mathematical results he uses 'We', whilst in discussing economic issues he uses 'I'. (3) He uses numerous metaphors and analogies. (4) He appeals to philosophical consistency. (5) He appeals to hypothetical, 'toy' economies to support his conclusions. It is devices such as these, McCloskey claims, not any demonstration that his conclusions were consistent with empirical data, that persuaded his audience.

Taking a more recent example, McCloskey examines the rhetoric of John Muth, the inventor of rational expectations, the concept that has done so much to transform macroeconomics in the past decade (see p. 162). In the article in which he first wrote about rational expectations Muth, like Samuelson, appeals to what McCloskey calls the 'modernist' methodology of empirical testing: 'The only real test, however, is whether theories involving rationality explain observed phenomena any better than any alternative theories.' Muth's real appeal, however, is very different. (1) He appeals to philosophical consistency: the usual models 'do not assume enough rationality'; 'rationality is assumed in all other aspects of entrepreneurial behaviour', and hence it ought to be applied to the formation of expectations. (2) He uses analogies, comparing information about future hog prices with any other good that can be bought and sold: 'information is scarce, and the economic system generally does not waste it'. (3) He appeals to 'purely theoretical arguments', such as the advantages of being able to model expectations in the same way in a large variety of models. These theoretical arguments are, McCloskey claims, purely aesthetic. When it comes to empirical testing, the data Muth cites are far from conclusive. McCloskey is thus led to the conclusion that,

The persuasiveness of Muth's paper comes from the richness and catholicity of its unofficial arguments, well beyond the official narrowness [i.e. falsificationism]. Among economists an argument from axiomatic demonstration, statistical test (regression in particular), or appeal to the competitive model all have prestige. None is logically compelling, nor even very persuasive by itself. One can object to each that garbage in implies garbage out. Yet the most hostile economist, if properly socialized, will want to yield to the form. He will be pleased by their success at a formal level – 'Gosh, what a clever argument that is: What a neat proof/statistical test/appeal to the intellectual traditions of economics' – even if he wants to disbelieve the substance. (McCloskey, 1985, p. 104)

Samuelson and Muth are clearly exceptional economic theorists, but the style of their arguments is, as any economist will testify, typical of much present-day theoretical work. Elegance is greatly prized. Theories are frequently not tested.

McCloskey argues that economists should stop pretending that they decide between theories according to the results of empirical testing. They should stop claiming that there is a single, correct way to undertake economic inquiries. Any prescriptive methodology is, he claims, presumptuous and laughable: 'Einstein remarked that "whoever undertakes to set himself up as a judge in the field of Truth and Knowledge is shipwrecked by the laughter of the gods." . . . Any methodology that is lawmaking and limiting will have this risible effect' (McCloskey, 1985, p. 20). The alternative to methodology is, for McCloskey, to study rhetoric: a literary way of understanding conversation, the conversation of economists and mathematicians as much as of poets and novelists. Economists are not experts; they are, McCloskey claims, basically persuaders, and instead of trying to fit their work into an out-of-date methodology they should analyse the methods they use to persuade. If economists were to do this, McCloskey claims, then their writing would be improved; their teaching would be more accessible; they would communicate better with practitioners in other disciplines and, above all, the nature of economic argument would be improved.

Many of McCloskey's points are undoubtedly very important. Economists are, in common with almost anyone who has something to say, persuaders. As such they use numerous rhetorical devices. His thesis, however, begs the all important questions of why economists find certain arguments persuasive and whether there is any rationale other than simply persuasion underlying what they do. It is certainly true, as McCloskey argues, that naive falsificationism is untenable, but this is not the same as saying that there is no underlying logic of discovery in economics. We need to turn, therefore, to the question of whether or not we can find an alternative rationale for the way economics is developing.

The methodology of scientific research programmes

As was mentioned above, economists frequently continue to support their theories in the face of empirical evidence which suggests that they are false. There are a number of reasons for this which are specific to economics. For example, economic data are always changing, which means that the testing of economic theories is always much more problematic than is the case in the natural sciences. More important than this, it can be argued that the vision of a science, whether economics or any other, as progressing by a series of 'crucial experiments', each of which leads to the rejection of one theory in favour of another, is inappropriate. Even in the natural sciences there are numerous examples of anomalies: empirical phenomena which are inconsistent with the ruling theory, but which are not regarded as refuting it. Such phenomena are regarded as puzzles that have not yet been solved.

One theory about how sciences develop, which takes account of such problems, is Imre Lakatos's 'Methodology of scientific research programmes'. According to this theory we should be concentrating not on individual theories, but on what he terms 'scientific research programmes'. Central to any research programme is its 'hard core', a set of assumptions and theories that must not be questioned if the research programme is to continue. Outside this hard core we have what Lakatos called the 'protective belt' of auxiliary hypotheses and assumptions. These are assumptions which we are free to change or modify as much as necessary in order to reconcile empirical evidence with the hard core. The way this works is clearly described by Lakatos:

the typical descriptive unit of great scientific achievements is not an isolated hypothesis but rather a research programme. Science is not simply trial and error, a series of conjectures and refutations. 'All swans are white' may be falsified by the discovery of one black swan. But such trivial trial and error does not rank as science. Newtonian science, for instance, is not simply a set of four conjectures – the three laws of mechanics and the law of gravitation. These four laws constitute only the 'hard core' of the Newtonian programme. But this hard core is tenaciously protected from refutation by a vast 'protective belt' of auxiliary hypotheses. And, even more importantly, the research programme also has a 'heuristic', that is, a powerful problem-solving machinery, which, with the help of sophisticated mathematical techniques, digests anomalies and even turns them into positive evidence. For instance, if a planet does not move as it should, the Newtonian scientist checks his conjectures concerning atmospheric refraction, concerning propagation of light in magnetic storms, and hundreds of other conjectures which are all part of the programme. He may even invent a hitherto unknown planet and calculate its position, mass and velocity in order to explain the anomaly. (Lakatos, 1978, I, p. 4)

Over time a scientific research programme will be modified in response to new facts. This may involve simply *ad hoc* adjustments, for which there is no clear rationale, with the theory becoming more and more complicated as a result. If this continues for too long the theory may become more complicated than the data it is trying to explain. The classic example of this is the Ptolemaic theory according to which all heavenly bodies moved in circles round the sun. When this was found inconsistent with the data, epicycles were introduced: planets were assumed to move in circles, the centres of which moved in circles round other circles which moved round the sun. As more and better observations were made, the number of such circles needed to explain the data increased very rapidly. Such a research programme is incapable of predicting new facts, and is labelled by Lakatos 'degenerating'. This is in contrast to the situation in a 'progressive' research programme. Progressive research programmes do change over time, but in such a way that their ability to predict new facts is enhanced, not reduced.

A research programme may go through several phases. If it is successful it will sooner or later become progressive, predicting new facts successfully, and with modifications to its theories increasing its predictive power. After a while, however, as new evidence emerges, the programme may start to degenerate, in that it may become possible to reconcile it with empirical evidence only by making arbitrary, *ad hoc*, modifications. If an alternative, progressive research programme emerges, scientists may abandon the old programme in favour of the alternative. The decision to abandon one programme in favour of another is, therefore, not because the old one is suddenly refuted, but because a better one appears. Scientists have to be persuaded that the new research programme is better than the old, such persuasion being achieved using all the rhetorical devices pointed out in the previous section.

When we come to interpret the history of economics in the light of these ideas we have to be careful, for a number of reasons. Although it has been shown to be an illuminating perspective from which to view certain episodes in the history of economic thought, it has not yet been established how far Lakatos's framework is an appropriate one for economics. In addition, there are a many levels at which Lakatos's methodology of scientific research programmes can be applied. We might, for example, view the whole of economics since Adam Smith (and maybe earlier) as comprising one large research programme. Alternatively we might focus on 'sub-programmes' within this larger programme: classical growth theory; Walrasian and neo-Walrasian economics; Keynesian economics; and so on. Or we might narrow things down still further, interpreting specific branches of the subject as scientific research programmes in their own right: human capital theory; the New Classical Macroeconomics.

A strong case can be made for regarding most contemporary, mainstream economics (the economics which forms the subject of this book) as comprising a single scientific research programme. It is often labelled either neoclassical economics or, after the economist who did most to establish it, 'neo-Walrasian' economics. Its central feature has been the progressive application of the principle of rational choice to all areas of economics, and to areas outside economics. Over the past few decades this programme has been extended to new areas, yielding new predictions and making sense of a wider and wider range of empirical phenomena. The pattern has emphatically not been one of a series of *ad hoc* adjustments, but rather the reverse. *Ad hoc* theories have been abandoned as economists have managed to explain more and more in terms of rational, maximizing behaviour. In one sense, therefore, economic theory today is simpler than it was. For example, in the 1950s it was possible to argue that macroeconomics and microeconomics were separate subjects, each based on a different set of assumptions. Today this is far less true, with both being based to a much greater extent on the assumption of individual maximizing behaviour.

One reason for the changes which have taken place in economic theory is changing intellectual standards. It is probably justifiable to say that most present-day economists expect theories to be mathematically more rigorous than did their predecessors, even 20 or 30 years ago. In addition, they attach much greater importance to theories' being based on maximizing behaviour than did their predecessors. But in addition, theories have changed in response to empirical evidence. Some of the best examples here are found in macroeconomics, where the demand-oriented theories of the 1950s and 1960s were found to be hopelessly inadequate when it came to analysing the supply shocks of the 1970s. Though important elements have been taken over from the earlier theories, supply-side factors are now given great prominence in any macroeconomic model. Similarly, the assumption of rational expectations, though introduced largely for theoretical reasons (it was an extension of the theory of rational behaviour to the problem of expectations), proved invaluable in making sense of observed empirical data, especially in the field of exchange rates.

7.3 THE STRENGTHS AND WEAKNESSES OF ECONOMICS

These arguments suggest that it is wrong to dismiss economics as being 'unscientific'. Learned journals certainly contain much that is going to be of little or no value to anyone, but despite this a strong case can be made that there is also much of great value, and that the subject is developing in a progressive manner. Thus although economists do use a large range of rhetorical devices when they seek to persuade each other, it is possible to discern a logic underlying the way the subject is developing.

This optimistic conclusion has, however, to be tempered with several notes of caution. The first is that the freedom allowed by Lakatos's methodology of scientific research programmes has two aspects. It allows fruitful ideas time to develop, recognizing that isolated tests of scientific theories can never, on their own, be completely persuasive. On the other hand, if the methodology is to mean anything at all it is necessary that there be an underlying commitment to the goal of producing, *in so far as this is possible*, successful predictions and, again *in so far as this is possible*, to test theories against empirical evidence. Certain things may be impossible to predict, and there are good reasons for saying that it is vital to understand, rather than simply to *outguess* our rivals: not only is understanding important for its own sake and as a means towards more reliable prediction, but it enables us to know something about the limits of our knowledge. We should thus take heed of Mark Blaug's admonition that,

> the ultimate question we can and indeed must pose about any research program is the one made familiar by Popper: what events, if they materialized, would lead us to reject that program? A program that cannot meet that question has fallen short of the highest standards that scientific knowledge can attain. (Blaug, 1980, p. 264)

Contrary to what McCloskey claims (see p. 188) there is nothing risible in this.

In addition to this danger of economic theories' losing touch with reality we have to face up to the limitations on what economists can achieve. These can be divided into two categories: limitations common to any type of economics, and limitations inherent in economics as it exists today. For many reasons economics lacks the relative certainty that can be found in the natural sciences. For all the progress that has been achieved over the past century in collecting and analysing empirical data (and this progress has been very substantial), economics lacks the solid empirical base characteristic of the natural sciences. Economics does not possess securely established empirical laws such as those that can be found in physics and chemistry. This situation may well be due, in part, to an overemphasis on theory at the expense of data collection, but it is also due to the nature of the subject matter with which economics deals: empirical regularities comparable with those found in the natural sciences may simply not be available.

Economic phenomena, as has been illustrated in previous chapters, change very substantially over time. Thus even if economists were to develop completely persuasive theories which generated successful predictions, they would sooner or later become out of date. In addition, economic phenomena are so complex that there will always be significant, apparently random, variations which limit our power to predict accurately. Possibly even more important than this, the world changes in response to new economic ideas. Governments change their policies when they discover something new about how the economy operates, and the rest of the economy may change its behaviour as a result. For example, in recent years many governments became converted to the idea that there was a link between the growth rate of the money supply and inflation, and as a result they introduced policies to restrict the money supply. In response to this the private sector's behaviour has changed, with new financial assets being created and with changes in relative interest rates inducing people to hold different assets. The result is that the relationship between money and income has become even less reliable. Thus even if there were a completely stable relationship between money and prices, its discovery might cause behaviour to change in such a way that the relationship disappeared.

These problems are particularly great in macroeconomics, where the interdependence of different parts of the economy cannot be ignored and expectations must be considered explicitly. Whereas in microeconomics we can frequently assume that the changes we are considering take place against a stable background, with substantially unchanged expectations, and that this background is not altered by the changes we are considering, this is hardly ever the case in macroeconomics. In addition macroeconomics is beset with aggregation and index number problems, which means that the theoretical foundation for most macroeconomic models is much weaker than is the case in most of microeconomics.

The limitations inherent in economics as it exists today concern problems that economists have shown no signs of ever being able to tackle successfully. Economics has proved itself immensely powerful where ways have been found to discern relatively mechanical functional relationships between variables. The calculus of maximizing behaviour has enabled economists to tackle not only 'economic' problems but also problems long thought the preserve of other social sciences, Gary Becker's work on the family and crime (Becker, 1968, 1976, 1981) being the most widely known (and controversial) example. Such work, together with a widespread resistance to considering ideas from other disciplines, has led to economists becoming, in the words of George Stigler, an eminent Chicago economist, 'the social science imperialists'. Some problems, however, have stubbornly resisted this advance, by far the most important one being the causes of economic growth. Many economic policies are advocated or opposed on the grounds that they will either promote or impede economic growth, but although economists, and especially economic historians, have had many insights into the problem, they have never been able to settle the matter, and there is no sign that they are likely to do so in the near future. Whenever we consider such issues, therefore, we must be very careful to make clear the limitations of our knowledge.

7.4 CONCLUSIONS

To a certain extent economics has deserved the criticism heaped upon it. Economists have clung on to out-of-date theories, claimed more than they were justified in claiming and have become carried away with abstract arguments to the detriment of common sense. Many controversies have generated heat rather than light, with the insights of earlier generations being forgotten. In part, confusions have arisen because economists have run up against the limitations of their subject: limitations on their ability to predict successfully and limitations imposed by the hard core of rational behaviour. Subject to these constraints, however, economics has made enormous progress. Whilst we would not go so far as Schumpeter (1982, p. 1052), who claimed that 'the more competent the economists are whom one consults, the less they disagree on fundamentals', it is true that there is substantial agreement amongst economists. For example, 'Monetarists' and 'Keynesians' reach different conclusions about how monetary and fiscal policy should be used, but the main reasons for these disagreements are not differences over economic theory so much as differences over value judgements and the interpretation of empirical evidence. Their underlying views of how the economy works have much in common. A major problem is that political and ideological issues are often mixed up with economic ones. When we turn to microeconomic issues (for example, the effects of taxation, or rent controls), there is even greater agreement amongst economists (see Heller, 1975; Frey, 1984).

One reason for these disagreements is that too much is claimed for economic theory. Advances in economic theory have, as we have seen in previous chapters, been central to the the progress of the subject over the past three to four centuries. However, economics comprises more than simply economic theory. To quote Alfred Marshall,

In my view 'Theory' is essential. No one gets any real grip of economic problems unless he will work at it. But I conceive no more calamitous notion than that abstract, or general, or 'theoretical' economics was economics 'proper'. It seems to me an essential but a very small part of economics proper: and by itself even – well, not a very good occupation of time. (Marshall, 1925, p. 437)

Elsewhere he pointed out that

There is scarcely any limit to the developments of economic theory which are possible: but of those which are possible only a small part are useful in having a direct relation to practical issues. (Marshall, 1885, p. 162)

Marshall also provided a clear statement of the limitations of economic theory:

that part of economic doctrine, which alone can claim universality, has no dogmas. It is not a body of concrete truth, but an engine for the discovery of concrete truth, similar to, say, the theory of mechanics.

He used an example from engineering to illustrate the dangers of claiming too much for theory:

The theory of mechanics contains no statement of fact as to the greatest strain which bridges will bear. Every bridge has its peculiarities of construction and material: and mechanics supplies a universal engine, which will help in determining what strain any bridge will bear. But it has no universal dogmas by which this strain can be determined without observation of the particular facts of the case.

Suppose that all the bridges over the canals of Venice were, as indeed most of them are, very nearly of the same material and general construction: suppose that there were a number of general dogmas with regard to all of them; and suppose some engineers had applied these dogmas to bridges built under different circumstances and in other places. When the breaking down of the new bridges had shown the folly of claiming universality for the practical dogmas of mechanics, impetuous people would rush to the conclusion that there was no universal organon of mechanical reasoning. (Marshall, 1885, p. 159)

Some of the critics of economic theory, Marshall claimed, had fallen into the same trap. A similar comment is true today.

Since Marshall's time the 'engine' of economic analysis, which according to Marshall '*can* claim universality', has been greatly refined, rendering it immensely more powerful, capable of being applied to an ever wider range of problems. When we look at how advances in economic theory have made it possible to clarify earlier ideas, to dispel false notions and to investigate problems previously considered beyond the scope of economic theory, we find evidence of enormous progress in economics. This, however, is only a part of economics.

In the all-important applied fields we have the problem that what we have to say is to a much greater extent contingent on prevailing circumstances, which are changing all the time. The problem is reinforced when we take account of the problem, characteristic of all social sciences, that developments in the subject can change the way the world works. When people learn something new about the economy they may try to take advantage of this by changing their behaviour. These arguments, however, must not be taken too far because, as we have seen in earlier chapters, whilst there have been enormous changes in the problems economists have sought to explain, not everything is different.

Over the past three centuries there has been a steady improvement in three aspects of economics. There has been continuous improvement in both the quantity and quality of the information available about the economy. In addition, there has been a dramatic improvement, especially over the past century, in the statistical techniques available for analysing these data. Equally important, however, has been the development of economic theory, for it is economic theory that has provided economists with a means to understand what is going on. This theory is, however, subject to severe limitations. If economists are to understand not only the power of economic theory but also its limitations, it is important that they do not lose touch with either economic history or the history of their discipline.

APPENDIX: TABLE OF MAIN EVENTS

This table shows the timing of some of the historical events discussed in the text. Other dates are included to provide 'landmarks'. Many entries are abbreviated.

Date	The world	Britain	United States	General economics	Money	Science and culture
1453	Fall of Constantinople					
1485		Accession of Henry Tudor				
1488	Diaz round Cape of Good Hope					
1498	Vasco da Gama to India					
1492	Columbus to America					
1507–47		Henry VIII				
1519–22	Magellan round world					
1544–51		Great debasement				
1549				Discourse of Commonweal		
1556					Navarrus *Commentario*	
1558–1603		Elizabeth I				
1563		Statute of artificers				
1588	Spanish Armada					

contd overleaf

Table of main events contd

Date	The world	Britain	United States	General economics	Money	Science and culture
1600	Dutch East India Company					
1602		East India Company				
1603–25		James I				Shakespeare *Hamlet*
1605						Bacon *Advancement of Learning*
1614						Napier invents logarithms
1620			Voyage of *Mayflower*			
1621		Commercial crisis			Mun–Misselden exchange	
1632						Galileo *Dialogue on World Systems*
1637						Descartes *Discourse on Method*
1642–6		Civil War				
1649		Execution of Charles I				
1651		Navigation Act				Hobbes *Leviathan*
1660		Restoration of Charles II				
1661–83	Colbert					
1662						Royal society founded
1664					Mun *England's Treasure*	
1686						Newton *Principia Mathematica*

1688	'Glorious Revolution'
1688–1702	William and Mary
1690	Petty *Political Arithmetic*
1691	Locke *Some Considerations*
1694	Bank of England
1696	Recoinage crisis
1703	Methuen Treaty
1705	Newcomen's first steam engine; Law *Money and Trade*
1709	Coke used for smelting iron
1716	Banque Générale
1717	Compagnie d'Occident
1719–20	Collapse of Law's schemes; South Sea Bubble
1742	Handel *Messiah*
1752	Hume *Political Discourses*
1755	Cantillon *Essai*
1760–1820	George III; Quesnay *Tableau Economique*
1764	
1769	Watt's steam engine
1770	Spinning Jenny
1773	Boston Tea Party
1776	Declaration of Independence; Smith *Wealth of Nations*

contd overleaf

Table of main events contd

Date	The world	Britain	United States	General economics	Money	Science and culture
1779		Crompton's mule				
1783			Treaty of Versailles			
1784		Puddling and rolling patented				
1789	French Revolution					
1793	Revolutionary War					
1798				Malthus *Essay*		
1802					Thornton *Paper Credit*	
1804	Napoleon crowned emperor					
1810				Report of Bullion Committee		
1815	Battle of Waterloo			Ricardo *Principles*		
1817						
1819		First Factory Act				
1825		Stockton–Darlington railway	Erie Canal completed			
1834	Zollverein formed	Tolpuddle martyrs		Cournot *Recherches*		
1836–1901		Victoria				
1838						
1844		Bank Charter Act				
1846		Repeal of Corn Laws				
1848	Revolutions of 1848		Californian gold rush	J. S. Mill *Principles*	*The Communist Manifesto*	
1849		Repeal of Navigation Act				

Year					
1851			Australian gold rush	Great Exhibition	
1859			First oil well		
1860				Cobden–Chevalier Treaty	
1861–5			Civil War		
1862	Juglar *Crises Commerciales*				
1863	Jevons Pamphlet on gold				
1867		Marx *Capital*, vol. I			
1869			First transcontinental railroad	Suez Canal opened	
1871		Jevons *Theory*		German Empire	
1873					
1874		Walras *Elements*			
1878			Bland-Allison Act		
1879			End of greenbacks		
1881			American Federation of labour		
1890		Marshall *Principles*	Sherman Anti-trust Act		
1897			Klondike gold rush		
1898	Wicksell *Interest and Prices*				
1909					Einstein's theory of relativity
1911	Fisher *Purchasing Power*				
1914			Clayton Anti-trust Act	Panama Canal opened	

contd overleaf

Table of main events contd

Date	The world	Britain	United States	General economics	Money	Science and culture
1914–18	World War I					
1917	Russian revolution					
1925		Return to gold standard				
1926		General Strike				
1929	The Great Crash					
1933			The New Deal			
1936					Keynes *General Theory*	
1939–45	World War II					
1944	IMF					
1945	United Nations					
1947	India/Pakistan independent	Nationalization of coal				
1950–53	Korean War					
1951	Steel and Coal Community			Samuelson *Foundations*		
1957	Ghana independent					
1958	Treaty of Rome (EEC)					
1960	Nigeria independent					
1967					Friedman Presidential Address	
1973	Arab-Israel war/oil price rise					
1978			Airline Deregulation Act			
1979	Iran revolution/oil price rise					
1984		Sale of British Telecom				

A Note on the Literature

The purpose of this note is twofold. It provides some suggestions for further reading on the material covered by each chapter and, just as important, it serves as an indication of the main sources I have used. In the interests of brevity this note does not mention primary sources discussed in the text. Virtually everything mentioned in this note has been a source of useful ideas. For more comprehensive bibliographies the reader is recommended to consult Blaug (1985), Spiegel (1983) or, for the classical period, O'Brien (1975), all of which contain excellent bibliographies.

There are many textbooks on the history of economic thought. Schumpeter (1954) is one of the greatest books ever written on the subject, its 1200 pages containing a wealth of information on economic ideas and numerous related topics. Spiegel (1983) is particularly good on earlier writings, covering many authors in much greater detail than most other books. Blaug (1985) and O'Brien (1975) (On the classical economists) cannot be too highly recommended. Finally, Backhouse (1985) is the only book which provides anything like a systematic coverage of the history of twentieth-century economic thought, including developments since 1945.

In this book I have, for a number of reasons, avoided providing bibliographical information on the economists discussed. A book which examines the history of economics from a different point of view, using biographical information to explain economists' ideas, is Heilbroner (1983).

Chapter 1

In addition to being worth reading in their own right, Heller (1975) and Coats (1971) contain, between them, references to many of the criticisms of economics which appeared in the early 1970s. The best concise discussion of different approaches to the history of economic thought is probably the opening chapter of Blaug (1985). See also the introduction to Schumpeter (1944). The best introduction to different approaches to the history of economic thought is probably the introduction to Blaug (1985). Absolutist interpretations of the history of economic thought include Schumpeter (1944), Blaug (1985) and Backhouse (1985). Extreme relativist positions are taken by, for example Dasgupta (1985) and Rogin (1956). Provocative introductions to the history of economic thought are to be

204 *A Note on the Literature*

found in Robinson (1962) and Dobb (1937). Finally, the importance of economic history for economists is addressed in Parker (1986).

Chapter 2

The classic study of British economic growth is Deane and Cole (1965), and the most recent is Crafts (1985), in which discussions of other work can be found. On French economic growth see Marczewski (1961). O'Brien and Keyder (1978) contains a more up-to-date discussion of the period after 1780. Crouzet (1966) compares France and Britain. Of the numerous attempts to explain Quesnay's *tableau*, Eltis (1984) is particularly useful, discussing not only the *tableau* itself but also its relation to the eighteenth-century economy as Quesnay perceived it.

Classical theories of growth are discussed in virtually all texts on the history of economic thought. A concise summary is in Samuelson (1978), though he minimizes the differences between Smith and Ricardo. On this see Hollander (1980). O'Brien (1975) is, as with most topics in classical economics, extremely lucid. Malthus's position is discussed in Gilbert (1980). For the historical background see Mathias (1983) and Crouzet (1982). Evidence on profits in the nineteenth century is taken from Blaug (1956) and the introduction to Church (1980). Marx is discussed in all the usual texts, Blaug's exposition being particularly recommended. See also Eltis (1984) and chapter 1 of Morishima and Catephores (1978). Robinson (1942) is straightforward and still repays reading.

Simple introductions to modern growth theory and the capital controversies are, because of the nature of the subject, hard to find. Backhouse (1985), chapter 25, provides one of the least technical accounts available. The classic account of the capital controversies is Harcourt (1972), written from the Cambridge (England) point of view. An account of the controversy which is critical of both sides is Blaug (1975).

Development economics is surveyed in Meier (1970). Two useful accounts, both from a neoclassical perspective, are Little (1982) and Lal (1983). Backhouse (1985) contains a brief history of development economics, and some further references to the literature on the subject. A very good way into the subject, however, is provided by the collection of articles in Meier and Seers (1984 and 1987). For these volumes a series of leading development economists were invited to provide a retrospective view of the subject and their contributions to it, and these are printed together with responses by younger contributors to the subject. Much of the information about developing economies is taken from the World Bank's *Development Reports*. Morawetz (1977) contains a useful account of progress from 1950 to 1975.

Chapter 3

Hill (1967) contains a useful, simple account of English economic policy in the seventeenth century. European mercantilism is discussed in Clough and Rapp (1975). A much more comprehensive coverage of the both mercantilist ideas and policies is contained in Heckscher (1955). Some of the issues raised by Heckscher's book are discussed in Coleman (1969). Many of the arguments about seventeenth-century ideas are taken from Appleby (1978). Many texts on the history of economic thought cover the period only briefly, an exception being Spiegel (1983). The eighteenth century is a neglected period, now comprehensively covered in Hutchison (1988).

On classical economic policy see Mathias (1983), Coats (1971), Taylor (1972) and O'Brien (1975), the last of these giving all the major references. The discussion of the factory acts owes much to Blaug (1959). Dupuit and the French engineers are clearly discussed in Ekelund and Hebert (1983). On List see Henderson (1983). The account of the tariff reform campaign is taken from Backhouse (1985), which contains full details of the sources on which it is based. Policy issues in the US, including both anti-trust policy and the New Deal, are discussed in Niemi (1975), Scheiber, Vatter and Faulkner (1976). Neale (1970) provides some useful information on anti-trust policy. Commons is discussed in Backhouse (1985), which contains further information on my sources. On the New Deal see Sternscher (1964) and Fusfeld (1956).

Debates over marginal cost pricing are well covered in Ruggles (1949). Reid and Allen (1970), Kay and Thompson (1986) and Curwen (1986) discuss problems relating to UK nationalized industries. US deregulation is covered by Bailey (1986).

Chapter   4

The classic study of sixteenth-century inflation is Hamilton (1923). A more up-to-date treatment is in Braudel and Spooner (1967), with English problems being covered by Outhwaite (1969) and Palliser (1982) which contain references to other literature. Spanish writers of the period are covered in Grice-Hutchison (1952), with the *Discourse of the Commonweal* being available in editions by Lamond (1893) and Dewar (1969). English monetary problems, including the recoinage crisis of 1696, are discussed in Horsfield (1960). The best source of information about Law's schemes is Murphy (1986). Cantillon's monetary thought, and its relation to mercantilism, is explored in Brewer (1988).

One of the best sources on early nineteenth-century British monetary controversies is still Viner (1937). More recent is Fetter (1965). Both are recommended. On US monetary problems after the Civil War see Scheiber, Vatter and Faulkner (1976).

Chapter   5

The account of the pre-industrial English economy is based on Supple (1959) and Mathias (1983). On nineteenth-century cycles see Mathias again and Rostow (1948). On the economic ideas, the main secondary sources I have used are to be found in the relevant sections of Backhouse (1985). Others include Davis (1972), Barber (1985) and Backhouse (1987).

Chapter 6

One of the few works on the history of economic thought to discuss the *Discourse of the Commonweal* in detail is Johnson (1938), though ideas on it can also be found in history texts such as Palliser (1982). See also the introductions by Lamond (1893) and Dewar (1969). On the seventeenth century see Appleby (1978). Petty, Locke and North are lucidly explained by Letwin (1963). The main study of Cantillon is Murphy (1986). For references on Smith and the classical economists see the bibliographies in O'Brien (1975) and Blaug (1985). On modern economics see the references given for chapter 1. A survey of much of this material, at a relatively non-technical level, is to be found in the relevant chapters of Backhouse (1985).

Chapter 7

The main references for this chapter are clearly McCloskey (1985) and Lakatos (1970). Though parts of the book are hard going for someone new to the ideas, Caldwell (1982) provides a thorough account of different approaches to economic methodology. A briefer account is provided in Blaug (1980), this book also having the merit that it applies these ideas to a number of areas of contemporary economics. For a good account of how theoretical ideas are developed, and of how they have evolved, see Weintraub (1985). See Hahn (1985) for a robust defence of economic theorizing, and Stigler (1982).

Bibliography

Abramovitz, M. (1952) 'The economics of growth', in *A Survey of Contemporary Economics*, volume II, edited by B. F. Haley. Homewood, Ill.: R. D. Irwin.

Akerlof, G. A. (1970) 'The market for "lemons": quality uncertainty and the market mechanism', *Quarterly Journal of Economics*, 84, pp. 488–500.

Aldcroft, D. H. and Fearon, P. (editors) (1972) *British Economic Fluctuations 1790–1939*. London: Macmillan.

Appleby, J. O. (1978) *Economic Thought and Ideology in Seventeenth-Century England*. Princeton: Princeton University Press.

Backhouse, R. (1983) *Macroeconomics and the British Economy*. Oxford: Martin Robertson.

Backhouse, R. (1985) *A History of Modern Economic Analysis*. Oxford: Basil Blackwell.

Backhouse, R. (1987) 'F. A. Walker's theory of "hard times"', *History of Political Economy*, 19, pp. 435–46.

Bailey, E. (1986) 'Price and productivity change following deregulation: the US experience', *Economic Journal*, 96, pp. 1–17.

Baily, M. N. (1981) 'Productivity and the services of capital and labour', *Brookings Papers on Economic Activity* 1, pp. 1–66.

Barber, W. J. (1985) *From New Era to New Deal: Herbert Hoover, the economists, and American economic policy, 1921–1933*. Cambridge: Cambridge University Press.

Barbon, N. (1690) *A Discourse of Trade*. Reprinted in Hollander (1903).

Baumol, W. J. (1982) 'Contestable markets: an uprising in the theory of industry structure', *American Economic Review*, 72(1), pp. 1–15.

Baumol, W. J., Panzar, J. C. and Willig, R. D. (1982) *Contestable Markets and the Theory of Industry Structure*. San Diego: Harcourt Brace Jovanovich.

Becker, G. (1968) 'Crime and punishment: and economic approach', *Journal of Political Economy*, 76, pp. 169–217.

Becker, G. (1976) *The Economic Approach to Human Behavior*. Chicago: Chicago University Press.

Becker, G. (1981) *A Treatise on the Family*. Cambridge, Mass.: Harvard University Press.

Blaug, M. (1956) 'The empirical content and longevity of Ricardian economics', *Journal of Political Economy*. Reprinted in Blaug (1986).

Blaug, M. (1958) *Ricardian Economics*. New Haven: Yale University Press.

Blaug, M. (1959) 'The classical economists and the factory acts: a re-examination', *Quarterly Journal of Economics*. Reprinted in Blaug (1986).

Blaug, M. (1975) *The Cambridge Revolution: Success or Failure?* London: Institute of Economic Affairs.

Blaug, M. (1980) *The Methodology of Economics*. Cambridge: Cambridge University Press.

Blaug, M. (1985) *Economic Theory in Retrospect*. Cambridge: Cambridge University Press.

Blaug, M. (1986) *Economic History and the History of Economics*. Brighton: Wheatsheaf Books.

Boulding, K. (1957) 'A new look at institutionalism', *American Economic Review*, 47 (supplement), pp. 1–12.

Braudel, F. P. and Spooner, F. (1967) 'Prices in Europe from 1450 to 1750', in *The Cambridge Economic History of Europe*, volume IV, edited by E. E. Rich and C. H. Wilson. Cambridge: Cambridge University Press.

Brewer, A. A. (1988) 'Cantillon and mercantilism', *History of Political Economy*, forthcoming.

Bullion Committee (1810) *The Paper Pound of 1797–1821: a Reprint of the Bullion Report*. Edited by E. Cannan, 1925. London: Frank Cass.

Cain, P. J. (1980) *Economic Foundations of British Overseas Expansion, 1815–1914*. London: Macmillan.

Caldwell, B. (1982) *Beyond Positivism*. London: George Allen and Unwin.

Cassel, G. (1923) *The Theory of Social Economy*, 2 volumes. Translated by J. McCabe. London: T. Fisher Unwin.

Cantillon, R. (1755) *Essay on the Nature of Trade in General*. Translated by H. Higgs. London, 1932. Reprinted in Monroe (1965).

Challis, C. E. (1978) *The Tudor Coinage*. Manchester: Manchester University Press.

Church, R. A. (ed.) (1980) *The Dynamics of Victorian Britain*. London: George Allen and Unwin.

Clark, C. G. (1940) *The Conditions of Economic Progress*. 2nd edition 1951; 3rd edition 1957. London: Macmillan.

Clark, J. B. (1907) *Essentials of Economic Theory*. New York: Macmillan.

Clark, J. M. (1934) *Strategic Factors in Business Cycles*. New York: National Bureau of Economic Research.

Clough, S. B. and Rapp, R. T. (1975) *European Economic History*, 3rd edition. New York: McGraw-Hill.

Coats, A. W. (ed.) (1971) *The Classical Economists and Economic Policy*. London: Longman; Methuen.

Coats, A. W. (1977) 'The current "crisis" in economics in historical perspective', *Nebraska Journal of Economics and Business*, 16, pp. 3–16.

Coleman, D. C. (ed.) (1969) *Revisions in Mercantilism*. London: Methuen.

Commons, J. R. (1924) *The Legal Foundations of Capitalism*. New York.

Commons, J. R. (1936) 'Institutional economics', *American Economic Review*, 26, pp. 237–54.

Crafts, N. F. R. (1985) *British Economic Growth during the Industrial Revolution*. Oxford: Clarendon Press.

Crouzet, F. (1966) 'England and France in the eighteenth century: a comparative analysis of two economic growths', in R. M. Hartwell (ed.) *The Causes of the Industrial Revolution in England*. London: Methuen.

Crouzet, F. (1982) *The Victorian Economy*. London: Methuen.

Curwen, P. (1986) *Public Enterprise*. Brighton: Wheatsheaf Books.

Dasgupta, A. K. (1985) *Epochs of Economic Theory*. Oxford: Basil Blackwell.

Davis, J. R. (1971) *The New Economics and the Old Economists*. Ames: Iowa State University Press.

Deane, P. and Cole, W. A. (1969) *British Economic Growth, 1688–1959*, 2nd edition. Cambridge: Cambridge University Press.

Debreu, G. (1959) *The Theory of Value*. New York: Wiley.

Denison, E. (1967) *Why Growth Rates Differ*. Washington DC: Brookings Institution.

Denison, E. (1979) *Accounting for Slower Economic Growth: the United States in the 1970s*. Washington DC: Brookings Institution.

Dewar, M. (ed.) (1969) *A Discourse of the Commonweal of this Realm of England* attributed to Sir Thomas Smith. Lexington, Va.: Virginia University Press.

Dobb, M. (1937) *Political Economy and Capitalism*. London: Routledge.

Domar, E. (1946) 'Capital expansion, rate of growth and employment', *Econometrica*, 14, pp. 137–47.

Dornbusch, R. and Fischer, S. (1984) *Macroeconomics*. London: McGraw-Hill.

Dupuit, J. (1844) 'On the measurement of the utility of public works', translated by R. H. Barback, *International Economic Papers*, 2, (1952), pp. 83–110.

Dupuit, J. (1853) 'On utility and its measure', *Journal des Economistes*, 1st series, 35, pp. 1–27.

Ekelund, R. B. and Hebert, R. F. (1983) *A History of Economic Theory and Method*. New York: McGraw-Hill.

Eltis, W. A. (1984) *The Classical Theory of Economic Growth*. London: Macmillan.

Fetter, F. W. (1965) *The Development of British Monetary Orthodoxy*. Cambridge, Mass.: Harvard University Press.

Fisher, I. (1911) *The Purchasing Power of Money*. New York: Macmillan.

Frey, B. *et al.* (1984) 'Consensus and dissension among economists: an empirical inquiry', *American Economic Review*, 74, pp. 986–94.

Friedman, M. (1953) 'The methodology of positive economics', in *Essays in Positive Economics*. Chicago: Chicago University Press.

Friedman, M. (1956) 'The quantity theory of money: a restatement', in *Studies in the Quantity Theory of Money*, edited by M. Friedman. Chicago: Chicago University Press.

Friedman, M. (1968) 'The role of monetary policy', *American Economic Review*, 58, p. 1–17.

Friedman, M. and Schwarz, A. J. (1963) *A Monetary History of the United States, 1867–1960*. Princeton: Princeton University Press.

Fusfeld, D. R. (1956) *The Economic Thought of Franklin D. Roosevelt*. New York: Columbia University Press.

Gilbert, G. (1980) 'Economic growth and the poor in Malthus' *Essay on Population*', *History of Political Economy*, 12, pp. 83–96.

Grice-Hutchison, M. (1952) *The School of Salamanca: Readings in Spanish Monetary Theory, 1544–1605*. Oxford: Oxford University Press.

Hahn, F. H. (1985) *In Praise of Economic Theory*, Jevons Memorial Fund Lecture, 1984. London: University College London.

Hamilton, E. J. (1923) *Spanish Treasure and the Price Revolution in Spain, 1501–1650*. Cambridge, Mass.: Harvard University Press.

Harcourt, G. C. (1972) *Some Cambridge Controversies in the Theory of Capital*. Cambridge: Cambridge University Press.

Harris, J. R. (1967) 'Steam power in the 18th century', *History*, 52, No. 175.

Harrod, R. F. (1939) 'An essay in dynamic theory', *Economic Journal*, 49, pp. 14–33.

Heckscher, E. F. (1955) *Mercantilism*, 2 volumes. Translated by M. Shapiro. London: George Allen and Unwin.

Heilbroner, R. (1983) *The Worldly Philosophers*. Harmondsworth: Penguin Books.

Heller, W. W. (1975) 'What's right with economics?', *American Economic Review*,

65(1), pp. 1–26.

Henderson, P. D (1985) *Ignorance and Design*. Oxford: Basil Blackwell.

Henderson, W. O. (1983) *Friedrich List*. London: Frank Cass.

Hill, C. (1967) *Reformation to Industrial Revolution*. London: Weidenfeld and Nicolson.

Hobson, J. A. (1896) *The Problem of the Unemployed*. London: Methuen.

Hollander, J. H. (1903) *A Reprint of Economic Tracts*, series 2. Baltimore, Md: The Lord Baltimore Press.

Hollander, S. (1980) 'On Professor Samuelson's canonical classical model of political economy', *Journal of Economic Literature*, 18, pp. 559–74.

Horsefield, J. K. (1960) *English Monetary Experiments, 1650–1710*. London: Bell.

Hoselitz, B. (ed.) (1960) *Theories of Economic Growth*. Glencoe, Ill.: The Free Press.

Hotelling, H. (1938) 'The general welfare in relation to problems of taxation and of railway and utility rates', *Econometrica*, 6, pp. 242–69.

Hume, D. (1752) *Writings on Economics*, edited by E. Rotwein. Edinburgh: Edinburgh University Press. Reprinted in Monroe (1965).

Hutchison, T. W. (1977) *Knowledge and Ignorance in Economics*. Oxford: Basil Blackwell.

Hutchison, T. W. (1981) *The Politics and Philosophy of Economics*. Oxford: Basil Blackwell.

Hutchison, T. W. (1988) *Before Adam Smith*. Oxford: Basil Blackwell.

Janssen, L. H. (1961) *Free Trade, Protection and Customs Union*. Stanfert Kreese.

Jevons, W. S. (1863) 'A serious fall in the value of gold ascertained and its social effects set forth'. Reprinted in Jevons (1884).

Jevons, W. S. (1884) *Investigations in Currency and Finance*. London: Macmillan.

Johnson, E. A. J. (1938) *Predecessors of Adam Smith*. London: King.

Juglar, C. (1862) *Des crises commerciales et leur retour périodique, en France, en Angleterre et aux Etats-Unis*. Paris: Guillaumin.

Kay, J. A. and Thompson, D. J. (1986) 'Privatisation: a policy in search of a rationale', *Economic Journal* 96(1), pp. 18–32.

Keynes, J. M. (1936) *The General Theory of Employment, Interest and Money*. London: Macmillan. Reprinted as Keynes (1971–83), volume VII. London: Macmillan, 1973.

Keynes, J. M. (1940) *How to Pay for the War*. Reprinted as Keynes (1971–83), volume XXII.

Keynes, J. M. (1971–83) *The Collected Writings of John Maynard Keynes*. 31 volumes. Edited by D. Moggridge. London: Macmillan.

Klein, L. R., and Goldberger, A. (1955) *An Econometric Model of the US, 1929–52*. Amsterdam: North Holland.

Kuznets, S. (1956) 'Quantitative aspects of the economic growth of nations', *Economic Development and Cultural Change*, 5, pp. 5–94.

Lakatos, I. (1970) 'The methodology of scientific research programmes', in *Criticism and the Growth of Knowledge*, edited by I. Lakatos and A. Musgrave. Cambridge: Cambridge University Press. Reprinted as chapter 1 of Lakatos (1978), volume 1.

Lakatos, I. (1978) *Philosophical Papers*. Volume 1: *The Methodology of Scientific Research Programmes*. Volume 2: *Mathematics, Science and Epistemology*. Cambridge: Cambridge University Press.

Lal, D. (1983) *The Poverty of Development Economics*. London: Institute of Economic Affairs (Hobart Paperback 16).

Lamond, D. (ed.) (1893) *A Discourse of the Common Weal of this Realm of England*. Cambridge: Cambridge University Press.

Landes, D. S. (1969) *The Unbound Prometheus*. Cambridge: Cambridge University Press.

Law, J. (1705) *Money and Trade Considered together with a Proposal for Supplying the Nation with Money*. Reprinted 1966. New York: Augustus M. Kelley.

Leontief, W. A. (1971) 'Theoretical assumptions and nonobserved facts', *American Economic Review*, 61; reprinted in Leontief, *Essays in Economics*, volume 2. Oxford: Basil Blackwell, 1977.

Letwin, W. (1963) *The Origins of Scientific Economics*. London: Methuen.

Lewis, W. A. (1954) 'Economic development with unlimited supplies of labour', *Manchester School* 22; reprinted in *The Economics of Underdevelopment*, edited by A. N. Agarwala and S. P. Singh. Oxford: Oxford University Press.

Lewis, W. A. (1955) *The Theory of Economic Growth*. London: Allen and Unwin.

Lewis, W. A. (1978) *Growth and Fluctuations, 1870–1913*. London: George Allen and Unwin.

Link, R. G. (1959) *English Theories of Economic Fluctuations, 1815–1848*. New York: Columbia University Press.

List, F. (1841) *The National System of Political Economy*. Translated by S. S. Lloyd, 1904. London: Longman Green & Co.

Little, I. M. D. (1982) *Economic Development*. New York: Basic Books.

Locke, J. (1691) *Some Considerations of the Lowering of Interest and Raising the Value of Money*. Reprinted in *The Works of John Locke*. 10 volumes. London: 1812.

Lucas, R. E. and Sargent, T. J. (1978) 'After Keynesian macroeconomics', in *After the Phillips Curve: Persistence of High Inflation and High Unemployment*. Federal Reserve Bank of Boston, Conference Series No. 19. Reprinted in *Rational Expectations and Econometric Practice*, edited by R. E. Lucas and T. J. Sargent. London: George Allen and Unwin, 1981.

Lundgren, N. (1969) 'Customs unions of industrialized west European countries', in *Economic Integration in Europe*, edited by G. R. Denton. London: Weidenfeld and Nicolson. Reprinted in *European Integration*, edited by M. Hodges. Harmondsworth: Penguin Books, 1972.

Malthus, T. R. (1798) *An Essay on the Principle of Population as it Affects the Future Improvement of Society*. 2nd edition, 1803.

Malthus, T. R. (1836) *The Principles of Political Economy*, 2nd edition. LSE Series of reprints of scarce works on political economy, No. 3.

Marczewski, J. (1961) 'Some aspects of the economic growth of France, 1660–1958', *Economic Development and Cultural Change*, 9, II, pp. 369–86.

Marshall, A. (1885) 'The present position of economics'. Inaugural lecture given at Cambridge. Reprinted in Marshall (1925).

Marshall, A. (1887) 'Remedies for fluctuations of general prices', *Contemporary Review*; reprinted in Marshall (1925).

Marshall, A. (1890) *Principles of Economics*. 8th edition, 1920. London: Macmillan.

Marshall, A. (1925) *Memorials of Alfred Marshall*, edited by A. C. Pigou. London: Macmillan.

Martyn, H. (1701) *Considerations on the East India Trade*. Reprinted in McCulloch (1856).

Marx, K. (1974) *Capital*. 3 volumes. German edition, 1873, 1885, 1894. English translation by S. Moore and E. Aveling. London: Lawrence and Wishart.

Mathias, P. (1983) *The First Industrial Nation*, 2nd edition. London: Methuen.

McCloskey, D. (1985) *The Rhetoric of Economics*. Brighton: Wheatsheaf Books, 1986.

McCulloch, J. R. (1856) *A Select Collection of Early English Tracts on Commerce*. Reprinted 1952. Cambridge: Economic History Society.

Meade, J. E. (1956) *The Theory of Customs Unions*. Amsterdam: North Holland. References are to the reprint of chapter 11 in *International Economic Integration*, edited by P. Robson. Harmondsworth: Penguin Books, 1972.

Meek, R. L. (1962) *The Economics of Physiocracy*. London: George Allen and Unwin.

Meier, G. M. (1970) *Leading Issues in Economic Development*. Oxford: Oxford University Press.

Meier, G. M. and Seers, D. (eds.) (1984) *Pioneers in Development*. Oxford and New York: Oxford University Press.

Meier, G. M. and Seers, D. (eds.) (1987) *Pioneers in Development*, 2nd series. Oxford and New York: Oxford University Press.

Mill, J. (1808) *Commerce Defended*, reprinted in *James Mill: Selected Economic Writings*, edited by D. Winch. Edinburgh: Oliver and Boyd, 1966.

Mill, J. S. (1844) *Essays on Some Unsettled Questions of Political Economy*. London: Parker.

Mill, J. S. (1848) *Principles of Political Economy*. London.

Mitchell, B. R. and Deane, P. (1962) *Abstract of British Historical Statistics*. Cambridge: Cambridge University Press.

Mitchell, B. R. (1983) *International Historical Statistics: The Americas and Australasia*. London: Macmillan.

Mitchell, B. R. (1978) *European Historical Statistics, 1750–1970*. London: Macmillan.

Mitchell, W. C. (1913) *Business Cycles*. New York: Burt Franklin.

Monroe, A. E. (1965) *Early Economic Thought*. Cambridge, Mass.: Harvard University Press.

Morawetz, D. (1977) *Twenty-five Years of Economic Development, 1950–1975*. Washington DC: The World Bank.

Morishima, M. and Catephores, G. (1978) *Value, Exploitation and Growth*. London: McGraw-Hill.

Mun, T. (1664) *England's Treasure by Forraign Trade*. Reprinted in McCulloch (1856) and in Monroe (1965).

Murphy, A. (1986) *Richard Cantillon*. Oxford: Oxford University Press.

Navarrus (1556) *Comentario Resolutio de Usuras*. Extracts translated in Grice-Hutchinson (1952).

Neale, A. D. (1970) *The Antitrust Laws of the United States of America*, 2nd edition. Cambridge: Cambridge University Press.

Nef, J. U. (1934) 'The progress of technology and the growth of large-scale industry in Great Britain, 1540–1640', *Economic History Review*, 5, pp. 3–24.

Nelson, R. L. (1959) *Merger Movements in American Industry, 1895–1956*. Princeton: Princeton University Press.

Niemi, A. W. Jr (1975) *US Economic History*. Chicago: Rand McNally.

North, D. (1691) *A Discourse on Trade*. Reprinted in Hollander (1903) and in McCulloch (1856).

O'Brien, D. P. (1970) *J. R. McCulloch: A Study in Classical Economics*. London: George Allen and Unwin.

O'Brien, D. P. (1975) *The Classical Economists*. Oxford: Oxford University Press.

O'Brien, P., and Keyder, C. (1978) *Economic Growth in Britain and France, 1780–1914*. London: George Allen and Unwin.

Outhwaite, R. B. (1969) *Inflation in Tudor England*. London: Macmillan.

Overstone, Lord (1857) *Tracts on Metallic and Paper Currency*. London.

Overton, M. (1987) *Agricultural Revolution in England: the transformation of the rural economy, 1500–1830*. Cambridge: Cambridge University Press.

Palliser, D. M. (1982) *The Age of Elizabeth*. London: Longman.

Parker, W. N. (ed.) (1986) *Economic History and the Modern Economist*. Oxford: Basil Blackwell.

Petty, W. (1899) *Economic Writings*, 2 volumes. Edited by C. H. Hull. Cambridge: Cambridge Univeristy Press.

Phelps-Brown, H. and Hopkins, S. V. (1956) 'Seven centuries of the price of consumables', *Economica*, 23, pp. 296–314.

Phillips, A. W. (1958) 'The relation between unemployment and money wage rates in the United Kingdom 1861–1957,' *Economica*, 25, pp. 283–99.

Reid, G. L. and Allen, K. (1970) *Nationalised Industries*. Harmondsworth: Penguin Books.

Ricardo, D. (1810) *The High Price of Bullion a Proof of the Depreciation of Banknotes, 1810–11*. Reprinted in Ricardo (1951), volume II.

Ricardo, D. (1817) *Principles of Political Economy and Taxation*, 3rd edition 1821. Reprinted in Ricardo (1951), volume I. Reprinted 1971, Harmondsworth: Penguin Books.

Ricardo, D. (1951) *The Works and Correspondence of David Ricardo*, 11 volumes. Edited by P. Sraffa. Cambridge: Cambridge University Press.

Riden, P. (1980) 'The iron industry', in Church (1980).

Robinson, J. (1942) *An Essay on Marxian Economics*. London: Macmillan.

Robinson, J. (1962) *Economic Philosophy*. Harmondsworth: Penguin Books.

Rogin, L. (1956) *The Meaning and Validity of Economic Theory*. New York: Harper.

Rosenstein-Rodan, P. (1984) 'Natura facit saltum: analysis of the disequilibrium growth process', in *Pioneers in Development*, edited by G. M. Meier and D. Seers. Oxford: Oxford University Press.

Rostow, W. W. (1948) *The British Economy in the Nineteenth Century*. Cambridge: Cambridge University Press.

Ruggles, N. (1949) 'Recent developments in the theory of marginal cost pricing', *Review of Economic Studies*, 17, pp. 107–26.

Sachs, J. D. (1979) 'Wages, profits and macroeconomic adjustment: a comparative study,' *Brookings Papers on Economic Activity*, 2, pp. 269–319.

Samuelson, P. A. (1947) *Foundations of Economic Analysis*. Cambridge, Mass.: Harvard University Press.

Samuelson, P. A. (1978) 'The canonical classical model of political economy', *Journal of Economic Literature*, 16, pp. 1416–34.

Say, J. B. (1803) *A Treatise on Political Economy*. Translated by C. R. Prinsep, 1821. London: Longman.

Scheiber, H. N., Vatter, H. G. and Faulkner, H. U. (1976) *American Economic History*. New York; Harper and Row.

Schumpeter, J. A. (1954) *History of Economic Analysis*. New York: Oxford University Press.

Schumpeter, J. A. (1982) 'The "crisis" in economics—fifty years ago', *Journal of Economic Literature*, 20, pp. 1049–59.

Seligman, E. R. A. (1925) *Essays in Economics*. New York: Macmillan.

Smith, A. (1776) *An Inquiry into the Nature and Causes of the Wealth of Nations*. Edited by E. Cannan. Chicago: University of Chicago Press, 1976.

Spence, M. (1973) 'Job market signalling', *Quarterly Journal of Economics*, 87, pp. 355–74.

Spiegel, H. W. (1983) *The Growth of Economic Thought*. Durham, NC: Duke University Press.

Sternscher, B. (1964) *Rexford Tugwell and the New Deal*. New Brunswick: Rutgers University Press.

Stigler, G. J. (1982) *The Economist as Preacher*. Oxford: Basil Blackwell.

Supple, B. (1959) *Commercial Crisis and Change in England, 1600–42*. Cambridge: Cambridge University Press.

Taylor, A. J. (1972) *Laissez Faire and State Intervention in 19th Century Britain*. London: Macmillan.

Thornton, H. (1802) *An Enquiry into the Nature and Effects of the Paper Credit of Great Britain*. Edited by F. A. Hayek, 1939. London: LSE.

United States, Bureau of the Census (1960) *Historical Statistics of the United States, Colonial Times to 1957*. Washington DC.

Verdoorn, P. J. (1954) 'A customs union for Western Europe—advantages and feasibility', *World Politics*, volume 6.

Viner, J. (1937) *Studies in the Theory of International Trade*. London: George Allen and Unwin.

Viner, J. (1950) *The Customs Union Issue*. London: Stevens.

Walker, F. A. (1879) *Money, Trade and Industry*. London: Macmillan, 1889.

Walras, M. E. L. (1874) *Elements of Pure Economics*. Translated by W. Jaffe, 1954. London: George Allen and Unwin.

Weintraub, E. R. (1985) *General Equilibrium Theory: Studies in Appraisal*. Cambridge: Cambridge University Press.

Wicksell, K. (1894) *Interest and Prices*. Translated by R. F. Kahn, 1936. London: Macmillan.

Wicksell, K. (1898) 'The influence of the rate of interest on commodity prices'. Translated in *Selected Papers on Economic Theory*, edited by E. Lindahl. London: George Allen and Unwin, 1958.

Winch, D. (1969) *Economics and Policy*. London.

World Bank (1978) *World Development Report, 1978*. Washington DC.

Wrigley, E. A. and Schofield, R. S. (1981) *The Population History of England, 1541–1871*. London: Edward Arnold.

Index